THE ORGANIZATIONAL RESPONSE TO PERSONS WITH MENTAL ILLNESS INVOLVED WITH THE CRIMINAL JUSTICE SYSTEM

RESEARCH IN SOCIAL PROBLEMS AND PUBLIC POLICY

Series Editors: William R. Freudenburg and
Ted I. K. Youn

Recently published volumes:

RESEARCH IN SOCIAL PROBLEMS AND PUBLIC POLICY

VOLUME 12

THE ORGANIZATIONAL RESPONSE TO PERSONS WITH MENTAL ILLNESS INVOLVED WITH THE CRIMINAL JUSTICE SYSTEM

EDITED BY

STEPHANIE W. HARTWELL

Department of Sociology, University of Massachusetts, Boston, USA

2005

ELSEVIER
JAI

Amsterdam – Boston – Heidelberg – London – New York – Oxford
Paris – San Diego – San Francisco – Singapore – Sydney – Tokyo

ELSEVIER B.V.
Radarweg 29
P.O. Box 211
1000 AE Amsterdam
The Netherlands

ELSEVIER Inc.
525 B Street, Suite 1900
San Diego
CA 92101-4495
USA

ELSEVIER Ltd
The Boulevard, Langford
Lane, Kidlington
Oxford OX5 1GB
UK

ELSEVIER Ltd
84 Theobalds Road
London
WC1X 8RR
UK

First edition 2005

British Library Cataloguing in Publication Data
A catalogue record is available from the British Library.

ISBN: 0-7623-1231-9
ISSN: 0196-1152 (Series)

∞ The paper used in this publication meets the requirements of ANSI/NISO Z39.48-1992 (Permanence of Paper).
Printed in The Netherlands.

CONTENTS

LIST OF CONTRIBUTORS

Beth Bjerregaard	Department of Criminal Justice, University of North Carolina at Charlotte, Charlotte, NC, USA
Carolyn S. Breda	Vanderbilt University, Nashville, TN, USA
Jonathan C. Clayfield	Psychiatry Department, University of Massachusetts, Worcester, MA, USA
Anne Marie Coté	Department of Sociology and Anthropology, Millersville University, Millersville, PA, USA
William H. Fisher	Psychiatry Department, University of Massachusetts, Worcester, MA, USA
Sondra J. Fogel	School of Social Work, University of South Florida, Tampa, FL, USA
Jorge O. Folino	Programa E.R.L., Procuración General, Buenos Aires, La Plata, Argentina
Christine Gagliardi	University of Massachusetts, Boston, NY, USA
Albert J. Grudzinskas, Jr.	Psychiatry Department, University of Massachusetts, Worcester, MA, USA
Stephanie W. Hartwell	Department of Sociology, University of Massachusetts, Boston, MA, USA
Arthur J. Lurigio	College of Arts and Sciences, Loyola University, Chicago, IL, USA
Kimberly A. Mahaffy	Department of Sociology and Anthropology, Millersville University, Millersville, PA, USA

Robert A. McMackin   Massachusetts Department of Public
                            Health, Jamaica Plain, MA, USA

Theodore I. Mutale   Bethlem Royal Hospital, Beckenham,
                            UK

Elliot Pittel   Massachusetts Department of Public
                            Health, Jamaica Plain, MA, USA

Kristen Roy-Bujnowski   Psychiatry Department, University of
                            Massachusetts, Worcester, MA, USA

M. Dwayne Smith   Department of Criminology, University
                            of South Florida, Tampa, FL, USA

James A. Swartz   Jane Addams College of Social Work,
                            University of Illinois at Chicago,
                            Chicago, IL, USA

INTRODUCTION

Since 1963, the promise of the Community Mental Health Centers Con-struction Act (1963), the planned provision of community-based mental health services, and advances in psychotropic medication and treatment suggested that the mentally ill might be better managed and served in the community than in hospital (Bachrach & Lamb, 1989; Grob, 1991). While "dehospitalization" proceeds today (Geller, 2000), large numbers of indi-viduals with mental illness also return to the community from correctional custody and bring with them complicated clinical profiles and service needs (Laberge & Morin, 1995; Rice & Harris, 1997; Lamb & Weinberger, 1998; Lamb et al., 1999). An increasing awareness of this phenomenon has re-sulted in estimates that prisons contain four to five times the rate of persons with mental illness found in the community (Morris & Tonry, 1990; Regier et al., 1990; Morris et al., 1997; Rice & Harris, 1997; Wolff et al., 1997). According to the 2000 Prison Census, about 150,900 or 1 in 10 state inmates were in mental health programs; 114,400 or 1 in 13 were receiving psycho-tropic medication; and 18,900 or 1 in 80 were in 24-hour psychiatric care (Bureau of Justice Statistics, 2000). While the recent estimates suggest that approximately 16% of all those incarcerated in state prisons (16% of all males and 24%of all females) have some sort of mental illness (Ditton, 1999), a meta-analysis examining the prevalence of mental disorder with a narrow criterion found that 10% of male and 18% of female inmates had an Axis I major mental disorder of thought or mood (Pinta, 2001).

Individuals with mental illness who engage in criminality receive longer sentences and serve them out due to legal representation, mandatory sen-tencing, parole conditions, and crime severity (Lamb & Weinberger, 1998; Healey, 1999; Travis, 2000). The vast majority is released from correctional custody without mandated correctional monitoring or transitional services aiding community re-entry or reintegration (Porporino & Motiuk, 1995; Healey, 1999; Travis, 2000; Piehl, 2002). Upon release, living in the com-munity with a mental illness and criminal history may be exacerbated by the social isolation fostered through lengthy incarceration. Release from long-term correctional custody signifies a change in structure, environment, and daily life that can be difficult to manage for a population that is already disenfranchised, disadvantaged, and stigmatized (Link et al., 1987, 1997;

Hartwell, 2002). Thus, their service needs and experiences are likely to be unique from mentally ill individuals without a criminal history.

This volume, *The Organizational Response to Persons with Mental Illness Involved with the Criminal Justice System*, explores the approaches (program development and evaluation), strategies (risk assessments and interventions), and institutions (courts, hospitals, community corrections, and prisons) responding to offenders with mental illness from arrest to release from incarceration. Policies regarding mentally ill offenders are played out differently by state and county, and the capacity of communities to support individuals with mental illness and criminal histories varies. Examination of quantitative and qualitative research on organizational responses to "mentally ill offenders" as well as responses to the institutional processes in their lives is the basis of this volume.

The chapters that follow demonstrate issues and approaches in the organizational and institutional response to mentally ill offenders and share themes including the importance of program evaluation; data collection; innovative programming and best practices in resource utilization; dispositions and the courts; screening; and, finally, a broader articulation of outcomes given the special needs of the population. Taken together, the chapters highlight where theory and practice meet programmatically and in the lives and experiences of adult and adolescent offenders with mental illness. From arrest to release, the organizational response to mentally ill offenders is continually evolving according to existing policies and resources. How organizations respond, how they should respond, and their ability to evolve is a central theme. The chapters in this volume offer cases with wide ranging policy implications regarding structural and functional changes institutions and organizations might consider given the confines of context and resources to improve the conditions of mentally ill offenders. Thus, the pathways and potential turning points presented herein offer guidance on how organizations and institutions could respond given their structure, function, and capacities to be effective.

Each section of the volume has two chapters. Part I examines efforts in programming and program evaluation for adolescents (McMackin & Pittel) and adults (Clayfield & colleagues). While McMackin and Pittel highlight the importance of a public health approach and the pitfalls of lacking an evaluation component, Clayfield and colleagues document that an integrated multi-organization structure is effective in serving offenders with mental illness through strong program evaluation. Part II features risk assessment. Both Mutale and Folino's assessment approaches offer secondary prevention tools supportive of re-entry. Part III highlights the importance of the court as a gatekeeper to services (Breda) and in offering final dispositions with the mitigating role of mental illness (Bjerregaard, Smith & Fogel). Part IV focuses on the role that prisons have in identification (Swartz) and intervention programming (Gagliardi). Much is currently done in prisons, but both chapters offer ideas to evolve practices behind bars. Finally, Part V features outcomes. Both chapters introduce life course theory to better understand the experiences of people with mental illness involved with the criminal justice system. They offer a broader view of what success means programmatically (Cote & Mahaffy) and to the offenders with mental illness themselves in the context of their organizationally and institutionally bound environments (Hartwell). All sections share important lessons in theory and practice to help develop the institutional and organizational response to mentally ill individuals involved with the criminal justice system.

Stephanie W. Hartwell
Editor

PART I:
PROGRAMMING AND PROGRAM EVALUATION – TWO CASES FROM MASSACHUSETTS

A PUBLIC HEALTH APPROACH TO ADDRESS THE MENTAL HEALTH NEEDS OF JUVENILE OFFENDERS

Robert A. McMackin and Elliot Pittel

ABSTRACT

The Lemuel Shattuck Hospital Youth Service Program adopted a public health approach to address the mental health needs of incarcerated juvenile offenders in Massachusetts. The program, which operated for 6 years, provided psychiatric care and neuropsychological assessment to delinquent youth as well as training for psychiatry residents, neuropsychology fellows and Massachusetts Department of Youth Services' staff. The program recognized and attempted to address the health care disparity of limited access to quality mental health services for incarcerated youth, particularly those from disadvantaged and minority backgrounds. The program was a collaborative venture among the Massachusetts Departments of Public Health and Youth Services, and Tufts-New England Medical Center. The scope of the problem of mental health care for incarcerated youth will be first outlined, followed by a history and evaluation of the program from a public health and system integration perspective.

The Organizational Response to Persons with Mental Illness Involved with the Criminal Justice System

Research in Social Problems and Public Policy, Volume 12, 3–25

Copyright © 2005 by Elsevier Ltd.

ISSN: 0196-1152/doi:10.1016/S0196-1152(05)12001-8

THE EPIDEMIOLOGY OF MENTAL ILLNESS AMONG JUVENILE OFFENDERS

The National Mental Health Association (1999) reported rates of mental health disorders as high as 60–75% for incarcerated adolescents. A recent study by Teplin et al. (2002) of 1,829 youth interviewed with the Diagnostic Interview Schedule for Children (DISC) at the Cook County Detention Center in Chicago, Illinois, found the prevalence of any mental disorder was 67% for males ($n = 1,172$) and 74% for females ($n = 657$). A notable finding in the Teplin study was that, even excluding Conduct Disorder, the overall prevalence of mental health disorders remained 60% in males and 70% in females. These rates of mental health disorders among criminally involved youth are two to six times those found in the general population (Breda, 1996) and hold up across cultures. Vreugdenhil, Doreleijers, Vermeiren, Wouoters, & Wim Vand Den Brink (2004), also using the DISC, found a 90% rate of mental health disorders among a population of incarcerated Dutch male youth, which was over three times the prevalence found in the normal Dutch adolescent population. Additionally, the co-morbidity rate among juvenile offenders, particularly of substance abuse and mental health disorders, has been reported as high as 67% (GAINS, 1999; Vreugdenhil et al., 2004).

Serious emotional disturbance can be defined as an emotional disturbance that leads to extreme functional impairment. Friedman, Katz-Leavy, Manderscheid, and Sondheimer (1996) reported the overall community prevalence for any diagnosable psychiatric disorder among children aged 9–17 is 20% and 5–9% for serious emotional disturbance. Cocozza and Skowyra (2000) estimated that the prevalence of serious emotional disorders among youth in the juvenile justice system is at least 20%. Not only is the prevalence of mental illness among juvenile offenders high, but one in five juvenile offenders experiences functional impairment such as learning disabilities, social skills deficits, or interpersonal problem-solving difficulties as a result of serious emotional disturbance or mental illness.

In some respects, this high prevalence of mental health problems among many youthful offenders is not surprising, considering the toxic environments in which many have been raised. The lives of many juvenile offenders are marked by inconsistent parenting, familial substance abuse, physical and/or sexual abuse, and exposure to community violence (Haapasalo & Kankkonen, 1997; Malinosky-Rummell & Hansen, 1993; McMackin, Morrissey, Newman, Erwin, & Daly, 1998; Rivera & Widom, 1990; Weeks & Widom, 1998; Widom, 1989, 1995).

The psychosocial stressors many delinquent youth must deal with are not evenly distributed across social classes. In a review of the impact of childhood poverty, Evans (2004) stated:

> The confluence of multiple psychosocial and physical risk factors may be a key, unique feature of childhood poverty. Adverse socioemotional and cognitive developmental outcomes are accelerated by exposure to multiple risks relative to singular risk exposure (Evans, 2004, p. 86).

When co-occurring, these personal, familial, economic and social stressors have a synergistic effect that impacts the mental health of a juvenile offender. Indications of the multiple stressors many juvenile offenders in Massachusetts face were outlined in an internal survey of youth committed to the Department of Youth Services (DYS) that indicated half of DYS committed youth had histories that include child welfare involvement and half required special education services. Additionally, a third of DYS youth reported weekly alcohol use, and close to half reported weekly marijuana use. Indicators of family psychosocial stress included 86% of youth were raised in broken homes, a parental unemployment rate of over 50%, and only half of biological parents had completed the 12th grade (Sylva, 1999).

An examination of boys held in secure treatment in Massachusetts, the highest level of security reserved for youth with the most severe or chronic offense histories, showed many additional stressors. Almost half of the boys in secure treatment reported a history of physical abuse and nearly a third reported sexual abuse. Exposure to violence was a predominate feature in the lives of many, with three quarters having had their lives seriously threatened, and almost half having been shot or stabbed. Over 80% had known someone murdered and over a quarter had seen someone murdered (McMackin et al., 1998).

PUBLIC HEALTH AND PSYCHIATRIC SERVICES FOR MENTALLY ILL JUVENILE OFFENDERS

The overall mission of public health is succinctly summarized by the adage "An ounce of prevention is worth a pound of cure." The Federal Healthy People 2000 and 2010 initiatives more extensively outlined the nation's prevention health care agenda for the prior and next 10 years. The overarching goals of the Healthy People initiatives have been to increase the span of healthy life, both in respect to quantity and quality for all Americans; to reduce health care disparities for all Americans; and to improve access to preventive health care services for all Americans.

The Healthy People 2000 Final Review (2000) illustrated how closely linked these goals are to issues of race and class. Between the years of 1990 and 1999, 23% of persons below the poverty level reported fair to poor health; whereas only 7% of persons above the poverty level reported fair to poor health. African-Americans die on average six years earlier than whites (71.3–77.3 years) and more strikingly African-Americans have 8.3 fewer years of a healthy life than whites (57.8–66.1 years).

Additionally, mental illness is a serious condition that contributes to decreased longevity as well as impairment to the quality of life at all points on the lifespan. The chronic mentally ill die almost 10 years earlier than the non-mentally ill. The comparison between age cohorts is even more alarming: the mentally ill in the 25–64 age group are six to seven times more likely to die from a cardiac event and two to six times more likely to die from pulmonary disease than their non-mentally ill counterparts (Sudders, 2002). According to a recent Surgeon General's Report on Mental Illness, impairments due to children's emotional and behavioral problems may lower their quality of life and increase their chances of not being fully functional members of the society (U.S. Public Health Service, 2000). These stressors are compounded for the mentally ill who become involved in the criminal justice system. Speaking directly to the plight of juvenile offenders, the Surgeon General's Report (2000) stated that juvenile justice agencies often do not recognize mental health problems. A 1995 report to Congress on mental illness in the criminal justice system, filed by a consortium of federal agencies, reported:

> Persons with mental illness who come into contact with the criminal justice system are particularly vulnerable. They bear a double burden: the stigma associated with their mental illness and the stress of potential arrest and confinement. Involvement with the criminal justice system may exacerbate the isolation and distrust often associated with mental illness (Center for Mental Health Services, Substance Abuse and Mental Health Service Administration, Public Health Service & U.S. Department of Health and Human Service, 1995, p. I).

Although the focus of this report was on adult offenders, this conclusion fits with juveniles as well.

The children most likely to go without appropriate services are poor and children of color (Satcher, 1999; National Mental Health Association Survey, 1999; Isaacs-Shockley, 1996). Researchers have also found that minority children are more likely to be referred to the juvenile justice system for disruptive behavior and white children are referred for mental health treatment (Cross, Bazron, Dennis, & Isaacs, 1989; Isaacs-Shockley, 1996; Thomas, Stubbe, & Pearson, 1999; Pumariega, 1999). Nationally, although minority youth represent only 32% of the 10–17 year olds in the general population, 68% of the youth held in juvenile justice facilities are minorities (Snyder, 1997). Some advocates have described the juvenile justice system as the "de-facto" mental health system, especially for disenfranchised, poor, minority youth. This has real implications for the provision of mental health diagnostic and treatment services. Farmer, Burns, Phillips, Angold, and Costello (2003) found that the juvenile justice system was the second most common point of entry for mental health care for youths between the ages of 14 and 16.

MENTAL ILLNESS AND RECIDIVISM

The data from the study by Teplin, Abram, McClelland, Dulcan, and Mericle (2002) indicated that the symptoms juvenile offenders experience do not ameliorate over time but rather compound. Children in the two older youth cohorts (age 14, 15 and 16 and above) of the study had higher prevalence in almost all diagnostic areas than those in the younger cohort (age 13 and below). Ditton (1999) showed adult mentally ill offenders recidivate more often than their non-mentally ill counterparts, yet there is little information on recidivism and mental illness among juveniles.

In Massachusetts, 66% of committed juvenile offenders were rearraigned within 1 year of discharge and of those, 72% were rearraigned within their first 6 months of release; however, there was no separate analysis of mental illness as a contributing factor (Corneliussen, Waters, & Taberner, 1996). Frederick (1999) examined the records of 2,763 youth discharged from the New York State Youth Authority. He identified 40 criminal risk factors that were collapsed into eight categories including mental health, substance abuse, behavior problems at school, educational handicaps, educational performance, household characteristics, family environment, and relations with parents. Almost half of the youth had at least one risk factor from the mental health category, but again mental health was not broken out as a separate variable related to recidivism.

Harris and Rice (1999) reported that for adult offenders, including individuals with and without mental disorders, the same risk factors impact on recidivism (e.g. prior criminal history, substance abuse, anti-social peers). The critical factor is that the mental disorder should be treated so that the individual can benefit from an intervention program. This is particularly important from an economic point of view. The cost of 10 years of criminal behavior, including victim cost, criminal justice costs and offender productivity loss, has been estimated between \$1.3 and \$1.5 million per offender (Snyder & Sickmund, 1999). Considering that higher rates of delinquent behavior is associated with higher levels of psychopathology (Breda, 1996); that adult mentally ill offenders recidivate at a higher rate than non-mentally ill offenders (Ditton, 1999); and when their mental illness is stabilized they can more fully benefit from offender-based treatments (Harris & Rice, 1999), it follows that treatment of the mentally ill offenders at the youngest possible age is paramount from both economic costs and human suffering perspectives.

PSYCHIATRIC CARE WITHIN THE DEPARTMENT OF YOUTH SERVICES PRIOR TO 1997

Massachusetts was the first state in the country to deinstitutionalize its juvenile justice system in the early 1970s, dismantling the training school system in favor of a greater reliance on community services. Small secure residential settings were reserved for the most serious or chronic offenders. Currently the Department of Youth Services operates, directly or under contract, 66 residential facilities for youth. Each program serves between 20 and 30 youth. Forty-one of these programs (33 for boys and 8 for girls) are considered "hardware secure," providing the highest level of security. The remaining 25 programs provide lesser levels of security, from partial secure to "open door." Each program has its own clinical service program staffed by a master's level (or above) clinical director and a number of clinicians who are generally at the master's level. Medical services are provided under regional sub-contracts with all programs having a registered nurse or physician assistant on site for all or part of the week. DYS places a strong emphasis on family reintegration. The current DYS Strategic Plan (1998) calls for the location of services, including secure facilities, in the home communities of offenders; collaboration with community resources and providers; and an emphasis on education, job training and employment programs tailored to the needs of the youthful offender.

Prior to the development of the Youth Service Program, psychiatric care was delivered through an informal network of community-based providers in each regional area. Communication among the providers was minimal, as was the integration of psychiatric care with the overall medical care a youth would receive. The responsibility to find psychiatric care was placed primarily on each individual program, with youth periodically taken out of high secure programs to see community providers, while in shackles and chains. DYS did have an independent psychiatric consultant who saw youth for specialized evaluations and followed a few youth for medication management.

The proportion of youth on psychotropic medications was quite low until the mid-1990s, when it began to rise rapidly and came to the attention of DYS health and clinical administrators. An internal survey of youth entering the DYS detention system in 1997 (Morrissey, 1997) revealed that 15% were prescribed psychotropic medications and 2–3% had a history of psychiatric hospitalization. This underscored the importance of developing a consistent care program to address psychiatric illness. In recognition of the scope of the problem, which included medication being discontinued due to a lack of providers, the DYS Director of Clinical Services identified the psychiatric needs of youth as a high priority problem and was receptive to a proposed collaboration with the Lemuel Shattuck Hospital (LSH) staff regarding the development of a psychiatric care program for youth in DYS care.

HISTORY AND DESIGN OF THE YOUTH SERVICE PROGRAM

LSH is the Massachusetts Department of Public Health (DPH) hospital providing services to disadvantaged populations in the greater Boston area. The hospital's mission is to "provide comprehensive health care and support services which meet the health and social needs of our community," as part of the overall DPH mission of ensuring all Massachusetts residents have access to quality health care. The teaching affiliate of LSH is Tufts New England Medical Center (Tufts-NEMC), which is affiliated with Tufts University School of Medicine.

In 1996, LSH administrators were concerned about the high prevalence and long-term impact of mental disorders among juvenile offenders, particularly among disadvantaged and minority populations. Considering that LSH is an important provider of health and mental health care to many adult correctional facilities, the LSH administration viewed a program for juvenile offenders as an opportunity to provide early intervention and hopefully reduce the burden of psychiatric illness among youth who were at risk to go on to become adult offenders. Thus, the psychiatric needs of youth placed in the juvenile justice system were viewed as a public health concern by the senior LSH staff.

The Youth Service Program (YSP) was conceptualized with four primary goals: (1) to improve access to and the quality of psychiatric care at DYS facilities; (2) to improve the continuity of services for youth who are transferred from facility to facility; (3) to provide training and consultation for DYS staff and child and adolescent psychiatry residents; and (4) to collect data on the mental health needs of offenders and apply for funds to conduct research on the best system of cost-effective mental health services for incarcerated youth. Crisis services were excluded from the YSP as there was a state-wide crisis management system administered through the Department of Mental Health.

There are four regional DYS areas within Massachusetts: Metro (Boston and the northern suburbs), Southeast, Central and Western. It was jointly decided with DYS that the YSP would focus its services on the Metro and Southeast Areas with some services provided to the Central Area and none to the Western Area, which had its own local provider. The programs most in need of services were determined by the DYS Director of Clinical Services and DYS regional clinical directors. With funding provided by DYS, DPH and third-party insurance (primarily Medicaid), the YSP began to see patients in December, 1997.

The YSP was initially staffed by a half-time board certified child and adolescent psychiatrist, a full-time clinical nurse specialist and a quarter-time psychologist who also served as the program director. Support services were provided by LSH and billing services provided by Tufts-NEMC. The YSP expanded both staff and facilities covered each year between 1997 and 2000. At the time of its closure in 2003, the YSP had provided care to 1,639 youth (1,287 boys and 352 girls). Staffing at the time of its closure included a full-time board-certified child and adolescent psychiatrist who was also the program medical director, a part-time board-certified child and adolescent psychiatrist who also coordinated training of Tufts-NEMC child and adolescent psychiatry residents, a full-time clinical nurse specialist who specialized in working with girls, a part-time child and adolescent psychiatry resident, a full-time neuropsychology post-doctoral fellow, a social worker to assist in case management, and a quarter time psychologist or program director.

The majority of services were provided on site at the DYS facility where the youth resided. The remaining services were provided by establishing a clinic at one secure DYS facility that permitted youth from less secure programs in the same DYS area to be transported to the clinic site. Procedures for making referrals were developed. Upon arrival at a facility, the YSP clinician held a triage meeting with the clinical directors from each program to be visited. Cases were reviewed and prioritized. About 50% of referrals arose from the triage meeting, while the other 50% were previously identified by program staff based on the youth's history of prior psychiatric care or his/her presentation on the unit. The triage meeting served several functions. First, it was valuable in identification of youth who had not previously been referred. It allowed the YSP clinician to quickly review all follow-up cases. It also provided an opportunity to provide informal training to DYS staff.

All patient services provided by YSP clinicians were voluntary. When needed, the DYS clinical staff often assisted the YSP clinician with contacting families to obtain permission to evaluate and then prescribe psychotropic medication. No youth were seen if they or their families refused to consent to care. No court ordered evaluations were performed to be used as possible aides to sentencing or for any other forensic reason. A decision by a youth to not take medication was never held against him or her by DYS staff through any type of program or other restriction of privileges.

PATIENT CHARACTERISTICS

A retrospective chart review was done of 102 patient records (80 male and 22 female) by selecting every fifth record from the central YSP alphabetical file between the letters A and H. This review represented 6% of the patients seen between 1997 and 2003. Table 1 presents the racial background of the sample.

Table 2 presents additional characteristics of the sample.

It should be noted that while 25% of the sample had a history of prior suicide attempts, 36% of the referred girls had at least one prior suicide attempt.

All youth served by the YSP had an initial psychiatric evaluation. As part of this evaluation, 95 of the youth in the sample (74 males and 21 females) were assigned a DSM IV (Diagnostic and Statistical Manual, 4th edition) Global Assessment of Functioning (GAF). This score can range from 0 to 100 and the average for the sample was 53. This GAF score represented a moderate severity in symptoms or moderate difficulty in a youth's social, occupational, or school functioning. The average number of psychiatric diagnoses each youth received was 2.6. A quarter of the youth were seen by more than one YSP provider during the time they received care from the YSP.

Table 1.   Race of the Sample.

	Males		Females		Total (%)
	N	%	N	%	
African–American	15	14.7	2	1.9	16.6
White	32	31.4	13	12.7	44.1
Hispanic	14	13.7	1	1.0	17.6
Other[a]	8	7.8	2	1.9	9.7
Unknown[b]	11	10.8	4	3.9	14.7
Total	80	78.4	22	21.6	100.0

[a]Youth of Cape Verdian, Asian or mixed racial descent.
[b]Data not available.

Table 2.   Characteristics of the Sample (80 Males and 22 Females).

	Males		Females		Total (%)
	N	%	N	%	
Detained by DYS	31	30.4	10	9.8	40.2
Committed to DYS	33	32.4	10	9.8	42.2
Committed while in treatment	16	15.7	2	1.9	17.6
Prior psych hospitalization	40	39.2	9	8.8	48.0
Prior suicide attempt	17	16.7	8	7.8	24.5
Serious substance abuse history	48	47.0	16	15.7	62.7

PROGRAM OUTCOMES

The principal program outcomes achieved and limitations of the YSP are presented in relation to each of the initial goal areas: improving the quality and access to care for youth; improving the continuity of care for youth; developing training opportunities for mental health professionals, and establishing a data base.

Improving Quality and Access to Psychiatric Services

Many youth with serious psychiatric illness who were placed in the DYS facilities received psychiatric care through the YSP as evidenced by the inpatient hospitalization rate for YSP referrals prior to incarceration being over 15 times that of the full DYS population (48% vs. 2–3%). Additionally, YSP referrals had a high suicide attempt rate prior to incarceration (25%), and an average GAF of 53 at the time of their initial YSP assessment.

Psychiatric care was provided at regularly scheduled times at over 25 DYS facilities by board certified child and adolescent psychiatrists as well as off-hours consultation available by page. This availability of psychiatric care meant that many youth did not have medication abruptly discontinued due to lack of access to a provider, which periodically took place prior to the advent of YSP services. Regular triage meetings were held with DYS program and clinical staff to identify youth in need of services and review the treatment plans of all youth in care. This close collaboration may have contributed to lowering psychiatric emergencies at programs served by the YSP as indicated by a reduction in emergency service utilization in the Metro Boston Area programs served by the YSP. Additionally, neuropsychological assessments were provided to 136 youth to assist in treatment and educational planning.

The YSP never developed an integrated medical record including psychiatric care. This lack of an integrated medical record interfered with the quality of care as initial assessments were repeated at times and it made collaboration with other medical providers difficult particularly around monitoring medication side effects and ordering tests.

African–American youth were underrepresented in the referral pattern for both males and females based on the percentage of the full DYS population they represented. This fits with the national mental health referral patterns previously noted for African–American youth (Cross et al., 1989; Isaacs-Shockley, 1996; Thomas et al., 1999; Pumariega, 1999), where they are less frequently referred for psychiatric care in comparison to white youth. It raises the question whether African–American psychiatric needs went unrecognized and therefore were being inadequately addressed.

Overall the access and quality of psychiatric care was notably improved for youth during the tenure of the YSP.

Continuity of Care

Continuity of care was initially addressed by establishing the YSP as the main provider for psychiatric care to over 25 separate DYS programs. Under this system of care, youth were able to receive services from the same provider as they moved from facility to facility. To illustrate, 18% of the

youth evaluated by a YSP clinician had their first encounter in a detention
facility and were later followed by the YSP as they moved to an assessment
and later a treatment facility for DYS committed youth. This indicated a
continuity of care as youth were seen not only in different facilities but as
they changed legal status from detained to committed. To ensure a continuity of care, YSP staff shared their diagnostic evaluations and follow-up
reports with DYS clinical staff and chaired regular triage meetings. This
helped both YSP and DYS staff to monitor patient symptoms and target
behaviors. Additionally, a program was developed for girls where one provider followed girls from detention to assessment and then to treatment
programs in the two DYS areas the YSP was contracted to cover. This
continuity of care was particularly important for females where 36% had a
prior history of suicide attempts and 41% a history of psychiatric hospitalization. By the provider following a patient from program to program the
provider could ensure continuity in the care by informing staff at each
program of a girl's psychiatric treatment plan and providing a stable caring
relationship for the girl.

Here again, limitations were faced regarding providing a continuity of
care in that services were only implemented for two of the four DYS areas,
Metro and Southeast, and partially for a third area, Central. There remained service shortfalls particularly at some Central Area programs the
entire time the YSP provided care. At times a youth would be transferred to
a program not covered by the YSP and on these occasions the assurance of
continuity in the treatment plan was less certain. Nonetheless, the continuity
of care provided to incarcerated youth was enhanced by the YSP.

Training

The training goal was considered important in the initial planning of the
YSP as a means to upgrade the understanding of psychiatric illness among
DYS providers as well as to enhance the training for medical professionals
entering psychiatry. As a step toward this all YSP professional staff held
clinical faculty appointments with the Department of Psychiatry at Tufts
University School of Medicine. A part time YSP/DYS 4-month rotation
was integrated into the Tufts-NEMC child and adolescent psychiatry res-
idency training program. Additionally, a YSP/DYS post-doctoral neuropsychology training position was developed as part of the LSH
neuropsychology training program. A benefit of the academic affiliation
with Tufts-NEMC and training opportunities provided through the YSP

was that it helped with recruitment of medical professionals who wanted to maintain an academic affiliation, have an academic professional peer group, and be involved in the teaching of residents.

The bulk of the YSP training of DYS personnel was done informally through the triage process. The YSP did schedule monthly in-service case presentations and rounds that DYS personnel were invited to but only few attended due to other responsibilities. While the training component associated with Tufts-NEMC successfully provided training to over 20 residents, the formal training of DYS personnel could have been more rigorous.

Data Collection

The program's weakest area, as is often the case in applied programming, was data generation, collection and organization. While administrative data was available for billing purposes, neither an integrated nor an electronic medical record was developed. This lack of an integrated medical record interfered with the continuity of care as previously mentioned and forced staff to hand carry records from program to program. Program planning was also impacted by not having an integrated electronic medical record. Data was not readily available for report preparation, planning meetings, research, and proposal development.

PROGRAM EVALUATION

The YSP will be evaluated by applying the program development guidelines outlined by the GAINS Center (1999)[1] in *The Courage to Change: A Guide for Communities to Create Integrated Services for People with Co-Occurring Disorders in the Justice System.* Their guidelines are meant to be applied to adult or juvenile offender programs designed to meet the needs of individuals with mental illness and co-occurring substance abuse disorders. Although 63% of the youth referred to the YSP had substance abuse problems, the YSP was designed to focus primarily on their mental health issues. Nonetheless, the GAINS Center guidelines provide a framework by which the YSP can be assessed.

The National GAINS Center recommends taking a "system integration" approach to collaboration among the various stakeholders as a program is developed. System integration in contrast to service integration represents a "new arrangement among the service organizations, including their treatment services, administration, management information systems, and staff training" (GAINS, 1999, p. 8). Service integration provides for an overlapping of services that may be coordinated by a caseworker often acting as the intermediary or advocate for a client among various independent agencies or providers. System integration is characterized by a spanning of the boundaries among the providers so services do not overlap but are integrated. A full integration of care may include a sharing of budgets, planning, and staff among the principal stakeholders. An integrated system leads to fewer seams or gaps among providers through which clients can slip. This is particularly important within the criminal justice sector where there may be a mandatory aspect to the treatment. Seams or gaps in the system of care among providers can contribute to noncompliance by clients or allow for clients to get lost among the various providers if there is no good communication among the providers.

The GAINS Center describes a two step process to the development of a system integration approach. These steps are Start-up and Implementation.

Start-up

Start-up is a time for coalition building and strategic planning. It is recommended that the key agencies be identified, consumer groups consulted and a common goal with a strategic plan determined. A strong leader, with good communication skills, should direct the process, and although the start may be small the group should "carry a big vision." The project must commit to cultural sensitivity, organize political support, and clarify a funding strategy.

Although not specifically designed to follow the GAINS plan from its inception, the YSP incorporated many of the GAINS' guidelines in the initial planning phase. The YSP Program Director worked closely with his DYS counterpart, the DYS Director of Clinical Services, meeting bi-weekly for the first three years of the program to develop trust, mutual respect of each other, shared objectives, and a clear understanding of the needs of youth. The YSP Program Director and the DYS Director of Clinical Services shared the leadership role through being persistent in keeping a work group organized, keeping senior administrators of LSH and DYS apprised of progress, preparing agendas and summaries of meetings, involving Medicaid representatives, and maintaining a larger vision for the YSP. There was a shared primary goal between YSP and DYS staff that consisted of improving the psychiatric care provided to incarcerated youth. However, there was some disagreement among the parties related to the secondary goals of training, research, and improving medical records. These goals were of particular interest to YSP/DPH staff due to our interest in improving the quality of care and program evaluation or impact. While political support for the program model was sought from the executive staffs of DPH and DYS, the planners did not seek additional political support from other public or private child welfare and mental health agencies nor from elected officials. Cultural sensitivity received close attention by all members, given that large percentage of the cases referred were expected to be minorities. LSH staff contacted the Department of Mental Health (DMH) and consulted with a senior DMH psychiatrist who was the primary DMH/DYS liaison. Consumer or patient advocate groups were not consulted in the early planning.

Implementation

The GAINS Center describes a four-phase approach to implementation as a program moves from informal to formal relationships among all the parties involved in the project. The implementation phases will first be presented, and then discussed in how they apply to the YSP. The phases are:

1. *Cooperation*: Key personnel from all cooperating agencies meet and share information on a regular basis.
2. *Coordination*: Representatives from each agency move to joint staff meetings and program planning to learn more about each group's operating procedures.
3. *Collaboration*: Representatives of each agency continue to have regular meetings, cross train staff and move to interagency agreements through memoranda of understanding.
4. *Integration*: Representatives share budgets, jointly fund key positions and view client care as a shared responsibility.

As a project moves through these four phases there are a number of tasks that need to be accomplished that include:

- Formal and informal agreements among all parties.
- A marketing strategy.
- Systems of information sharing.
- Accessibility to services by clients.
- Cross training.

- Boundary-spanning positions.
- Outcome evaluations.
- Respect for each system's stage of development.

During the first three years of the YSP steady progress was made through the Cooperation, Coordination and Collaboration Phases of the GAINS model. The principal planners worked closely together as the YSP moved from Start-up to the Cooperation Phase. The initial survey of psychotropic usage among youth entering DYS detentions (Morrissey, 1997) was jointly designed by the YSP Program Director and the DYS Director of Clinical Services who together identified the programs where services were first piloted.

During the first three years quarterly meetings were held with regional DYS administrators in the two target areas the YSP served, Metro and Southeast. Bi-weekly meetings were held between the YSP Program Director and the DYS Director of Clinical Services and a semi-annual meeting was held with senior DYS and LSH staff. These regular systems of communication helped the YSP move into the Coordination Phase.

YSP staff developed referral protocols as well as on-site protocols for where and how patients would be seen and how records would be shared with DYS clinical and medical staff. YSP staff also conducted up to six trainings per year for DYS staff as part of the regular DYS statewide training program. Additionally, other stakeholders, particularly the Department of Psychiatry of Tufts-NEMC and the Medicaid management company for Massachusetts were brought more fully into the process. Tufts-NEMC child and adolescent psychiatry residents began a voluntary rotation at DYS facilities. Discussions regarding reimbursement rates were opened with the Medicaid management company. DYS recognized the need for psychiatric services and as the DYS programs that were served expressed satisfaction with the YSP, the YSP expanded to 25 sites by the end of the third year. These all represented Coordination Phase achievements.

The Collaboration Phase is characterized by the development of formal agreements, a process that was begun in the third year of the YSP. The most notable achievement in this area was a formal Memorandum of Understanding (MOU) signed by the Commissioners of DYS and DPH in the fourth year of the program. This MOU outlined the extent of the mental health needs of incarcerated youth and how DYS and DPH would collaborate to address those needs. The MOU stressed not only the service needs of the youth but called on the two agencies to collaborate on infrastructure development for data systems, addressing training or academic needs, and collaborative research. Additionally, agreements were reached with the two other major program partners, the Department of Psychiatry of Tufts-NEMC and the Medicaid management company for Massachusetts. The voluntary training rotation of Tufts-NEMC children and adolescent psychiatry residents became a formal part of the psychiatry-training program for all children and adolescent psychiatry residents. A billing rate that took into account staff travel time, the complexity of the cases, and family consultation was negotiated with the Medicaid management company. This billing rate allowed for the YSP to recover increased revenue, particularly for initial evaluations. Entering its fourth year the YSP was in the Collaborate Phase of the GAINS model. Unfortunately, the YSP failed to make the transition to the Integration Phase.

Inherent to the Integration Phase is a sharing of decision-making and responsibilities. Dual tracks of accountability, sharing of budgetary resources, and boundary-spanning positions are cornerstones of this phase. The YSP was impacted by a number of key personnel changes in 2001 that negatively impacted on the program making a smooth transition to the Integration Phase. The DPH and DYS commissioners, who had shown an active interest in and support for the YSP program, both resigned. Additionally, the resignation of the DYS Director of Clinical Services, who was active in the planning of the YSP from inception, was a key loss for the collaboration. These resignations created a leadership vacuum. The YSP Program Director went from a bi-weekly program review meeting with a DYS counterpart to almost a year with no DYS counterpart to meet with. Although YSP staff continued to meet regularly with DYS area staff, the ongoing communication with the DYS central office was never fully reestablished. An example of the difficulties caused is that in the early planning of the YSP there were a number of discussions concerning the competing priorities of service to youth and the research and training needs of an academic institution (Tufts-NEMC). The initial planners came to view these priorities as complementary rather than competitive. However, with new DYS administrators the discussions of balancing service delivery with other interests again came to the fore as competitive rather than complementary goals. That concern was never resolved.

The transition into the Integration Phase was also complicated by the YSP incurring a budget deficit most years. Initial financial projections made during the Start-up phase turned out to be inaccurate because many implementation costs were underestimated. Reasons for this included YSP staff downtime while in facilities because some youth were unable to be seen for security, staff coverage or space reasons. In addition, the amount of time it took to complete an initial patient evaluation was underestimated by at least an hour per evaluation.

The GAINS guideline calls for the establishment of a clear funding strategy with a funding leader who will help blend the existing funding streams. The YSP operated out of LSH, but under the umbrella of Tufts-NEMC services. All funding was channeled through the Tufts-NEMC Department of Psychiatry, which was the institutional funding leader. The funding streams provided by DYS, DPH and the Medicaid management company never fully covered the salaries of direct care providers resulting in several breakeven budgets or deficits of up to $30,000 annually. Although the Medicaid management company had agreed to enhance reimbursement rates, the majority of that revenue was never realized due to billing code errors and computer problems both at Tufts-NEMC and the Medicaid management company. There was often confusion as to who was fiscally responsible for the YSP deficits. These deficits ended up being covered by LSH through surpluses in other areas of its comprehensive Tufts-NEMC contracts. The chronic under funding of the YSP, particularly for any initiative not related to immediate care, such as establishing a database system or an electronic patient record, hindered the transition to the Integration Phase.

The YSP continued to operate into 2002 when, due to a change in the academic affiliation for forensic psychiatry at LSH, the YSP began planning a change of its academic affiliation from Tufts-NEMC to the University of Massachusetts Medical School (UMass), which would become the funding leader. The Department of Psychiatry at UMass was interested in incorporating the YSP into their child and adolescent psychiatry and forensic training programs. A series of meeting were held with senior LSH, UMass, and DYS administrators regarding the transfer of the YSP to UMass. All parties were concerned at how the YSP budget deficits interfered with it achieving its service, research and academic goals. A cost analysis showed it would require more than a doubling of the DYS/DPH financial commitment to the YSP (up to $400,000 from $135,000) for UMass to absorb the YSP, expand staffing to cover the DYS Central Area of the state and establish a patient data system. Unfortunately, this request came simultaneously with a contracting state budget that saw both DPH and DYS suffering budget cutbacks. In light of conflicting priorities, DYS and DPH were unable to increase funding. The YSP closed in August 2003.

CONCLUSION

The GAINS Center program development guidelines contain a section on "Sustaining Successful Programs" once they have been established. They note five "Key Survival Strategies" identified as:

1. Plan for the future from day one
2. Data, data, data
3. Some cost data are helpful
4. Political vs. financial stability
5. Market shamelessly (GAINS, 1999, p. 23)

What went wrong with the Youth Service Program?

First, the YSP did plan for the future from day one by working and planning with the primary stakeholders; however, it did not receive the necessary finances to develop the infrastructure support that could sustain the program into that future.

Next, data systems, which are critical for program evaluation and planning, were never established. Steady progress was made in other departments and services of LSH and Tufts-NEMC during the late 1990s in the development and implementation of electronic medical records, but the YSP made no progress in that area. The Tufts-NEMC electronic medical record system was reviewed and could have been adapted for the YSP but there were never adequate funds to work on that project. Additionally, there was no way to integrate an electronic record within the DYS record keeping system, which was manual and varied from program to program. As a result there was no formal collection of data on outcome indicators to demonstrate the YSP' was an effective program at providing needed mental health care to the incarcerated youth. However, although formal data collection did not occur, the Boston Emergency Service Team, which handled all mental health emergencies at Metro Boston DYS facilities, reported anecdotally a reduction of emergency calls from programs serviced by the YSP. This would lead to a lowering of psychiatric hospitalizations for DYS youth and associated cost savings, but this data could not be properly documented. Additionally, most DYS facility administrators reported a lowering of mental health related incidents, particularly suicide gestures and youth on precautionary watches, after the introduction of YSP services. Without any formal data collection and scientifically planned program evaluations, reductions in mental health related incidents could not be presented as documenting program effectiveness.

The program never established broad political support within the human service, academic, and political arenas, and as a result could not solicit support from those areas during a time of fiscal crisis. There was strong local support of the YSP from DYS program and area administrators as well as from LSH medical and administrative staff. That local support did not travel upwards into the respective DYS and DPH central office administrations, especially after the resignations of the two commissioners that supported the development of the YSP. This led to not having a political constituency within the DYS and DPH hierarchy that enthusiastically supported the program and would ensure that financial resources were available during a time of constricting budgets.

Although innovative in design, the YSP remained parochial in operation. The program director focused on facilitating day to day operations but did not vigorously market the program's achievements. The DPH/DYS MOU was the high-water mark of the program, but it did not lead to further strategic planning among stakeholders. Rather than being a starting point for further collaboration it became an end point.

The YSP never achieved system integration. Service integration was achieved but when the fiscal pressures mounted, there was not enough cohesion to sustain the program. The MOU outlined a number of boundary-spanning functions, including the YSP Medical Director providing monthly consultation to DYS senior administrators on issues related to mental illness and health care, but although available, this consultation service was never utilized. System integration would have led to a joint budget and a broad range of shared goals with boundary-spanning positions that may have allowed the program to endure in a time of fiscal crisis. However, when the heavy winds of budgetary cutbacks blew and managers reassessed priorities and core functions, the overlapping of service integration could not stand up to the fiscal pressure. Had the knitting of a system integration approach been achieved, the Youth Service Program may have been better able to sustain such a buffeting.

The mental health problems of incarcerated youth represent a need that if unmet will often contribute to future disorders, disabilities and incarceration as adults for many youth. The public health approach of identification and treatment of these disorders at the earliest possible time is the most efficacious means to address the problem. The Youth Service Program provided a model to address the psychiatric needs of incarcerated youth, but without full institutional support and funding it was unable to be sustained. Nonetheless, the history of the program illustrates the depth of the problem and highlights the area that must be addressed for such a program to succeed.

NOTES

1. The National GAINS Center was established in 1995 to collect and disseminate information on persons with mental illness and co-occurring substance abuse disorders within the criminal justice system. The GAINS Center is supported by numerous funders including the Substance Abuse and Mental Health Service Administration, the National Institute of Corrections, the Office of Justice Programs, and the Office of Juvenile Justice and Delinquency Prevention.

ACKNOWLEDGMENTS

The Lemuel Shattuck Hospital (LSH) Youth Service Program (YSP) was a collaborative effort of many professionals, who dedicated time in making it successful, particularly Joseph Cohen, MD, LSH VP of Medical Services; Carole Johnson, MD YSP Medical Director; Carl Fulwiler, MD, PhD, Associate Professor, Departments of Psychiatry, UMass Medical Center & Tufts University School of Medicine; David Gansler, PhD, LSH Chief of Psychology; and Carlo Morrissey, EdD, DYS Director of Clinical Services (ret.).

REFERENCES

Breda, C. S. (1996). Delinquency and mental illness: the intersection of problems and systems. In *Proceedings of the 8th Annual Research and Training Center Conference*, Dept of Child and Family Studies, Florida Mental Health Institute, University of South Florida, 1–4.

Center for Mental Health Services, Substance Abuse and Mental Health Service Administration, Public Health Service & U.S. Department of Health and Human Service. (1995). *A Report to Congress – Double Jeopardy: Persons with Mental Illness in the Criminal Justice System.* Rockville, MD.

Cocozza, J., & Skowyra, K. (2000). Youth with mental health disorders: Issues and emerging responses, *Juvenile Justice. Journal of the Office of Juvenile Justice and Delinquency Prevention*, 3(1), 3–13.

Corneliussen, E., Waters, C., & Taberner, S. (1996). *Recidivism analysis of committed juveniles discharged in 1990–1992.* Boston, MA: Massachusetts Department of Youth Services.

Cross, T., Bazron, B., Dennis, K., & Isaacs, M. (1989). *Towards a culturally competent system of care: A monograph on effective services for minority children who are severely emotionally disturbed.* Washington, DC: Georgetown University Child Development Center.

Ditton, P. M. (1999). *Bureau of Justice Statistics, special report, Mental health and the treatment of inmates and probationers.* (NIJ Publication No. 1744). Washington, DC: U.S. Justice Department, Office of Justice Programs, 1–11.

Evans, G. W. (2004). The environment of childhood poverty. *American Psychologist*, 59(2), 77–92.

Farmer, E., Burns, B., Phillips, S., Angold, A., & Costello, E. J. (2003). Pathways into and through mental health services for children and adolescents. *Psychiatric Services, 54*, 60–66.

Frederick, B. (1999). *Factors contributing to recidivism among youth placed with the New York State Division for Youth. Albany, NY.* New York: New York State Division of Criminal Justice Services.

Friedman, R., Katz-Leavy, J., Manderscheid, R., & Sondheimer, D. (1996). Prevalence of serious emotional disturbance in children and adolescents. In: R. W. Manderscheid & M. A. Sonnenschein (Eds), *Mental health, United States, 1996* (pp. 77–91). Washington, DC: U.S. Government Printing Office.

GAINS Center. (1999). *The courage to change: A guide for communities to create integrated services for people with co-occuring disorders in the justice system.* Washington, DC.

Haapasalo, J., & Kankkonen, M. (1997). Self-reported childhood abuse among sex and violent offenders. *Archives of Sexual Behavior, 26*, 421–431.

Harris, G. T., & Rice, M. E. (1999). Mental disordered offenders: what research says about effective services. In: C. Webster & M. Jackson (Eds), *Impulsivity* (pp. 361–393). New York: Guilford Press.

Isaacs-Shockley, M., Cross, T., Bazron, B. J., Dennis, K., & Benjamin, M. (1996). Framework for a culturally competent system of care. In: B. A. Stroul (Ed.), *Children's mental health: Creating systems of care in a changing society* (pp. 23–40). Baltimore: Paul H. Brookes.

Malinosky-Rummell, R., & Hansen, D. J. (1993). Long-term consequences of childhood physical abuse. *Psychological Bulletin, 114*, 68–79.

McMackin, R., Morrissey, C., Newman, E., Erwin, B., & Daly, M. (1998). Perpetrator and victim: Understanding and managing the traumatized young offender. *Corrections Management Quarterly, 2*(1), 35–44.

Morrissey, C. (1997). *Psychotropic medication use rates for youth committed or detained by the Massachusetts Department of Youth Services.* Unpublished raw data.

National Mental Health Association. (1999). *Factsheet: Children with emotional disorders in the juvenile justice system.* Washington, DC.

Pumariega, A., Atkins, D., Rogers, K., Montgomery, L., Nybro, C., Caesar, R., & Millus, D. (1999). Mental health and incarcerated youth. II: Service utilization. *Journal of Child and Family Studies, 8*(2), 205–215.

Rivera, B., & Widom, C. S. (1990). Childhood victimization and violent offending. *Violence and Victims, 5*, 19–35.

Satcher, D. (1999). *Mental health: A report of the Surgeon General.* Washington, DC: U.S. Government Printing Office.

Snyder, H. N. (1997). Juvenile arrests 1996. *Juvenile Justice Bulletin*, (NCJ Publication No. 167578). Washington, DC: US Department of Justice, Office of Juvenile Justice and Delinquency Prevention.

Snyder, H. N., & Sickmund, M. (1999). *Juvenile Offenders and Victims: 1999 National Report.* Washington, DC: Office of Juvenile Justice and Delinquency Prevention.

Sudders, M. (2002). *Department of Mental Health Mortality Report 2000.* The Commonwealth of Massachussetts Executive Office of Health and Human Services Report, October.

Sylva, M. (1999). *DYS public information packet.* Boston, MA: Massachusetts Department of Youth Services.

Teplin, L. A., Abram, K. M., McClelland, G. M., Dulcan, M. K., & Mericle, A. A. (2002). Psychiatric disorders in youth in juvenile detention. *Archives of General Psychiatry, 59*, 1133–1143.

Thomas, W. J., Stubbe, D. E., & Pearson, G. (1999). Race, juvenile justice, and mental health: new dimensions in measuring pervasive bias. *Journal of Criminal Law and Criminology, 89,* 615.

U.S. Public Health Service (2000). *Report of the Surgeon General's Conference on Children's Mental Health: A national action agenda.* Washington, DC.

Vreugdenhil, C., Doreleijers, T. A. H., Vermeiren, R., Wouoters, L. F. J. M., & Den Brink, W. V. (2004). Psychiatric disorders in a representative sample of incarcerated boys in the Netherlands. *Journal of the American Academy of Child and Adolescent Psychiatry, 43*(1), 97–104.

Weeks, R., & Widom, C. S. (1998). Self-reports of early childhood victimization among incarcerated adult male felons. *Journal of Interpersonal Violence, 13,* 346–361.

Widom, C. S. (1989). Does violence beget violence? A critical examination of the literature. *Psychological Bulletin, 106,* 3–28.

Widom, C. S. (1995). Victims of childhood sexual abuse-late criminal consequences. *Research in brief: National Institute of Justice, 3,* 1–8.

E PLURIBUS UNUM: CREATING A MULTI-ORGANIZATIONAL STRUCTURE FOR SERVING ARRESTEES WITH SERIOUS MENTAL ILLNESS

Jonathan C. Clayfield, Albert J. Grudzinskas, Jr., William H. Fisher and Kristen Roy-Bujnowski

ABSTRACT

Large numbers of adults with mental illness detained by police, seen in the courts, and confined in prisons and jails has been a longstanding concern of officials in the mental health and criminal justice systems. Diversion programs represent an important strategy to counteract the criminalization of persons with mental illness. The challenge is to identify and integrate resources in such a way that an organization bridging the police, courts, mental health, substance abuse, homelessness, welfare and entitlements agencies would evolve that would effectively and appropriately serve offenders with mental health issues, keeping them stable in the community and reducing recidivism.

The Organizational Response to Persons with Mental Illness Involved with the Criminal Justice System
Research in Social Problems and Public Policy, Volume 12, 27–49
ISSN: 0196-1152/doi:10.1016/S0196-1152(05)12002-X

INTRODUCTION

The presence of large numbers of adults with severe mental illness detained by police, seen in the courts, and confined in prisons and jails has been a longstanding concern of officials in both the mental health and criminal justice systems. In the criminal justice system, police officials complain that their officers spend too much time dealing with problems surrounding mental illness – a role that they see as tangential to their law enforcement function and not within their purview (Fry & O'Riordan, 2002; Lamb, Weinberger, & DeCuir, 2002; Borum, 2000). Administrators of jails and prisons claim that inmates with mental illness constitute both an expense and a management burden (Human Rights Watch, 2003; Open Society Institute, 1996). These expenses include the cost of psychotropic medications that they are often mandated by law to provide. Additional expenses, which they measure in staff time, arise from the fact that inmates with severe psychiatric illness may sometimes be disruptive, incite disorder among other inmates, be easily victimized or exploited by other inmates, and require disproportionate amounts of staff time for suicide watches and other special attention.

The mental health community has its own set of concerns. A number of years ago a survey was conducted by the National Association of State Mental Health Program Directors (NASMHPD), asking its mental health agency administrator members to prioritize their concerns. In roughly three-quarters of the responses, criminal justice involvement among clients of their agency was cited as one of the top three concerns (Noel Mazade, personal communication). These concerns center on a range of issues, among them the potentially deleterious effects of exposure to incarceration, inadequate and/or interrupted psychiatric treatment, little if any follow-up treatment upon release, and the loss of housing and benefits, in particular Medicaid, following conviction and incarceration. In addition, traditionally poor link-ages have existed between correctional and mental health organizations, with the result that little continuity is seen to exist between psychiatric treatment provided individuals while incarcerated and that available fol-lowing release.

There are probably few actors (i.e., officials, advocates, policy makers, etc.) in either the mental health or criminal justice communities who view the current system for managing arrestees with mental illness in a favorable light. Developing mechanisms and organizational structures that conform to this agreed upon view may be harder, however, because effective strategies for dealing with persons who have mental health, substance abuse, medical, housing and other problems are not simply the foci of one or two systems. The increasingly fragmented human services systems found in many locales has tended to locate responsibility for these issues in an array of ever more specialized public and private agencies. For example, in Worcester, Massachusetts, a person dealing with both mental health issues and substance abuse can be treated by one of several inpatient or outpatient mental health providers (with access depending on health insurance coverage or lack of health insurance), but has to go elsewhere to receive treatment for the substance abuse issue from a substance abuse treatment provider, with little to no treatment coordination or communication between providers. Each of these agencies operates in the context of its own clientele, referral network and funding stream, and is staffed by professionals having specialized interests and expertise. These organizations may share clientele with other agencies that deal with different aspects of their clients' needs, but they may or may not be connected with them if their routine operations do not cause them to interact. Thus, in some cases, such as the one we describe here, actors seeking to develop organizational structures for addressing the problems posed by arrestees with mental illness and substance abuse have sometimes found both the will and, in many cases, even the resources necessary to manage this problem. They may be equally likely to find, however, that these resources are not linked or integrated in a way that can address the needs of this specific multi-problem population. The Surgeon General's report on mental health in America noted that

> Another of the defining trends has been the transformation of the mental illness treatment and mental health services landscapes, including increased reliance on primary health care and other human service providers. Today, the U.S. mental health system is multifaceted and complex, comprising the public and private sectors, general health and specialty mental health providers, and social services, housing, criminal justice, and educational agencies. These agencies do not always function in a coordinated manner. (U.S. Department of Health and Human Services (USHHS), 1999)

The challenge, then, is to identify and integrate these resources in such a way that an organization bridging the police, courts, mental health, substance abuse, homelessness, welfare and entitlements agencies would evolve that would effectively and appropriately serve arrestees with mental health issues. This paper is, in essence, a case study describing such an effort in Worcester, Massachusetts, a medium-sized post-industrial city with a population of approximately 170,000.

CONSTRUCTING A SOCIAL PROBLEM AND
ITS SOLUTION

Solutions to social problems are of necessity grounded in a social and professional construction of the individuals involved, the causal factors that bring about these individuals' situations, and the potential effectiveness of various solutions (Friedson, 1970). The belief structure that derives from this construction is woven together into an overarching definition of the problem that then drives social action, in some cases spurring "moral entrepreneurs" (i.e., aggressive advocates for specific causes) and their communities to devise remedies (Becker, 1963).

In the case of the person with mental illness involved in the criminal justice system, much attention has been focused on persons who also are homeless and likely to have a co-occurring substance abuse disorder as both homelessness and substance abuse among people with mental illnesses are associated with higher arrest and incarceration rates (Council of State Governments, 2002; USDHHS, 2002; GAINS, 2001). These individuals' involvement with the criminal justice system tended to be in the form of arrest for low-level, non-violent offenses, such as trespassing and disorderly conduct. These arrests were seen as arising from three discrete but interrelated issues (Hiday, 1999). Officers feeling the need to remove individuals whose behavior posed problems in the community, but whose presentation was seen as not rising to the level required for hospitalization could use arrest as a means to "clear the call." Related but perhaps differently motivated are the so-called "mercy bookings" of persons viewed by police officers as likely to freeze or starve to death if allowed to remain in their observed circumstances. Finally, individuals may be arrested for the so-called "survival crimes" – stealing a candy bar when hungry or a piece of clothing when cold, or trespassing to find shelter (Wolff, Diamond, & Helminiak, 1997; Hiday, & Wales, 2003).

The current crisis of the "criminalization of the mentally ill" has been recognized in the social science literature since 1972 (Abramson, 1972). It is said to have its origins in the "deinstitutionalization" movement of the 1950s. The phenomenon, however, was first recognized in the 1930s by Penrose who identified the "hydraulic model" of social control. Penrose studied several European countries and discovered that an inverse corollary existed between the size of the prison population and the size of the committed mental health population in each of the countries he studied (Penrose, 1939). This approach locates the cause of criminal behavior in the mentally ill in the inadequacy of mental health services (Torrey et al., 1992).

Deinstitutionalization, or perhaps more properly "dehospitalization," was a complex set of concurrent developments, including legal reforms in the 1950–1960s spurred by the civil rights movement; changing funding streams for the care and treatment of mental illness (including the development of social security disability income (SSDI) in 1956 and Medicaid and Medicare in 1965); and advances in pharmacological treatment (the development of Thorazine). These factors all contributed to relocate persons with serious mental illness from state hospitals to community settings (Grob, 1991). Today, legal advances including the passage of the Americans with Disabilities Act and cases interpreting that act; the evolution of funding streams including the managed care of mental health services delivery; and pharmacological advances including the development of the new generation of so-called "atypical antipsychotic medications" are further changing the face of community-based care (Grudzinskas & Clayfield, 2004). While many have benefited from being moved from long-term hospitals into community-based care, others have not fared so well. This may be reflected in increasing reliance on other (non-mental health) public human services and increased barriers to service access (USHHS, 1999). A well-known outcome, and one well documented over the last 20 years, is homelessness (Interagency Council on the Homeless, 1992). A more recently described outcome, but one that was originally set out 65 years ago (see Penrose, 1939) is the housing of persons with severe mental illness in jails and prisons once long-term treatment beds are no longer available (Council of State Governments, 2002; Center for Court Innovation, 2001). We do not mean to suggest that these complex social problems can be attributed solely to the movement of persons with mental illness from inpatient to outpatient settings, but rather to suggest that some clear relationship likely exists between these phenomena. Additional factors such as mandated sentencing and draconian sentencing policies for drug offenses may also be a factor.

Virtually no one, including the police, views jail as the optimal setting for managing such cases. Social constructions of the problem, its causes and its potential solution vary, but mental health advocates have been sufficiently active and outspoken on the "mentally ill offender" that it is their definition that has gained hegemony. These advocates define this problem as one of mental health system failure (Torrey et al., 1992). The life situations and resulting arrests of the individuals we have described are seen as resulting from failures in the organization and financing of mental health services and, perhaps, standards for hospitalization that are too stringent (Fisher et al., 2002, 2004). The interim report of the President's New Freedom Commission on Mental Health acknowledged that "adults with serious mental illness, one of our Nation's most vulnerable groups, suffer greatly from the fragmentation and failings of the system. The evidence of our failure to help them is most apparent and most glaring on our Nation's streets, under our bridges, and in institutions like nursing homes and jails." (p. 8). The Commission's Final Report concluded that "highly categorical federal funding streams (*silos*) for mental health, housing, substance abuse, and other health and social welfare programs greatly contribute to the fragmentation and failure to comprehensively address the multiple service needs of many people with serious mental illnesses" (New Freedom Commission on Mental Health – Final Report, 2003, p. 31). Given this belief structure, the appropriate remedy is thought to be a restructuring of mental health services and better linkages between the mental health and criminal justice systems. At the "person" level, the social construction of the plight of these individuals locates its cause in the person having become disconnected from the mental health service system. The solution, therefore, is to restore these individuals to their place in the treatment system and to devise appropriate measures to prevent repetition of the factors that brought about the undesirable circumstances.

THE DIVERSION OF POLICE DETAINEES WITH MENTAL ILLNESS

To operationalize this belief system actors within local mental health systems have worked with their counterparts in the criminal justice system to devise and implement an "intercepts" for persons with mental illness identified at various points within the criminal justice process. Some of these take the form of crisis interventions imposed by police in concert with various components of local mental health systems (Borum, Deane, Steadman, & Morrissey, 1998). Others, referred to collectively as "jail diversion" mechanisms, identify and shift arrestees with mental illness from the "criminal justice" track to the "mental health" track, either prior to arrest (i.e., "pre-booking" diversion), after arrest ("post-booking" diversion), or after arraignment ("pre-trial" diversion). (Appelbaum, 2000; Borum, 2000; Dupont & Cochran, 2000; Steadman, Davidson, & Brown, 2001; Watson, Hanrahan, Luchins, & Lurigio, 2001). The potential solution to the "arrestee with mental illness problem" offered by these diversion mechanism approaches gave them national prominence. Assessing their effectiveness was the focus of a multi-site research/demonstration project funded by the Substance and Mental Health Services Administration (SAMHSA) in the mid-1990s (Steadman et al., 1999). But even before the evaluative data from this project became available, jail diversion for arrestees with mental illness gained significant support from a diverse array of organizations, including the Soros Foundation (Soros Foundation Center on Crime, Communities and Culture, 1996) and the American Pubic Health Association (American Public Health Association APHA Resolution, 1999).

POLICING APPROACHES: CRISIS INTERVENTION TEAMS

Concurrent with these efforts in the mental health arena were new developments within police practice. The literature on police management of persons with mental illness, which spans more than four decades (Bittner, 1967; Borum, 2000; Cordner, 2000; Fyfe, 2000), indicates that police have exercised broad discretion in this area, and have preferred "informal" resolutions over "formal" ones such as arrest or emergency hospitalizations (see Lamb et al., (2002) for an overview of this literature). Evolution in practice in this area led to police departments' developing specialty units, often termed "crisis intervention teams" (CITs), for managing situations involving persons with mental health issues (Cochran, Deane, & Borum, 2000).

In most jurisdictions the CIT consists of a cadre of officers who undergo extensive training in the management of persons with mental illness and of other crises involving what police term "emotionally disturbed persons" or EDPs.[1] Police departments employing this approach deploy CIT officers who can be summoned by dispatchers or other officers to manage situations involving EDPs during every shift. The "national model" of the CIT is that developed by the Memphis Tennessee Police Department, a model that has been evaluated extensively (Dupont & Cochran, 2000; Steadman, Deane, Borum, & Morrissey, 2000) and widely replicated, either partially or in full. The Memphis CIT program "...has been designated as a model program by the National Alliance for the Mentally Ill and the American Association of Suicidology....[and] has been replicated in a number of jurisdictions, including Albuquerque, New Mexico; Portland, Oregon; and Seattle" (Steadman et al., 2001).

CIT AND JAIL DIVERSION: WHAT WERE THE OUTCOMES?

CIT and jail diversion mechanisms represent different approaches to deflecting arrestees or potential arrestees with mental illness away from the criminal justice system and into mental health services. What these mechanisms arguably share are results that can best be described as "mixed."

If we define the success of these interventions in terms of the psychiatric status and continuity of system involvement, the Memphis model appears not to have achieved its desired result, despite the effectiveness of the police model itself. During the time this model was being implemented and evaluated, Tennessee's public mental health system was experiencing severe budget cuts, and the state's managed Medicaid system known as "Tenn-Care" was unable to provide its psychiatrically disabled beneficiaries the array of services required for stabilization in the community (Chang et al., 1998). The lesson of the Memphis CIT initiative, which also could be gleaned from scrutinizing any of a number of jail diversion programs, is that these services can be effective only if the mental health system that is to receive and serve those diverted from the criminal justice system has adequate resources to meet these individuals' needs.

MENTAL HEALTH DIVERSION IN WORCESTER: A CASE STUDY IN SYSTEM INTEGRATION

"Much of the research on mental health service systems has been carried out in the context of service demonstration programs that are attempting to deliberately alter interagency relationships in a community care system by making them more coordinated and more responsive to meeting the multiple needs of clients with serious mental disabilities." (Morrissey, Johnsen, & Calloway, 1998, p. 305). This statement reflects the main goal of the Massachusetts Mental Health Diversion & Integration Program (MMH-DIP) in its efforts to work with Massachusetts communities interested in developing integrated treatment alternatives for persons with mental health, substance abuse, and/or homelessness issues who become involved with law enforcement (our population of interest). The MMHDIP, located within the Department of Psychiatry at the University of Massachusetts Medical School in Worcester, began talks with the Worcester Police Department (WPD) in 2001 regarding the potential of developing within WPD a "Memphis-like" CIT program that would also include the establishment of a community coalition, the Worcester Diversion Consortium, to include representatives of the WPD and community care representatives. The Worcester network includes: WPD, the Central Area Office of the Department of Mental Health, the Central Regional Office of the Department of Public

Health Bureau of Substance Abuse Services, UMass Memorial Medical Center, Massachusetts Behavioral Health Partnership (a Medicaid "carveout" managed care agency), Community Health Link (multi-service outpatient provider system), Spectrum Health Systems Inc. and Adcare Hospital (substance abuse treatment programs), Worcester Persons In Peril Shelter (a homeless shelter and detoxification program), the Center for Health and Development (the Worcester District Court Forensic Evaluation Clinic), a Department of Corrections-funded Community Resource Center (a re-entry resource for persons transitioning from prison to the community); the Massachusetts Chapter of NAMI and various consumer members including members of Genesis Club Inc. (a psychosocial clubhouse). WPD has a long history (official police policy first adopted in 1992) of providing officers with discretion to ignore non-serious criminal activity (defined as non-felony and without injury to persons) if they believe the behavior is the result of mental impairment. While they were interested in working with providers of mental health, substance abuse, and shelter/housing services to better deal with a fragile population of persons with severe mental illness whom they encounter with a fairly high frequency, they were not interested in having a specialized group of CIT officers. Significant potential problems included lack of funding, specialization issues with their police unions (e.g., a cadre of officers receiving specialized training would qualify for increased pay), and staffing issues. Therefore, WPD requested that MMHDIP train the entire police department from the chief to the civilian dispatchers (over 440 personnel) as part of their police in-service training. The one and one-half hour crisis intervention and risk management training curriculum developed by the MMHDIP involved recognizing the signs and symptoms of mental illness, de-escalation techniques, and an introduction to treatment resources in the community that officers could access in lieu of arrest. This training was delivered over a period of 10 weeks, 2 trainings per week, starting in November, 2002. This in-service curriculum was developed from a 12-hour crisis intervention and risk management training curriculum created by the UMass Medical School's MMHDIP that is currently part of the Worcester Police Academy new recruit training program.

In addition to the generalist training provided to WPD, MMHDIP continues to convene the Worcester Diversion Consortium (WDC), which meets on a monthly basis to problem-solve around treatment issues related to our population of interest. This consortium has provided a forum, which did not previously exist, for all stakeholders involved to communicate around a number of social service issues. Some examples of issues solved by the WDC include:

- The inappropriateness of having persons with mental illness (PMI) with co-occurring substance abuse disorders detoxify in a WPD jail cell. At one WDC meeting, at the request of the police, the Director of UMass Memorial Medical Center (UMMC) visited the jail cells and determined that they were not an appropriate place for PMI to sober up. As a result, police now transport intoxicated offenders to the UMMC's Emergency Department.
- The discovery of 10 federally funded transitional beds for step down from acute inpatient mental health care. At a WDC meeting, the Director of an emergency department stated the need for transitional beds to serve as a step down for PMI transitioning from acute inpatient care to outpatient services. The Executive Director of an outpatient provider of mental health, substance abuse, and housing services, stated that it had received federal funding for 10 transitional beds, which were only filled to 60% capacity. Subsequently, these beds were filled to capacity.
- The Worcester Public Inebriate Program (PIP) Shelter had difficulty contacting a provider for sub-acute detox bed availability after 5 p.m. At a WDC meeting, the Director of the PIP shelter stated that he had instructed workers at his shelter not to bother calling the provider after 5 p.m. because the provider's telephones were put on voice mail. The Executive Director of the provider stated that he was unaware that this practice was occurring. Subsequently, the provider no longer puts their telephones on voice mail after 5 p.m.

These examples represent just a few of the issues that have been resolved in large part because of the establishment of WDC. Community mental health, substance abuse, housing/shelter, and law enforcement systems have been able to use this forum to problem-solve around communication and integration issues, in order to make the best use of the current services available. Despite their separate funding streams, these organizations have realized that PMI with co-occurring substance abuse and/or homelessness issues have multiple service needs that each organization is ultimately involved with at some point in time.

USING NETWORK ANALYSIS TO INFORM SYSTEM INTEGRATION

In order to gauge the level of interagency coordination among the members of the WDC and identify those organizations in the consortium that needed to be better integrated within the system, MMHDIP employed a Network Analysis Survey (NAS) utilizing Ucinet 6.0 Social Network Analysis software. This type of analysis was performed on a relatively small number of key stakeholders (13) in the Worcester community that are active in meeting the needs of our target population. Other research using network analysis has focused the evaluation of programs that are specifically aimed at altering the structure of an existing service system over time, and for comparing systems (Morrissey et al., 1994, 1998, 2002; Morrissey, Calloway, Johnsen, & Ullman, 1997). For purposes of this case study, we chose to utilize network analysis techniques to paint a picture of how organizations in the WDC were integrated. We identified weak links (those organizations that needed to be better integrated in the network) and determined other stakeholders that needed to be part of the WDC. We then helped to determine better ways to access resources in the community. This information was incorporated into our generalist police training curriculum to inform police of alternative resources in the community and how to access them. We ultimately sought to get WDC member "buy-in" in recognizing the need to better integrate existing services for our target population.

At the time the network analysis was performed, the organizations in WDC were comprised of representatives of the local mental health authority ("DMH"), local public health authority ("DPH"), emergency mental health services ("EMHS"), the local court clinic ("CHD"), a local correctional community resource center ("CRC"), a psychosocial rehabilitation clubhouse-model program ("Genesis"), substance abuse providers ("Adcare" and "Spectrum"), a substance abuse shelter program ("PIP"), the local homeless coalition ("WCH"), a large multi-service provider ("CHL"), a managed Medicaid organization ("MBHP"), and the local police department ("WPD").

A representative from each organization that best knew their organization's operations and working relationships (both formal and informal) with each other member organization in WDC was asked to complete the self-administered survey. Respondents were encouraged to consult other staff in their organizations when completing the survey. The Worcester Network Analysis Survey comprised of six questions (see Table 1). Questions one through five were intended to assess the strengths of relationships between the organizations in the consortium in terms of how they were currently dealing with persons with mental illness who commit crimes, often as a result of their symptoms of mental illness. As mentioned earlier, many of these individuals also suffer with co-occurring issues of substance abuse and homelessness, which further complicates how their service needs are met.

Table 1.   Worcester Network Analysis Survey Questions.

1. To what extent do you, or does other staff in your agency, *interact with staff* from this other provider or agency?
2. To what extent do you, or does other staff in your agency, *send client referrals* to this other provider or agency?
3. To what extent do you, or does other staff in your agency, *receive client referrals from* this other provider or agency?
4. How well *coordinated* are your activities, or those of your agency, with those of this other provider or agency?
5. Does your relationship, or that of your agency, with this other provider or agency include a *formal agreement, such as a contract, memo of understanding, a liaison, and/or a legal mandate*?
6. To promote an *ideal service system,* with which providers or agencies would it be critical for you or your agency to work?

Question six asked each member organization to envision the "ideal" service system and which organizations were critical to work with regard to our target population, even if no such relationship currently existed.

Organizations rated how strong a relationship they had with one another on a Likert-type scale from "0", indicating no relationship at all, to "4", indicating a very strong relationship. This resulted in a closed response matrix for each question (see Table 2). For the network analysis of the organizations in WDC, we chose responses of "3" or higher to indicate a fairly strong working relationship between the organizations (Morrissey et al. (1998) considered tie strengths of 3 or 4 on a 0–4 scale to be a more demanding test when analyzing system change). It has been demonstrated elsewhere in network analysis literature that these procedures (i.e., the demonstration of strong ties between organizations) do yield reliable estimates of interagency relationships (Morrissey et al., 1998; Calloway, Morrissey, & Paulson, 1993; Marsden, 1990).

Utilizing Ucinet 6.0 Social Network Analysis software, a resulting response matrix for each question can be graphed to illustrate the relationships among the organizations. In our analysis of these organizations, we joined or "stacked" the matrices of responses to questions 1 through 5 (see Fig. 1) in order to obtain an overall picture of how the organizations currently related to one another, since all of these questions deal with aspects of their current working relationships. Each circle or node represents an organization in WDC network. The position of these nodes in the network indicates their relational importance in the system relative to one another – the more central the organizations (those depicted as closer to the center of

Table 2. Response Matrix for Each Survey Question.

Question #1. To what extent do you, or does other staff in your agency, *interact with staff* from this other provider or agency?

		Agency A	Agency B	Agency C	*Agency X*→
	Agency A	-	3	0	...
Responses	Agency B	2	-	2	...
	Agency C	1	4	-	...
	Agency X ↓	...	...	...	-

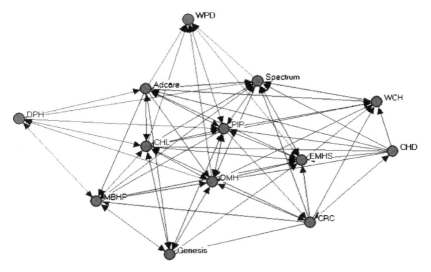

Fig. 1. Joined or "Stacked" Response Matrices (questions 1–5).

the network or system) are, the more richly connected they are in the system, while organizations on the periphery reflect less involvement (fewer connections) in the system. The arrows show communication and resource sharing coming in and/or going out of each organization.

Densities – the number of ties divided by the total number of possible ties, expressed as a percentage – were calculated for each question (1–5), with the average density across all five questions being approximately 34% (see Table 3). The highest density among the five questions was 42.95%,

Table 3.   Densities for Each Survey Question (actual ties divided by possible ties expressed as a percentage).

	Density (%)	
Question 1: *interact with staff*	42.95	
Question 2: *send client referrals*	28.21	
Question 3: *receive client referrals*	23.72	33.98% (average of all 5 questions assessing "current" level of network integration)
Question 4: *coordinated activities*	39.74	
Question 5: *formal agreement*	35.26	
Question 6: *ideal service system*	58.97	

which corresponded to the question (question #1) containing the least restrictive criteria of the five questions assessing the current level of services integration, essentially asking whether staff had any interaction with staff at another organization, regardless of what that interaction involved. The next highest densities (39.74%, question #4; 35.26%, question #5) involved coordinated activities and formal agreements, respectively, among the organizations in WDC. The fact that the densities for these questions were higher than the densities for either "sending" client referrals (28.21%, question #2) or "receiving" client referrals (23.72%, question #3), suggests that, at the time of this analysis, WDC had been working for well over a year in more of a planning phase, rather than an implementation phase, with regard to developing strategies to better integrate services for our target population.

Question 6 of the Worcester NAS asked organizations to envision what the "ideal" service system would look like, and with which organizations it would be critical to work, regardless of whether they currently had a relationship with those particular organizations (see Fig. 2). The density for the resulting matrix to this question was approximately 59% (58.97%), suggesting that further improvement in communications and resource sharing among these organizations was both needed and desired. A separate open-ended question (Question #7) on the Worcester NAS asked what barriers were needed to overcome if their organization was not currently working with these providers. Responses to this question included:

> Barriers are lack of health insurance (once incarcerated benefits are gone), homelessness and, especially, mentioning any involvement in the criminal justice system which

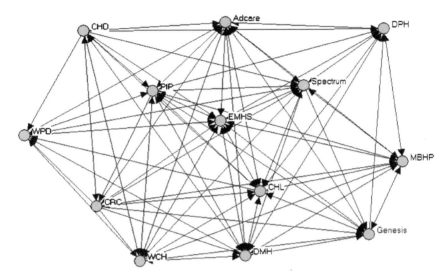

Fig. 2. Response to Question 6 of the Worcester Network Analysis Depicting the "Ideal" Service System.

oftentimes shuts doors. I need to not mention 'from the court.' This affects many of the programs listed – need to talk one-to-one to someone to decrease fears on their part.

The barrier to overcome is to have a better communication system. Each provider or agency can benefit each other some way, whether it is referrals or just general feedback. The population being served should have many outlets for services and right now some clients do fall in this shuffle.

Not being familiar with other organizations or the services they provide. Lack of faith that other organizations actually do what they say. Totally unrelated sets of services.

Restrictive eligibility criteria (e.g., to qualify for Department of Mental Health services).

A blockmodel analysis was performed to provide a clearer look at the current "stacked" network information as well as the "ideal" network information. Blockmodel analysis aggregates "organizations into social positions wherein member organizations have similar relationships within the system. It summarizes the complexity found in a system by focusing on a smaller number of social positions and their interconnections" (Morrissey et al., 1998, p. 310). In other words, it groups together organizations with similar or equivalent roles in the system. As Fig. 3 illustrates, a blockmodel analysis of the current stacked network (questions 1–5) revealed that the court-related services in cluster #2 (consisting of the court clinic ("CHD") and Department of Correction-funded Community Resource Center ("CRC") lack a strong working relationship with any of the other clusters (Cluster #1

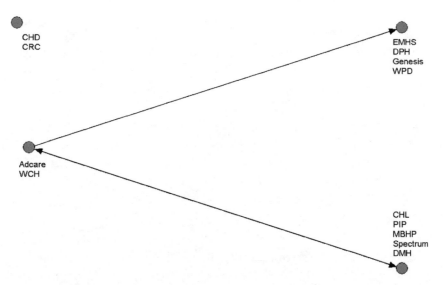

Fig. 3.   Blockmodel Analysis of "Stacked" Response Matrices of Questions 1–5.

containing a substance abuse treatment provider ("Adcare") and an emergency shelter offering sub-acute detoxification services ("PIP"); Cluster #3
consisting of the Department of Mental Health ("DMH"), "CHL" a large
multi-service (mental health, substance abuse, housing) provider, a managed-
Medicaid organization ("MBHP"), Emergency Mental Health Services
("EMHS"), and Genesis (a Department of Mental Health-funded psychosocial rehabilitation clubhouse-model program); and Cluster #4 consisting of
a substance abuse treatment provider ("Spectrum"), a community homelessness coalition ("WCH"), the Department of Public Health's Bureau
of Substance Abuse Services ("DPH"), and the Worcester Police Department ("WPD"). In addition, clusters 3 and 4 also lack strong communication
and resource sharing around our target population.

While the blockmodel analysis results of the "ideal" network has each
cluster connected (see Fig. 4), it is interesting to note that the communication and resource sharing between the court-related services ("CHD" and
"CRC") and the other clusters is only "one-way," with resources and communication flowing out as indicated by the direction of the arrows.
This means that there is no flow of information feeding back to the court-
related services. In order for the court to divert offenders to critical mental
health and other community-based services, "Court staff need to be able to

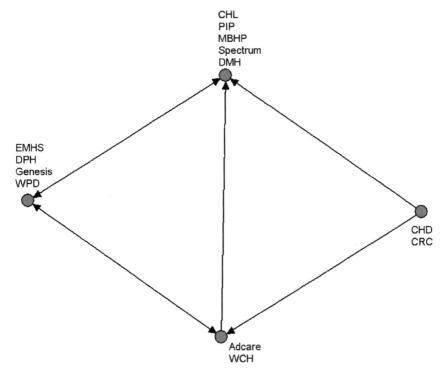

Fig. 4.   Blockmodel Analysis of "Ideal" Service System (question 6).

collaborate with community providers to implement a therapeutic inter-vention that may include medication management, substance abuse treat-ment, housing, job training, and psychosocial rehabilitation" (Watson et al., 2001, p. 477). It is critical for court staff to be able to monitor offender compliance in such therapeutic interventions in order to prevent further criminalization and recidivism.

Presenting these results to our WDC allowed members to visualize how they were currently relating to one another with regard to our target pop-ulation, as well as pinpoint those organizations in the consortium which need to be better integrated. In this case, the network analysis conducted revealed the need for better integration of court-related services within the current system. As demonstrated in the studies of drug treatment court functioning (Hora, 2002), integrating the court and making use of its ther-apeutic jurisprudence provides motivation to offenders to remain treatment compliant. Another factor that supports the need for better integration of the courts involves reentry issues, where inadequate transition planning leads to high recidivism rates of mentally ill offenders (New Freedom Commission on Mental Health – Final Report, 2003). "Such transition planning can only work if justice, mental health, and substance abuse systems have a capacity and a commitment to work with one another" (Osher, Steadman, & Barr, 2003, p. 81).

THE NEED FOR SYSTEMS INTEGRATION

"Each of these programs (organizations) has its special purpose, its unique sources of funding, its particular eligibility requirements, its own mode and standards of operation, and sometimes, its own geographic catchment area. Together, these features define system fragmentation" (Morrissey et al., 1998, p. 297). Recognizing that many of these individuals experiencing a mental health crisis have co-occurring issues of substance abuse and homelessness, any community-based intervention developed needs to identify and address any and all combinations of these issues in a coordinated and integrated fashion. This approach is supported by a growing body of research documenting literature regarding the need to integrate mental health and substance abuse services to effectively treat dually diagnosed individuals effectively (Drake & Mueser, 2000). In addition, the police need to be part of any coordinated system of care that is developed. They are often the first responders to persons in crisis and have the authority to exercise discretion, if appropriate, and seek treatment in lieu of arrest. Lack of funding for the development of community-based services necessary to permit safe transition of persons with mental illness from inpatient treatment to community-based settings has lead to difficulties in accessing services and ensuring a seamless continuum of care. Police, since they are available at all times, have become the de facto access point for service delivery. Only by promoting cultural change in the various stakeholders' cultures can they come to see the need to integrate the criminal justice system into the service delivery continuum.

Individuals with co-occurring disorders challenge both clinicians and the treatment delivery system (Hills, 2000). They most frequently use the costliest services (emergency rooms, inpatient facilities, and intensive outreach services), and often have poor clinical outcomes. The combination of problems increases the severity of their psychiatric symptoms and the likelihood for suicide attempts, violent behaviors, legal problems, medical problems, and periods of homelessness. Studies show that few providers or systems that treat mental illnesses or substance use disorders adequately address the problem of co-occurring disorders. As we recently noted in the New Freedom Commission report, "Only 19% of people who have co-occurring serious mental illnesses and substance dependence disorders are treated for both disorders; 29% are not treated for either problem" (New Freedom Commission on Mental Health – Final Report, 2003, p. 59).

The benefit of integrating treatment modalities and service delivery systems has been identified in a number of different disciplines (Human Rights Watch, 2003). The Surgeon General's Report observed that,

> Effective functioning of the mental health service system requires connections and co-ordination among many sectors (public-private, specialty-general health, health-social welfare, housing, criminal justice, and education). Without coordination, it can readily become organizationally fragmented, creating barriers to access. Adding to the system's complexity is its dependence on many streams of funding, with their sometimes competing incentives. (USHHS, 1999)

Widespread barriers impede effective treatment for people with co-occurring disorders at all levels, including Federal, State, and local governments, and individual treatment agencies (New Freedom Commission on Mental Health – Final Report, 2003).

While diversion programs represent an important strategy to counteract the criminalization of PMI, systems integration between the criminal justice, mental health, and social service systems needs to occur for any diversion effort to be fully realized. The criminal justice system and the police are players at two stages in dealing with mentally ill offenders – pre-booking diversion, where police often have discretion if the crime is of a minor nature to seek treatment for the offender in lieu of arrest, and post-booking (post-arrest) diversion, where judges can consider pre-and post-adjudication diversion options when appropriate. Courts are developing mental health court sessions (Steadman et al., 2001; Watson et al., 2001) to address the complex issues that mentally ill offenders present to the courts, offering a motivational component (therapeutic jurisprudence) proven successful in drug court programs (Hora, 2002) in helping to keep offenders engaged in the treatment services to which they are diverted.

Providing police and court officials with training on how to effectively deal with persons experiencing mental health and/or drug-related crises allows for these criminal justice officials to take appropriate action in accommodating the needs of this vulnerable population. In addition, such training has played a significant role in reducing injuries to police officers and to offenders experiencing such crises (Cochran et al., 2000).

The Worcester NAS that was conducted helped to pinpoint a major issue: poor linkages between the court and community-based services of all kinds. As a result, Worcester court officials, including judges and probation officials, are presently working with members of the WDC to improve upon these linkages.

WDC is also planning to analyze Worcester Police incident reports involving emergency mental health commitment evaluations, and match these reports to the Emergency Mental Health treatment records at the University of Massachusetts Medical Center (which receives all Worcester Police emergency mental health commitment transports) to determine the precipitants and dispositions of these evaluations, and the community service needs of these individuals. In addition, studies are underway at the UMMS Center for Mental Health Services Research to determine the longitudinal involvement of persons with severe mental illness (PSMI) with the criminal justice and social service systems to examine criminal career trajectories (e.g., nature of offending patterns of PSMI vs. non-mentally ill offenders); and, finally, to share the results of these studies with criminal justice officials, health and social service providers, and policy makers to help establish future funding priorities.

NOTES

1. The proliferation of CIT models notwithstanding, their future as the "model of choice" is clouded. Access/adequacy questions, changing views of specialty units within police departments, and police union issues all may serve to dissuade police officials from adopting this model. The access/adequacy issue has to do with the sheer volume of EDP calls taken by some large urban police department. For example, a police official within a large northeastern city told the authors that his department receives an average of one EDP call every 8 min. No CIT could possibly handle this volume of calls in a large urban area. Some police officials also question the wisdom of lodging all the knowledge and training on policing issues in small specialty units, preferring instead to adopt a "generalist" model in which all officers are well trained to handle the situations they will encounter. Finally, most police union contracts stipulate that officers with specialized skills and training, such as CIT members, be paid at a somewhat higher rate. This fact alone may be a strong disincentive for police administrators in cash-strapped municipalities to adopt a CIT model.

ACKNOWLEDGMENTS

Special thanks are due to Denine Northrup, Ph.D., of the Vanderbilt Institute for Public Policy Studies for giving us permission and support to adapt the network analysis survey used in the Nashville Connection Evaluation Study, and special thanks to Matthew Johnsen, Ph.D., at our own Center for Mental Health Services Research for providing technical assistance to us during analysis of the Worcester network survey data.

REFERENCES

American Public Health Association APHA Resolution. (1999). APHA Policy Statement 9929: *Diversion from jail for non-violent arrestees with serious mental illness.* APHA Policy Statements: 1948–present, cumulative. Washington, DC: American Public Health Association. Retrieved on May 7, 2004 at http://www.apha.org/legislative/policy/99policy.pdf

Abramson, M. (1972). The criminalization of mentally disordered behavior: Possible side effects of a new mental health law. *Hospital and Community Psychiatry, 23,* 101–105.

Appelbaum, K. L. (2000). Police encounters with persons with mental illness: Introduction. *Journal of the American Academy of Psychiatry and the Law, 28*(3), 325.

Becker, H. S. (1963). *Outsiders: Studies in the sociology of deviance.* New York: The Free Press.

Bittner, E. (1967). Police discretion in the apprehension of mentally ill persons. *Social Problems, 14,* 278–292.

Borum, R. (2000). Improving high-risk encounters between people with mental illness and the police. *Journal of the American Academy of Psychiatry and the Law, 28*(3), 332–337.

Borum, R., Deane, M. W., Steadman, H. J., & Morrissey, J. (1998). Police perspectives on responding to mentally ill people in crisis: Perceptions of program effectiveness. *Behavioral Sciences and the Law, 16,* 393–405.

Calloway, M., Morrissey, J., & Paulson, R. (1993). Accuracy and reliability of self-reported data in interorganizational networks. *Social Networks, 15,* 377–398.

Center for Court Innovation. (2001). *Rethinking the revolving door: A look at mental illness in the courts.* New York, NY: State of New York Unified Court System.

Chang, C. F., Kiser, L. J., Bailey, J. E., Martins, M., Gibson, W. C., Schaberg, K. A., Mirvis, D. M., & Applegate, W. B. (1998). Tennessee's failed managed care program for mental health and substance abuse services. *Journal of the American Medical Association, 279*(11), 864–869.

Cochran, S., Deane, M. W., & Borum, R. (2000). Improving police response to mentally ill people. *Psychiatric Services, 51*(10), 1315–1316.

Cordner, G. W. (2000). A community policing approach to persons with mental illness. *Journal of the American Academy of Psychiatry and the Law, 28*(3), 326–331.

Council of State Governments. (2002). *Criminal justice/mental health consensus project.* Lexington, KY.

Drake, R. E., & Mueser, K. T. (2000). Psychosocial approaches to dual diagnosis. *Schizophrenia Bulletin, 26*(1), 105–118.

Dupont, R., & Cochran, S. (2000). Police response to mental health emergencies – Barriers to change. *Journal of the American Academy of Psychiatry and the Law, 28*(3), 338–344.

Fisher, W. H., Dickey, B., Norman, S. L. T., Packer, I. K., Grudzinskas, A. J., & Azeni, H. (2002). Medicaid managed mental health care and use of a state's inpatient forensic system. *Psychiatric Services, 53,* 451–457.

Fisher, W. H., Normand, S. L., Dickey, B., Packer, I. K., Grudzinskas, A. J., & Azeni, H. (2004). Managed mental health care's effects on arrest and forensic commitment. *International Journal of Law and Psychiatry, 27*(1), 65–77.

Freidson, E. (1970). *Profession of medicine: A study of the sociology of applied knowledge.* New York: Harper & Row, Publishers, Inc.

Fry, A. J., & O'Riordan, D. P. (2002). Social control agents or front-line careers for people with mental health problems: Police and mental health services in Sydney, Australia. *Health and Social Care in the Community, 10*(4), 277–286.

Fyfe, J. J. (2000). Policing the emotionally disturbed. *Journal of the American Academy of Psychiatry and the Law, 28*(3), 345–347.

Grob, G. N. (1991). *From asylum to community.* Princeton, NJ: Princeton University Press.

Grudzinskas, A. J., & Clayfield, J. C. (2004). Mental health courts and the lessons learned in juvenile court. *Journal of the American Academy of Psychiatry and the Law, 32*, 223–227.

Hiday, V. A. (1999). Mental illness and the criminal justice system. In: A. V. Horwitz & T. L. Scheid (Eds), *A handbook for the study of mental health: Social contexts, theories, and systems* (pp. 508–525). New York: Cambridge University Press.

Hiday, V. A., & Wales, H. W. (2003). Civil commitment and arrests. *Current Opinion in Psychiatry, 16*(5), 575–580.

Hills, H. A. (2000). *Creating effective treatment programs for persons with co-occurring disorders in the justice system.* The GAINS Center, Delmar, NY. Available at: http://www.gains-ctr.com/pdfs/monographs/Creating_Effective_TX_Prog.pdf.

Hora, P. F. (2002). A dozen years of drug treatment courts: Uncovering our theoretical foundation and construction of a mainstream paradigm. *Substance Use & Misuse, 37*(12–13), 1469–1487.

Human Rights Watch. (2003). Ill-equipped: U.S. prisons and offenders with mental illness. Available at http://www.hrw.org/reports/2003/usa1003/

Interagency Council on the Homeless. (1992). *Federal task force on homelessness and severe mental illness: Outcasts on main street.* (ADM) 92-1904. Washington, DC.

Lamb, H. R., Weinberger, L. E., & DeCuir, W. J., Jr. (2002). The police and mental health. *Psychiatric Services, 53*(10), 1266–1271.

Marsden, P. V. (1990). Network data and measurement. In: W. R. Scott & J. Blake (Eds), *Annual Review of Sociology* (pp. 435–463). New York: Annual Reviews.

Morrissey, J. P., Calloway, M. O., Bartko, W. T., Ridgely, M. S., Goldman, H. H., & Paulson, R. I. (1994). Local mental health authorities and service system change: Evidence from the Robert Wood Johnson Program on chronic mental illness. *The Milbank Quarterly, 72*(1), 49–80.

Morrissey, J. P., Calloway, M. O., Johnsen, M. C., & Ullman, M. (1997). Service system performance and integration: A baseline profile of the ACCESS demonstration sites. *Psychiatric Services, 48*(3), 374–380.

Morrissey, J. P., Calloway, M. O., Thakur, N., Cocozza, J., Steadman, H. J., & Dennis, D. (2002). Integration of service systems for homeless persons with serious mental illness through the ACCESS program. *Psychiatric Services, 53*(8), 949–957.

Morrissey, J. P., Johnsen, M. C., & Calloway, M. O. (1998). Methods for system-level evaluations of child mental health service networks. In: M. H. Epstein, K. Kutash & A. Duchnowski (Eds), *Outcomes for children and youth with emotional and behavioral disorders and their families: Programs and evaluation best practices* (pp. 297–327). Austin, TX: PRO-ED, Inc..

National GAINS Center for People with Co-Occurring Disorders in the Justice System. (2001). *The prevalence of co-occurring mental health and substance abuse disorders in jails.* Fact Sheet Series. Delmar, NY: Author.

New Freedom Commission on Mental Health. (2003). *Achieving the promise: Transforming mental health care in America.* Interim Report. DHHS Pub. No. SMA-03-3832. Rockville, MD.

New Freedom Commission on Mental Health. (2003). *Achieving the promise: Transforming mental health care in America.* Final Report. DHHS Pub. No. SMA-03-3832. Rockville, MD.

Open Society Institute. (1996). *Mental illness in U.S. jails: Diverting the nonviolent, low-level offender.* Research Brief. The Center on Crime, Communities and Culture. Occasional Paper Series 1.

Osher, F., Steadman, H. J., & Barr, H. (2003). A best practice approach to community reentry from jails for inmates with co-occurring disorders: The APIC model. *Crime & Delinquency, 49*(1), 79–96.

Penrose, L. S. (1939). Mental disease and crime: Outline of a comparative study of European statistics. *British Journal of Medical Psychology, 18,* 1–15.

Soros Foundation Center on Crime, Communities and Culture. (1996). Research brief. *Mental illness in US jails: Diverting the non-violent, low-level offender.* Occasional Paper Series, No. 1. Author.

Steadman, H. J., Davidson, S., & Brown, C. (2001). Law & psychiatry: Mental health courts: Their promise and unanswered questions. *Psychiatric Services, 52*(4), 457–458.

Steadman, H. J., Deane, M. W., Borum, R., & Morrissey, J. P. (2000). Comparing outcomes of major models of police responses to mental health emergencies. *Psychiatric Services, 51*(5), 645–649.

Steadman, H. J., Deane, M. W., Morrissey, J. P., Westcott, M. L., Salasin, S., & Shapiro, S. (1999). A SAMHSA research initiative assessing the effectiveness of jail diversion programs for mentally ill persons. *Psychiatric Services, 50*(12), 1620–1623.

Steadman, H. J., Stainbrook, K. A., Griffin, P., Draine, J., Dupont, R., & Horey, C. (2001). A specialized crisis response site as a core element of police-based diversion programs. *Psychiatric Services, 52*(2), 219–222.

Torrey, E. F., Steiber, J., Ezekiel, J., Wolfe, S. M., Sharfstein, J., Nobel, J. H., & Flynn, L. M. (1992). *Criminalizing the seriously mentally ill: The abuse of jails as mental hospitals.* Washington, DC: Public Citizen's Health Research Group.

U.S. Department of Health and Human Services. (1999). *Mental health: A report of the surgeon general.* Rockville, MD: U.S. Department of Health and Human Services, Substance Abuse and Mental Health Services Administration, Center for Mental Health Services, National Institutes of Health, National Institute of Mental Health.

U.S. Department of Health and Human Services. (2002, November). *Report to Congress on the prevention and treatment of co-occurring substance abuse disorders and mental disorders.* U.S. Department of Health and Human Services, Substance Abuse and Mental Health Services Administration.

Watson, A., Hanrahan, P., Luchins, D., & Lurigio, A. (2001). Mental health courts and the complex issue of mentally ill offenders. *Psychiatric Services, 52*(4), 477–481.

Wolff, N., Diamond, R. J., & Helminiak, T. W. (1997). A new look at an old issue: People with mental illness and the law enforcement system. *Journal of Mental Health Administration, 24*(2), 152–165.

PART II:
RISK ASSESSMENT – TWO CASES
FROM AROUND THE GLOBE

RAMBO: THE EVALUATION OF AN INTERVENTION PROGRAM FOR UK MENTALLY ABNORMAL YOUNG OFFENDERS

Theodore I. Mutale

ABSTRACT

This chapter offers a prospective and naturalistic study of the impact of a risk-assessment and risk-management program on mentally abnormal young offenders admitted to a medium secure adolescent psychiatric in-patient unit in the United Kingdom (U.K.) because of violent, dangerous or self-harming behaviour. As a result of the risk assessment, there was a reduction in their violent, dangerous or self-harming behaviour that was significantly associated with a reduction in the number of risk factors. About 80% were discharged directly back into the community.

Public concerns over the dangerous behaviour of some people with mental disorder and the introduction of the Care Program Approach in the U.K. has put risk assessment at the centre of public safety debates (HMSO, 1989; Duggan, 1997). Risk assessment instruments and procedures that have been developed in response to these public concerns are applicable mainly to

The Organizational Response to Persons with Mental Illness Involved with the Criminal Justice System
Research in Social Problems and Public Policy, Volume 12, 53–73
Copyright © 2005 by Elsevier Ltd.
ISSN: 0196-1152/doi:10.1016/S0196-1152(05)12003-1

adults. A further important development is that some investigators now regard risk management as an integral part of a comprehensive risk assessment (Heilbrun, 1997) because some do not regard a one-time risk prediction as adequate (Steadman et al., 1993). With very few exceptions (Hoge & Andrews, 1996) risk assessment linked to risk management in adolescents has received less attention.

The aim of this study is to determine the impact of a structured risk management program targeted at risk factors identified by an adolescent risk-assessment checklist in a medium secure unit for mentally disordered young offenders. The study was conducted in a U.K. national medium secure or locked adolescent psychiatric inpatient unit that received patient referrals from England, Wales, Scotland and Northern Ireland.

The risk-assessment checklist, RAMBO (Risk Assessment Multi-system Behavioural Outcomes), is a questionnaire comprising of 63 risk and protective factors (18 static and 45 dynamic) for adolescent antisocial, offending, dangerous and self-harming behaviour derived from the literature (Burgess, Hartman, & McCormack, 1987; Cornell, Peterson, & Richards, 1999; Hoge, Andrews, & Leschied, 1996; Mossman, 1994; Lynam, 1996; Lewandowski & Westman, 1996; Rodham, Hawton, & Evans, 2004). The 63 items reflect risk and protective factors in the three subsystems to which most young people belong to – family, school and peer group. In order to ensure that there was a systematic inquiry of risk and protective factors, operational definitions for most items were included in a manual that accompanies the checklist. Risk factors reflected childhood adversity, substance misuse, current and past antisocial or offending behaviour, current and past self harm, individual characteristics such as empathy and impulse control and psychopathology.

The definition and rating of optimal parenting is similar to that adopted by the Parenting Bonding Instrument (Parker, Tupling, & Brown, 1979). The definition of emotional abuse used in the checklist has previously been described in the literature (Glaser, 1995). The definitions and rating of anxiety, depression, suicidal thoughts, passivity and paranoid ideation were similar to corresponding items in the Brief Psychiatric Rating Scale (Ventura, Lukoff, & Nuechterlein, 1993). The definition and rating of the symptoms of post-traumatic stress disorder was similar to the items in the post-traumatic stress disorder scale of the Trauma Symptom Checklist for Children (Briere, 1996). In all, the checklist was simply a structured and systematic extension of history taking and determined the number of risk factors present and was not meant to be a risk prediction schedule (see the appendix).

DESCRIPTION OF THE STRUCTURED RISK MANAGEMENT PROGRAM

The risk management program was structured in that it comprised of 24 modules that set out the application of specific cognitive behavioural techniques to reducing risk factors or strengthening protective factors. Multidisciplinary staff were trained by the author to deliver each module. Fig. 1 shows the 24 RAMBO modules. These were delivered in a group, individual or family setting. Each module focused on one topic or domain and comprised of 3 to 10 group or individual sessions. Each topic or domain addressed more than one risk or protective factor. Sessions included a scenario and role play, a quiz, a game, a practical project, a creative activity such as music, drawing or poetry, a review of newspaper, magazine or television items and sport.

The aim of each session was to challenge and change cognitive distortions, develop or improve cognitive processes such as problem-solving, attention and concentration, teach pro-social or positive self talk and develop a range of distraction techniques and other coping skills. Sessions included psycho education, relapse prevention and social skills training. More recently, the 'So what' and the 'Ethnicity and Culture' modules have been added. The 'So What' module was aimed at young people who are unable to show empathy and do not care about the adverse impact of their violent or offending behaviour on others or society. A second target group were young people who had gained insight into how their emotional distress arose from childhood abuse and, as a consequence of this insight did not see why other people should not suffer as they did. Such young people are likely to increase their violent behaviour as they gain insight and pose a challenge to services that are aimed at victims rather than perpetrators of violence. The 'So what' modules focused on the benefits and positives for the young person rather than the impact of their behaviour on others or society. The 'Ethnicity and Culture' module explored the impact of difference on attitudes, behaviour and response to interventions through the use of role-play, games and quizzes.

The author ran the initial modules as a training exercise in a group setting with three multidisciplinary co-facilitators: a teacher, an occupational therapist and a nurse. The RAMBO manual was the basis for the training exercise and all subsequent RAMBO sessions. Other professionals who have been trained by participating as co-facilitators include psychiatrists, assistant psychologists, social workers and nursing assistants. Thus, a multidisciplinary team now delivers the program.

The RAMBO group program was supported by individual sessions and family work that targeted risk factors identified by the RAMBO risk checklist. Family meetings focused on family strengths, problem solving, relapse prevention, psycho education and positive reframing of the young person's behaviour to reduce hostility and criticism. Furthermore, multidisciplinary meetings with professionals from the young person's home area were used to promote a multiagency or multidisciplinary approach – accommodation or a placement was organised; an appointment with the local mental health service prior to discharge was arranged; social services sorted out benefits or initiated a leaving care package if the young person had been accommodated by social services, and a social worker or a youth justice officer arranged a college placement or work experience in conjunction with the unit's education service.

METHODOLOGY

Consecutive young people admitted under the author's care between 1998 and 2003 had a RAMBO risk checklist interview done shortly after admission by the author or an associate specialist (doctor) who had had appropriate training. Twenty consecutive admissions were seen by both the author and the unit associate specialist, and agreement was good for all 63-checklist items with kappa values ranging from 0.78 to 0.97. Given the gravity of crimes committed and the severity of high-risk behaviour present, it was thought to be unethical or inappropriate to exclude young people from a potentially effective intervention. Thus, there were no exclusion criteria and young people acted as their own controls in that their RAMBO risk scores in the week leading up to admission were compared to RAMBO risk scores in the last week of admission. Furthermore, behavioural data detailing incidents 4 weeks prior to admission and throughout the inpatient period was made available to the author by the psychology department who monitored the young offenders independent of the RAMBO program.

The RAMBO group program was run once a week by a multidisciplinary staff team who had attended a RAMBO training program arranged by the author. The ward shut down for 90 min while all nursing staff on duty, occupational therapists, the ward teacher, the ward social worker, assistant psychologists, psychiatrists and all the young people participated in the group session. The session began with the whole group together. The use of techniques learned in the previous session was reviewed and the topic for the session introduced. Staff members were divided into three or four subgroups and each subgroup took on three or four young people. Most of the work was done in the subgroups. The larger group reconvened for the last 15 min of the session and each of the subgroups reported back on work done.

An element of competition was introduced in that subgroups competed to determine who had come up with the best responses. One of the young people was chosen to take the role of a judge and, with the help of a staff member, asked to decide which subgroup had the most appropriate answers, the most relevant role play, the best poem or song, the most striking drawing, the most effective self talk, the most effective distraction techniques and the most effective coping strategies. This element of competition encouraged young people to work hard at their tasks. At the beginning of each session one young person was chosen to act as the 'Enforcer'. The 'Enforcer' gave each young person marks out of a maximum of 10 at the end of the session depending on how well the young person had kept to the group rules. The group rules had been set by the young people and were reviewed regularly. Young people who scored 10 points on 3 consecutive occasions were awarded a series of special certificates – bronze, silver, gold and platinum. Three platinum certificates entitled a young person to a mystery prize chosen by group leaders. Other roles included the Host and Hostess whose job was to organise refreshments at the end of each session. Every fourth session was a recreational slot and the young people and staff organised a fun event such as music, a video film, a sporting event or a meal.

As previously indicated, Fig. 1 shows the structured RAMBO risk management modules. The modules targeted both the socio-maturational risk factors for offending behaviour and psychopathology such as command hallucinations, flashbacks and paranoid ideas or delusions. Each module addressed several RAMBO risk or protective factors. The types of modules chosen depended on the nature of risk and protective factors identified by the RAMBO risk checklist and decision tree. The modules were delivered in group, individual and family sessions.

The offence or offending behaviour cycle module enabled the construction of a behaviour cycle or formulation for each young person. All RAMBO individual, group and family interventions were based on the cycle or formulation created by the multidisciplinary unit team at a weekly formulation meeting. The behaviour cycle or formulation formed a vital link between the RAMBO risk assessment interview and other unit interventions such as education, the workshop, sport and community outings, ;and enabled the integration and targeting of all interventions in the unit. Additionally, the

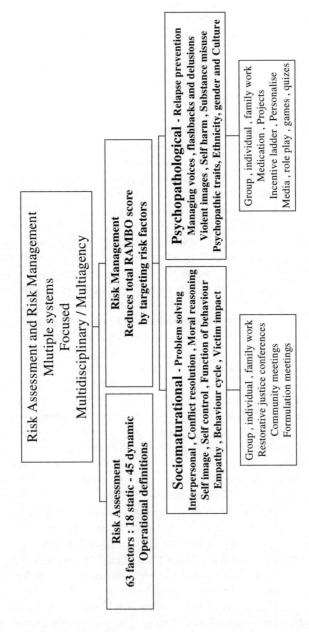

Fig. 1. RAMBO Program.

RAMBO restorative justice module helped unit staff address antisocial or dangerous behaviour on the unit by organising restorative justice conferences at which the perpetrator was brought face to face with the victim (other young person or staff member), confronted with the consequences of their behaviour and asked to make a written apology or some other appropriate reparation. At each conference, one staff member spoke on behalf of the unit staff. Another staff member sought the views of young people and reported these at the conference. Other staff members' role played the victim's parents, a member of the community, a policeman or any other community figure depending on the nature of the antisocial or dangerous behaviour perpetrated. This element of role-play intensified the impact of the conference by putting the young person's behaviour on the unit within a wider social context.[1]

The young offenders in this present study were divided into two categories: incarcerated young people referred from the youth justice system (youth prisons and youth justice section of secure or locked social services children's homes) and young offenders referred from the National Health Service inpatient units (public hospitals) or social services locked units (welfare section of secure children's homes) who had been diverted away from the youth justice system (diverted group). All young people had a mental disorder whose nature or severity warranted a mental health section and were deemed by referring professionals to have required treatment within a secure or locked setting because of their dangerous or high-risk behaviour. Those referred from the youth justice system were on mental health sections for mentally disordered offenders while those referred from health or social services were on civil mental health sections. Young people could appeal against their section by asking a Mental Health Tribunal (panel made up of a doctor, social worker and a lawyer) to review their case. The Mental Health Review Tribunal is appointed by the secretary of State for Health, is independent of the hospital and can discharge a mental health section (The Stationery Office Ltd, 2001). In this present study all young people appealed against their mental health section for several reasons. Young people transferred from prison wanted to leave once their date of release passed. Young people on civil orders were encouraged by advocacy services that visit the unit to seek transfer to an open unit. Finally, some young people had no insight into their illness and wanted to be discharged home. All appeals were supported by our unit social workers that made sure the young person had appointed a solicitor to represent them at the appeal hearing.

Several outcome measures were determined. First, the total number of risk factors as determined by the RAMBO checklist at the admission interview was compared with the total number at the discharge interview. The admission interview was conducted in the first week of admission and the discharge interview in the last week of admission. Second, the frequency of violence against others or property and suicidal behaviour or self harm in the 4 weeks before admission was compared to that in the last 4 weeks of admission. In the majority of cases the last 4 weeks were spent on a 4-week pre-discharge trial leave in an open community setting. The last 4 weeks were, therefore, an early trial of transition into the community. Behaviour on the unit was recorded by the Behaviour-Monitoring System run by the psychology service independent of the RAMBO program team.

RESULTS

The mean number (or average number per young person) of risk factors (or mean RAMBO score) at discharge was significantly lower than the mean number of risk factors at admission (12.2 (5.1) vs. 34.3 (5.2), $t = 17.9$, $p = 0.0000$). The reduction in the mean RAMBO score was due to the reduction in the number of dynamic risk factors.

The number of young people who had perpetrated dangerous behaviour (violence, sexually abusive behaviour or arson) during the last 4 weeks of admission was significantly lower than during the 4-week pre-admission period (2/34 vs. 26/34, Fisher's exact test, $p < 0.0000$). The number of young people who had self harmed or attempted suicide during the last 4 weeks of admission was significantly lower than during the 4-week pre-admission period (2/34 vs. 25/34, Fisher's exact test, $p < 0.0000$). Thus, admission to the program had reduced the need for young people to be transferred to adult or other medium secure setting.

Tables 1–3 compare the characteristics of the two categories of mentally disordered young offenders – adjudicated youth referred from the criminal or youth justice system, and young people on civil mental health orders because of dangerous behaviour referred from health or social services. The χ^2 test or Fisher's exact test was used as appropriate for differences in frequency between youth referred from the youth justice system (adjudicated) and those diverted from criminal disposal and referred by health or social services. The Student's t-test was used for differences in means.

Table 1 shows socio-demographic and clinical characteristics while Table 2 shows ICD 10 research diagnostic categories (World Health

Table 1. Socio-demographic and Clinical Characteristics of Adjudicated Youth (Youth Justice) Compared with Mentally Ill Young Offenders Diverted from the Criminal Justice System and on Civil Mental Health Treatment Orders.

	Mental Health Section			
	Criminal disposal ($N = 21$)	Civil orders ($N = 13$)	All ($N = 34$)	Statistics
Characteristics				
Male	14 (66.7)	5 (38.5)	19 (55.9)	
Female	7 (33.3)	8 (61.5)	15 (44.1)	
Mean age (years)	16.2 (1.3)	15.9 (1.0)	16.1 (1.2)	
Residence at admission				
Prison	11 (52.4)	0 (0.0)	11 (32.4)	$\chi^2 = 10.1, p = 0.002$
Secure hospital	5 (23.8)	6 (46.2)	11 (32.4)	
Secure SSD unit	2 (9.5)	0 (0.0)	2 (5.9)	
Open hospital	3 (14.3)	6 (46.2)	9 (26.5)	
Home	0 (0.0)	1 (7.6)	1 (2.9)	
Reason for referral				
Risk to others	21 (100.0)	9 (75.0)	30 (88.2)	
Risk to self	14 (73.7)	11 (91.7)	25 (80.7)	
Compulsory Treatment Order				
Civil	0 (0.0)	12 (92.3)	12 (35.3)	$\chi^2 = 30.0, p = 0.000$
Criminal	21 (100.0)	0 (0.0)	21 (61.8)	$\chi^2 = 34.0, p = 0.000$
Informal	0 (0.0)	1 (7.7)	1 (2.9)	
Family history				
Mental illness	9 (42.9)	10 (76.9)	19 (55.9)	$\chi^2 = 5.8, p = 0.030$
Substance misuse	7 (33.3)	6 (46.2)	13 (38.2)	
Crime	7 (33.3)	6 (46.2)	13 (38.2)	
Placements				
>2 placements	19 (90.5)	12 (92.3)	31 (91.2)	
mean number	5.5 (3.7)	2.3 (1.9)	4.3 (3.5)	$t = 2.74, p = 0.0052$
Mean length of stay (months)	14.6 (9.7)	21.4 (11.0)	17.29 (9.7)	$t = 1.78, p = 0.0424$
Childhood abuse				
Sexual	9 (42.9)	11 (84.6)	20 (58.8)	$\chi^2 = 5.8, p = 0.030$
Physical	10 (47.6)	5 (38.5)	15 (44.1)	
Emotional	17 (81.0)	11 (84.6)	28 (82.4)	
All types	18 (85.7)	12 (92.3)	30 (88.2)	
Substance misuse	17 (79.0)	5 (33.3)	22 (64.7)	$\chi^2 = 6.4, p = 0.025$

Table 2. ICD 10 Diagnostic Categories, Medication and RAMBO Variables.

	Mental Health Section			
	Criminal disposal ($N = 21$)	Civil order ($N = 13$)	All ($N = 34$)	Statistics
Medication in 4 week pre-admission period				
Mood stabilisers	11 (52.4)	11(84.6)	22 (64.7)	$\chi^2 = 5.8, p = 0.024$
Anxiolytics	3 (14.3)	5 (38.5)	8 (23.5)	$\chi^2 = 5.2, p = 0.017$
Antipsychotics	18 (85.7)	11 (84.6)	29 (85.3)	
Antidepressants	10 (47.6)	11 (84.6)	21 (61.8)	$\chi^2 = 6.4, p = 0.025$
Antimascurinics	7 (33.3)	5 (38.5)	12 (35.3)	
Final ICD 10 diagnostic categories				
Schizophrenia	8 (38.1)	2 (15.4)	10 (29.4)	
Bipolar disorder	3 (14.3)	0 (0.0)	3 (8.8)	
Depression	3 (14.3)	3 (23.1)	6 (17.7)	
PTSD	4 (19.1)	6 (46.2)	10 (29.4)	$\chi^2 = 5.3, p = 0.015$
Personality disorder	2 (9.5)	2 (15.4)	4 (11.8)	
OCD	1 (4.8)	0 (0.0)	1 (2.9)	
RAMBO program				
Yes	19 (90.5)	11 (84.6)	30 (88.2)	
No	2 (9.5)	2 (15.4)	4 (11.8)	

Organisation, 1998), medication prescribed in the 4 weeks leading up to admission. The poly pharmacotherapy reflects the difficulties referring youth justice, health and social service units had in stopping or reducing dangerous, violent or suicidal behaviour. Table 3 shows elements of the transition into the community program. The medium secure service had a pre-discharge unit that offered more intensive rehabilitation for young people with more severely impaired psychosocial functioning. In the U.K. any person previously on a mental health section must have a multidisciplinary pre-discharge meeting before discharge. At the meeting follow-up arrangements are made and a care coordinator identified to organise services for the patient post discharge. The psychiatrist responsible for a person on a mental health section is termed the responsible medical officer or RMO. Anyone previously on a mental health section must be followed up by a community RMO when discharged. The care coordinator and the RMO usually belong to a community mental health team and ensure that the patient is given

Table 3. Elements of Pre-discharge Program Aimed at Achieving Successful Resettlement or Discharge Back into the Community.

| | Mental Health Section | | | |
	Criminal disposal ($N = 21$)	Civil order ($N = 13$)	All ($N = 34$)	Statistics
Characteristics				
Pre-discharge unit				
Yes	9 (42.9)	10 (76.9)	19 (55.9)	$\chi^2 = 6.4, p = 0.025$
External college	5 (23.8)	6 (46.2)	11 (32.4)	
Work experience	6 (28.6)	3 (23.1)	9 (26.5)	
Escorted community leave				
Hospital grounds	19 (90.5)	13 (100.0)	32 (94.1)	
Local town area	17 (81.0)	12 (84.6)	29 (85.3)	
Unescorted community leave				
Hospital grounds	14 (66.7)	11 (84.6)	25 (73.5)	
Local town area	13 (61.9)	11 (84.6)	24 (70.6)	
Home leave				
Escorted	17 (81.0)	10 (76.9)	27 (79.4)	
Unescorted	16 (76.2)	9 (69.2)	25 (73.5)	
Face-to-face contact with parents during inpatient stay				
Mother	19 (90.5)	13 (100.0)	32 (94.1)	
Father	12 (57.1)	7 (53.9)	19 (55.9)	
Discharge arrangements				
4-week trial leave	16 (76.2)	11 (92.3)	27 (79.4)	
Discharged to new area	8 (38.1)	7 (53.9)	15 (44.1)	
New RMO	7 (33.3)	8 (61.5)	15 (44.1)	
117 meeting home or new area	19 (90.5)	12 (92.3)	31 (91.2)	
Home or new area				
College	8 (38.1)	8 (61.5)	16 (47.1)	
Day hospital/centre	8 (38.1)	8 (61.5)	16 (47.1)	
Discharge destination				
Community based group home	9 (42.9)	7 (53.8)	16 (47.1)	
Home	9 (42.9)	3 (23.1)	12 (35.3)	
Open hospital	2 (9.5)	1 (7.7)	3 (8.8)	
Secure unit	2 (9.5)	1 (7.7)	3 (8.8)	

appropriate care following discharge. A day centre is usually run by social services while a day hospital is usually run by a community mental health team. Both provide daytime activities. The majority of young offenders were discharged back into the community because they no longer required care in a secure or locked unit.

Table 4 shows the frequency of static risk factors. The χ^2 test or Fisher's exact test was used for differences in frequency between incarcerated youth referred from the youth justice system and youth on civil mental health orders. Young people referred from the youth justice system had a significantly higher proportion of youth who had a current or past conviction for violent, sexualised or fire-setting behaviour (18/21 vs. 0/13, Fisher's exact test, $p < 0.0000$) and three or more previous convictions (16/21 vs. 2/13, Fisher's exact test, $p < 0.0000$). Despite having no current charges or past convictions young people on civil mental health orders had a history of

Table 4.   Frequency of Static Risk Factors. Figures refer to numbers (%) of people.

Risk factor	Number of youth ($N = 34$)
Recorded or reported physical, sexual or emotional abuse	29 (85.3)
Left both birth parents, aged < 16 years	27 (79.4)
Past history of self harm	25 (73.5)
First onset of non-violent antisocial behaviour, aged < 11 years old	22 (64.7)
Birth parents separated when < 11 years old	20 (58.8)
Family history of domestic violence	20 (58.8)
Family history of psychiatric disorder	19 (55.9)
History of self mutilation	19 (55.9)
History of antisocial behaviour but has no convictions	19 (55.9)
Past or current conviction for violent, sexualised or fire-setting behaviour	18 (52.9)
Three or more previous convictions	18 (52.9)
Other self harm, excluding overdoses or self laceration	18 (52.9)
History of overdose	18 (52.9)
First onset of problem violent, sexualised Fire-setting behaviour, aged < 11 years	16 (47.1)
No convictions but history of violent, sexualised or fire-setting behaviour	13 (38.2)
Use of a weapon in past one year	13 (38.2)
Family history of drug or alcohol abuse	13 (38.2)
Family history of criminality	12 (35.3)

serious antisocial behaviour (11/13 or 84.6%) or violent, sexualised or fire-setting behaviour (10/13 or 76.9%).

Table 5 shows the frequency of dynamic risk factors. The χ^2 test or Fisher's exact test was used for differences in frequency between incarcerated youth referred from the youth justice system and youth on civil mental health orders. Young people referred from the youth justice system had a significantly higher proportion of youth who had reported substance misuse in the past year (17/21 vs. 4/13, Fisher's exact test, $p<0.01$), not attending school or college (15/21 vs. 3/13, Fisher's exact test, $p<0.0000$) and exclusively antisocial activities or interests (15/21 vs. 3/13, Fisher's exact test, $p<0.01$). Young people on civil mental health orders had a significantly higher proportion of youth who communicated by self harming (12/13 vs. 13/21, Fisher's exact test, $p<0.01$), had suicidal ideation (13/13 vs. 12/21, Fisher's exact test, $p<0.01$), used self harm to relieve tension (11/13 vs. 10/21, Fisher's exact test, $p<0.05$), believed no one cared (9/13 vs. 6/21, $\chi^2 = 5.4$, df $= 1$, $p<0.02$) and were full of guilt or self blame (9/13 vs. 4/21, Fisher's exact test, $p<0.01$).

Of the 21 incarcerated youth referred from the youth justice system, 18 (85.7%) had been convicted of violence to another person (Actual bodily harm (ABH), Grievous bodily harm (GBH) or assault), 8 (38.1%) of theft, 7 (33.3%) of burglary, 6 (28.6%) of robbery, 3 (14.3%) of sexual offences, 2 of taking cars without the owners consent, 1 (4.8%) of manslaughter and 1 (4.8%) of kidnap and false imprisonment. The median number of current offences was 3.

DISCUSSION

The findings of this study have several important implications for the assessment and management of mentally disordered young offenders presenting with dangerous, suicidal or persistent offending behaviour. First, the finding that the structured risk management program was associated with a significant reduction in the total number of RAMBO risk checklist items and, in turn, a subsequent reduction in the frequency of actual violent or suicidal behaviour suggested that the targeting of and development of program interventions with items identified by the RAMBO risk checklist was effective.

Second, the finding that at least 80% of young people in this present study were discharged from a medium secure setting directly into the community suggests that a program that linked risk assessment to risk management had

Table 5.   Frequency of Dynamic Risk Factors. Figures refer to numbers
(%) of people.

Risk Factor	Number of Youth ($N = 34$)
Does not confide in family members	31 (91.2)
Hopeless and/or helpless	30 (88.2)
No response to past interventions	30 (88.2)
Anxiety symptoms	30 (88.2)
Impulsive behaviour	30 (88.2)
Hostility to professionals	30 (88.2)
Poor parental care or over involvement	29 (85.3)
Resides in an institution	29 (85.3)
Two or more placements in the past one year	29 (85.3)
Does not confide in at least one peer	28 (82.4)
Denial/lack of remorse or empathy	28 (82.4)
Depression	27 (79.4)
Communicates by self harming	25 (73.5)
Suicidal ideation	25 (73.5)
Has no confidant	25 (73.5)
Seeking revenge or making threats	23 (67.7)
Paranoid delusions or ideas	23 (67.7)
Post-traumatic stress disorder symptoms	21 (61.8)
Uses self harm to relieve tension	21 (61.8)
Does not want help or is not co-operative	21 (61.8)
Substance misuse in the past one year	21 (61.8)
History of absconding in the past one year	20 (58.8)
Command hallucinations	20 (58.8)
Violence to person in last one month	20 (58.8)
Not attending school or college	18 (52.9)
Friend or close associates have history of criminality	18 (52.9)
Exclusively antisocial activities or interests	18 (52.9)
Does not confide in any professional	18 (52.9)
Damage to property in the past one month	17 (50.0)
Bullies others	16 (47.1)
Victim of bullying	15 (44.1)
Believes no one cares	15 (44.1)
Full of guilt or self blame	13 (38.2)
Desired intervention not available or possible	10 (29.4)
Reports being let down by a confidant	10 (29.4)
Passivity or controlled by external agent	8 (23.5)
School phobia	7 (20.6)
Fantasies of sexual or physical violence	7 (20.6)
Special educational needs	7 (20.6)
Identifies with fictional or real-life criminal	4 (11.8)

Table 5. (*Continued*)

Risk Factor	Number of Youth ($N = 34$)
Sadistic behaviour in the past one year	4 (11.8)
Sexually abusive behaviour in the past one month	3 (8.8)
Arson or fire setting in past one month	3 (8.8)
Prefers or seeks custody or prison	3 (8.8)
Cruelty to animal in the past one month	0 (0.0)

made a significant contribution to a successful and safe transition from hospital into the community of very disturbed, dangerous or suicidal young people. This finding is further supported by the fact that the majority of youth had been admitted from secure settings where violent or self-harming behaviour had remained major problems despite the secure setting and the prescription of medication such as antipsychotics, mood stabilisers, antidepressants and anxiolytics. Indeed, 88% of young people in this study had not responded to previous pharmacological and psychological interventions. Thus, the significant reduction in the frequency of dangerous behaviours reported in this present study was unlikely to be mainly due to the medium secure setting or the prescription of medication. The innovative addition of the RAMBO program is likely to have made a significant contribution to the stopping or reduction of violent or self-harming behaviour.

Third, the risk factors identified by the RAMBO risk checklist, such as childhood abuse, inadequate parenting, poor impulse control, substance misuse and school non-attendance, were consistent with the findings of previous reports (Burgess et al., 1987; Cornell et al., 1999; Hoge et al., 1996; Mossman, 1994; Lynam, 1996; Lewandowski & Westman, 1996). Furthermore, the RAMBO checklist demonstrated that confiding behaviour and optimal parenting were important protective factors in line with previous reports (Mak, 1994; Rutter & Quinton, 1984; Lewandowski & Westman, 1996; Bigam & Power, 1998). The importance of early detection and intervention was highlighted by the finding that in nearly two-thirds of young people in this study, the reported first onset of antisocial behaviour was before the age of 11 years. A striking finding was that hopelessness or helplessness was reported by at least 88% of young people in this study.

It is important to note that both youth referred from the youth justice system and individuals on civil mental health orders had very high proportions of young people with a history of antisocial, sexualised, violent or fire-setting behaviour and that the main difference was that young people on civil mental health orders had a significantly higher proportion of youth who had suicidal ideation, used self harm to communicate or relieve tension and were full of guilt or self blame. This finding suggested that young offenders with self-harming behaviour, suicidal ideation or a capacity for guilt were significantly more likely to be diverted away from the youth justice system even if they had violent, sexualised or fire-setting behaviour.

Fourth, despite some significant differences in characteristics, the young people referred from the youth justice system (adjudicated) had similar positive outcomes to those diverted from the criminal or youth justice system. This finding suggests that a youth justice disposal may be inappropriate and is consistent with a recent report that found that 10% of young offenders in prison had serious mental health problems (Office for National Statistics, 2000). In the U.K. services or structures for diverting mentally disordered young offenders from the criminal justice system are poorly developed. The situation is exacerbated by the paucity of community and inpatient adolescent forensic services. This study suggested that public health policies and the provision of mental health services in the U.K. have to be reviewed to ensure that all mentally abnormal young offenders are offered treatment rather than prison, whether or not suicidal ideation or capacity for guilt is present.

This study has some limitations. It was not possible to determine how well the program prevented re-offending behaviour because the likelihood of committing non-violent crimes such as burglary, theft or robbery was greatly reduced in the secure setting. The young people were used as their own control group because it did not seem ethical to deny one group of disturbed, violent or suicidal youth effective treatment. A possible solution to this problem would be to compare RAMBO with another intervention such as multisystemic therapy (MST) (Borduin & Henggeler, 1990). One difficulty with this suggestion is that MST has exclusion criteria that would result in the majority of young people in this present study being ineligible, particularly those with a serious psychotic or mental illness. The study was conducted in a secure setting and gains made in such a setting do not necessarily transfer into the community. However, it is important to note that the majority of the young people spent the last 4 weeks of their admission in the community on trial leave. Therefore, the incidence of dangerous, re-offending or suicidal behaviour in the last 4 weeks of admission reflected actual behaviour in a community setting. A 2-year followup study is in progress.

NOTES

1. Full details of the structured RAMBO risk management program and training are available from the author.

REFERENCES

Bigam, F. H., & Power, K. G. (1998). The quality of perceived parenting experienced by a group of incarcerated Scottish young offenders and its relation to psychological distress. *Journal of Adolescence, 25*, 161–176.

Borduin, C. M., & Henggeler, S. W. (1990). Multisystemic approach to the treatment of serious delinquent behaviour. In: R. J. Mcmahon & DeV. Peters (Eds), *Behaviour disorders of adolescence.* New York: Plenum Press.

Briere, J. (1996). *Trauma symptom checklist for children.* FL, USA: Odessa.

Burgess, A. W., Hartman, C. R., & McCormack, A. (1987). Abuser to abuser: Antecedents of socially deviant behaviours. *American Journal of Psychiatry, 144*, 1431–1436.

Cornell, D. G., Peterson, C. S., & Richards, H. (1999). Anger as a predictor of aggression among incarcerated adolescents. *Journal of Consulting Clinical Psychology, 67*, 108–115.

Duggan, C. (1997). Assessing risk in the mentally disordered. *British Journal of Psychiatry, 17*(suppl. 37), 1–39.

Glaser, D. (1995). Emotionally abusive experiences. In: P. Reder & C. Lucy (Eds), *Assessment of parenting: Psychiatric and physiological contributions* (pp. 73–86).

Heilbrun, K. (1997). Prediction versus management models relevant to risk assessment: The importance of the legal decision-making context. *Law and Human Behaviour, 21*, 347–359.

HMSO. (1989). *Caring for people in the community for the next decade and beyond.* London: HMSO.

Hoge, R., & Andrews, D. (1996). *The Youth Level of Service/Case Management Inventory (YLS/CM).* Ottawa, Ontario: Carleton University.

Hoge, R. D., Andrews, D. A., & Leschied, L. W. (1996). An investigation of risk and protective factors in a sample of youthful offenders. *Journal of Clinical psychology and Psychiatry, 37*, 419–424.

Lewandowski, L. M., & Westman, A. S. (1996). Social support desired vs. received by high school students in or not in a delinquency prevention program. *Psychological Reports, 78*, 111–114.

Lynam, D. R. (1996). Early identification of chronic offenders: Who is a fledgling psychopath? *Psychological Bulletin, 120*, 209–234.

Mak, A. S. (1994). Parental neglect and overprotection risk factors in delinquency. *Australian Journal of Psychiatry, 62*, 107–111.

Mossman, D. (1994). Assessing prediction of violence: Being accurate about accuracy. *British Journal of Consulting Clinical Psychology, 62*, 783–792.

Office for National Statistics. (2000). *Psychiatric morbidity among young offenders in England and Wales.* London: Office for National Statistics.

Parker, G., Tupling, H., & Brown, L. B. (1979). A parental bonding instrument. *British Journal of Medical Psychology, 52*, 1–10.

Rodham, K., Hawton, K., & Evans, E. (2004). Reasons for deliberate self harm: Comparison of self poisoners and self cutters in a community sample of adolescents. *Journal of the American Academy of Child and Adolescent Psychiatry, 43*, 80–87.

Rutter, M., & Quinton, D. (1984). Parental psychiatric disorder: Effects on children. *Psychological Medicine, 14*, 853–880.

Steadman, H. J., Monahan, J., Robbins, P. C., Appelbaum, P., Grisso, T., Klassen, D., Mulvey, E. P., & Roth, L. (1993). From dangerousness to risk assessment: Implications for appropriate research strategies. In: S. Hodgins (Ed.), *Mental disorder and crime* (pp. 39–62). London: Sage.

The Stationery Office Ltd. (2001). *The Mental Health Act 1983 (Remedial) Order.* London: HMSO.

Ventura, J., Lukoff, D., Nuechterlein, K., Liberman, R. P., & Green, M. F. (1993). Brief Psychiatric Rating Scale (BPRS) expanded version (4.0): Scales, anchor points, and administration manual. *International Journal of Methods in Psychiatric Research, 3*, 227–243.

World Health Organisation. (1998). *ICD-10 classification of mental and behavioural disorders: Diagnostic criteria for research.* Geneva, Switzerland: WHO.

APPENDIX

RAMBO
   RISK ASSESSMENT, MULTISYSTEM, BEHAVIOURAL OUTCOMES
INDEX SCORE☐ ☐   **REPEAT SCORE** ☐ ☐
Date   **Date**

The RAMBO checklist was developed to assist professionals to manage young people aged 12 to 21 years at risk of developing or repeating: **Dangerous behaviour** – violence arson and sexualised behaviour; **Suicidal behaviour** – self-harm, self-poisoning, self-mutilation; hanging or any form of self-injury; **Repeated or persistent offending** – non-violent offences such as theft, burglary and stealing cars. The checklist provides a structured and systematic way of determining the number of risk factors or the absence of protective factors. Items identified as present should be targeted for intervention using the RAMBO risk management program. A reduction in the number of dynamic items present when the assessment is repeated is the aim of the risk management program.

The scales are completed in two stages. Firstly, the semi-structured interview detailed in the instruction manual is carried out and items endorsed if appropriate. Secondly, available health, social services, school and other official records are scrutinised for relevant items. Further items are endorsed or modified provided this is in line with the operational definition and exclusion criteria.

Items are scored 0, 1 or 2 as set out in the manual. A total score is calculated by adding the scores for all the 63 items.

> RAMBO scales cannot be completed without the semi-structured interview detailed in the instruction manual. The manual can be obtained from the author: Dr T.I.R. MUTALE, Consultant Psychiatrist, South London and Maudsley NHS Trust, Adolescent Medium Secure Unit, Bethlem Royal Hospital, Monks Orchard Road, Beckenham, Kent, BR3 3BX, UK.

☐ 0 ☐ 1 SF1
Previous or current conviction for
Physical or sexual violence or arson

☐ 0 ☐ 1 SF2
Previous history of self-harm on two or more occasions

☐ 0 ☐ 1 SF3
At least 3 or more cautions or convictions

☐ 0 ☐ 1 SF4
No convictions or cautions for dangerous behaviour, but has a history of violent, sexual or fire-setting behaviour

☐ 0 ☐ 1 SF5
Overdose

☐ 0 ☐ 1 SF6
No convictions or cautions for non-dangerous offences, but has a history of non-dangerous antisocial behaviour

☐ 0 ☐ 1 SF7
Onset < 11 years of problem violent, sexual or fire-setting behaviour

☐ 0 ☐ 1 SF8
Self-mutilation

☐ 0 ☐ 1 SF9
Onset < 11 of non-violent antisocial behaviour

☐ 0 ☐ 1 ☐ 2 SF10
Recorded or self-reported physical, sexual or emotional abuse

☐ 0 ☐ 1 SF11
Family history of domestic violence

☐ 0 ☐ 1 SF12
Birth parents separated, < 16 years

☐ 0 ☐ 1 SF13
Family history of criminality

☐ 0 ☐ 1 SF14
Use of a weapon in the past one year

☐ 0 ☐ 1 SF15

Other selfharm, excluding overdoses and self-laceration e.g. ligatures, hanging, guns, jumping off buildings

☐ 0 ☐ 1 SF16

Left both birth parents, < 16 years

☐0 ☐1 SF17
Family history of depression or other psychiatric illness

☐0 ☐1 SF18
Family history of drug or alcohol abuse

☐0 ☐1 DF1
Denial or lack of remorse

☐0 ☐1 DF2
Full of guilt or self-blame

☐0 ☐1 DF3
Hostility to professionals

☐0 ☐1 DF4
Depression

☐0 ☐1 DF5
Friend or associate has a history of criminality or problems with police

☐0 ☐1 DF6
Does not want help or is not co-operative

☐0 ☐1 DF7
Hopeless and helpless

☐0 ☐1 DF8
History of absconding or running away

☐0 ☐1 DF9
Communicates via self-harm

☐0 ☐1 DF10
No response to previous interventions

☐0 ☐1 DF11
Anxiety symptoms

☐0 ☐1 DF12
Seeking revenge, making threats or very angry

☐0 ☐1 DF13
Post-traumatic stress disorder symptoms

☐0 ☐1 ☐2 DF14
Command hallucinations

☐0 ☐1 ☐2 DF15
Paranoid ideation or delusion

☐0 ☐1 DF16
Believes self-harm relieves tension

☐0 ☐1 ☐2 DF17
Believes controlled by external agent

☐0 ☐1 DF18
Low parental care or high parental control – affectionless control

☐0 ☐1 DF19
Does not confide in family members

☐0 ☐1 DF20
Has no confidant

☐0 ☐1 DF21
Not attending school or truanting or pretending to go to school

☐0 ☐1 DF22
Refusing to go to school and has somatic symptoms on school days but often well on weekends – school phobia

☐0 ☐1 ☐2 DF23
Fantasies of sexual or physical violence or fascination with violent films, videos or computer games

☐0 ☐1 DF24
Suicidal ideation

☐0 ☐1 **DF25**
Exclusively antisocial or criminal interests

☐0 ☐1 **DF27**
Victim of bullying

☐0 ☐1 **DF29**
Identifies with fictional or real-life criminal figures or criminal gangs

☐0 ☐1 **DF31**
Desired intervention not available or possible

☐0 ☐1 **DF33**
Does not confide in peers

☐0 ☐1 **DF35**
Has special educational needs or input

☐0 ☐1 **DF37**
Resides in an institution

☐0 ☐1 **DF39**
Destruction of property in previous one month

☐0 ☐1 **DF41**
Arson in previous one month

☐0 ☐1 **DF43**
Cruelty to animals in previous one month

☐0 ☐1 ☐2 **DF45**
Alcohol and drug misuse

☐0 ☐1 **DF26**
Bullies others

☐0 ☐1 **DF28**
Impulsive

☐0 ☐1 **DF30**
Believes no one wants, loves or cares for him or her

☐0 ☐1 **DF32**
Does not confide in any professional

☐0 ☐1 **DF34**
Reports being let down by a confidant

☐0 ☐1 **DF36**
Has had >2 placements

☐0 ☐1 ☐2 **DF38**
Prefers or seeks custodial or secure care or prison

☐0 ☐1 **DF40**
Sexually abusive behaviour in previous one month

☐0 ☐1 **DF42**
Physical violence directed at other people in previous one month

☐0 ☐1 ☐2 **DF44**
Sadistic behaviour in previous one year

TOTAL SCORE
☐☐

RISK ASSESSMENT AND VIOLENT RECIDIVISM RISK MANAGEMENT IN CONVICTS FROM ARGENTINA

Jorge O. Folino

ABSTRACT

In the year 2001, the Risk Assessment Pilot Program was implemented in Argentina with the aims of establishing a systematic manner of assessing risk for violent recidivism in conditional release candidates and contributing to the design of intervention programs that help to reduce the criminal recidivism rate. The baseline assessment showed that conditional release candidates had a high-risk profile: 72.5% had severe or moderate substance abuse problems; 62% had failed in previous probation, conditional release or discharge from a mental institution; 85% had serious or moderate employment problems before incarceration. Individuals who were substance abusers were incorporated to the Drug Abuse Biochemical Control Program. Variations in dynamic factors were assessed with conditionally released subjects. Some encouraging results were obtained through December 2003 and their initial impact on judicial and penitentiary institutions is already seen.

The Organizational Response to Persons with Mental Illness Involved with the Criminal Justice System
Research in Social Problems and Public Policy, Volume 12, 75–88
ISSN: 0196-1152/doi:10.1016/S0196-1152(05)12004-3

INTRODUCTION

In the province of Buenos Aires, Argentina, convicts released before they serve their sentence are kept under the jurisdiction of the Court of Penal Execution belonging to the Judicial Power – institution in charge of granting release – and under the assistance/supervision of the *Patronato de Liberados Bonaerenses* (Province of Buenos Aires Parole Board) belonging to the Executive Power. On the other hand, mentally ill patients who committed crimes and were acquitted by reason of insanity are also kept under the jurisdiction of the Court of Penal Execution, and when there is no family members responsible for them, their assistance and guardianship are given by the *Curaduría Oficial de Alienados* (Public Guardianship Office), also belonging to the Judicial Power. Public health institutions depending upon the Executive Power render different health services to both, ex convicts and offenders acquitted by reason of insanity.

Traditionally, different social and assistance supervision functions were precarious. Some of the most relevant obstacles within the system were the miscommunication and the uncoordinated work among institutions, the inadequate systematisation, the idiosyncratic assessment methods, the absence of outcomes assessment and the lack of resources. To sum up, the assessment and supervision system of conditionally released subjects were characterised by the services' deficiency and the lack of scientific studies. In the year 2001, the Risk Assessment Pilot Program (RAPP) was implemented with the aims of establishing a systematic manner of assessing risk for violent recidivism in conditional release candidates and contributing to the design of intervention programs that help to reduce the criminal recidivism rate. The aim of this study is to describe the program's technical aspects and its legal context, as well as the results of the baseline assessment, the dynamic risk factor assessment and the Drug Abuse Biochemical Control Program.

THE PROGRAM AND BASELINE ASSESSMENT RESULTS

Since the 1990s, efforts around the world have been made to develop several programs with the aim of finding a systematic way of assessing and managing risk for violence. According to our review of the literature, some of the most relevant international programs include the Penetanguishene Mental Health Centre Program, in Ontario, Canada (Rice & Harris, 1993; Harris,

Rice, & Cormier, 1993a; Quinsey, Harris, Rice, & Cormier, 1999; Webster, Harris, Rice, Cormier, & Quinsey, 1994; Quinsey, Rice, & Harris, 1995; Rice, Harris, & Cormier, 1992; Harris & Rice, 1990); the MacArthur Risk Assessment Study in three different U.S. cities (Monahan et al., 2000; Appelbaum, Robbins, & Monahan, 2000; Steadman et al., 2000; Monahan & Steadman, 1994; Steadman et al., 1998; Steadman et al., 1994); the collaborative program between the Mental Health, Law, and Policy Institute at Simon Fraser University; the British Columbia Forensic Psychiatric Services Commission in Canada (Webster, Eaves, Douglas, & Hart, 1997; Ross, Hart, & Webster, 1998; Kropp & Hart, 1997); and several of the projects carried out at the Centre for Violence Prevention, Karolinska Institute in Sweden (Tengstrom, 2001; Hare, Clark, Grann, & Thornton, 2000; Tengstrom, Grann, Langstrom, & Kullgren, 2000; Grann, Langstrom, Tengstrom, & Kullgren, 1999).

There was no program of such characteristics in Argentina until the year 2001. The Argentinean RAPP, which was implemented that year, consists of a case detection phase, which starts when a convict or an acquitted offender by reason of insanity requests the Court of Penal Execution some form of early release or discharge from an institution (Folino, Marengo, Marchiano, & Ascazibar, 2004c). If the offender is eligible for conditional release for having served the amount of time in prison required by law, the case is referred to the program director for the assessment to be conducted. Information from several sources is collected for the baseline assessment: criminal records review, previous expert psychiatric assessment, psychological and social studies; reports from the Penitentiary Service (often including behavioural assessment, adjustment to the institutional environment and multidisciplinary assessments); psychiatric interviews; interviews with family members or friends or acquaintances willing to receive the candidate in community. Finally, the program director produces a report addressed to the Judge of Penal Execution consisting of an expert opinion about the risk and management suggestions. The judge decides whether to release the subject or not and the decision is informed to the program director in order to establish the assessment plan for the follow-up period in community.

The baseline assessment includes the following instruments, among other measures: the *The Hare Psychopathy Checklist – Revised* (PCL-R) (Hare, 1990) (Spanish version designed for research purposes by the author of the present study), which is an instrument suitable for assessing the degree to which the subject coincides with the construct of psychopathy; the HCR-20, a guide for assessing violence risk factors concerning three dimensions corresponding to the historical, clinical and risk management factors

(Webster, 1997) (Folino, 2003); the *Violence Risk Appraisal Guide* (VRAG) (Quinsey et al., 1999), which is an actuarial violence risk assessment tool; and some items of the *Iterative Classification Tree* (ICT) (Steadman et al., 2000).[1]

From September 2001 to December 2003, 129 male candidates released from the Court of Penal Execution of the Judicial Department of La Plata were assessed as part of the program. This jurisdiction covers a population of about one million inhabitants, and the head operates in La Plata, the capital city of the Province of Buenos Aires. The sample of this study included the 129 male candidates for conditional release. Although women and cases from other departments were also assessed, they were excluded in order to avoid altering the representativeness of the geographical area.

Eighty-six per cent were convicted offenders and 14% were offenders acquitted by reason of insanity. In 80% of the cases, the index offence was some type of robbery; in 10%, homicide or attempted homicide; in 8%, physical injuries or threats and, in 2%, sexual abuse. Eighty-two per cent had committed a crime against an unknown victim. At the time of the evaluation, the study population had served 992 days on average in prison. (S.D. = 342; range = 27–1,785). Fifty-eight per cent of the convicts were granted conditional release 563 days on average before completing the term. (S.D. = 293.7; range = 7–1,653). Eight per cent of the convicts were released when the term was actually completed. By the end of this study, the rest of the convicts were still serving their sentences in prison. Thirty-three per cent of the offenders acquitted by reason of insanity were discharged from a psychiatric hospital.

Table 1 depicts the descriptive statistics for risk measures. Total PCL-R score has a maximum of 40; the mean measure obtained in the present study was 20, which corresponds to a moderate severity level and it is close to the 22.1 informed by Hare in his descriptive statistics of 5,408 cases collected from several samples of male offenders (Hare, 2003). The HCR-20 mean score does not allow to estimate the population's risk for violence in a direct manner since a final conclusion of risk does not rely exclusively on total score. On the contrary, the final conclusion is reached through the qualitative examination of the identified risk factors. Therefore, the reported mean score should only be considered for research and sample comparison purposes. On the other hand, the VRAG mean score reflects the sample's degree of risk, taking the population that was used for developing the instrument as reference; according to its value of 10.78, the sample could be placed, on average, in the sixth place out of nine risk categories, being the first, the lowest risk category and the ninth, the highest one.

Table 1. Risk Measures ($N = 129$).

Risk Measure	Minimum	Maximum	Mean	Standard Deviation
Adjusted total PCL-R	1	37	20.02	8.26
HCR-20	2	34	19.59	7.22
VRAG	−13	37	10.78	10.41

Note: PCL-R = The Hare Psychopathy Checklist – Revised (Hare, 1990); HCR-20 = HCR-20 Assessing Risk for Violence (Webster, 1997; Folino, 2003); VRAG = Violence Risk Appraisal Guide (Quinsey et al., 1999).

Some risk factors were highly represented in the population, for which they deserve special mention: 30% of the participants had been arrested before the age of 16; 25% had been in a penal institution for youth offenders; 62% had failed in previous probation, conditional release, or discharge from a mental institution; 28% had a close relative in prison; and 85% had serious or moderate employment problems before incarceration. The mean years of formal education was 6.95 years (S.D. = 2.84).

Additionally, a high prevalence of drug abuse disorders was registered. A history of severe drug abuse problems was registered by 50% of the population, and 22.5% had a history of moderate drug abuse problems, according to the H5 item of the HCR-20 (Webster et al., 1997). The percentage of cases with a DMS IV Axis I major mental disorder diagnosis (APA, 1994) was 5.4%. In all, 55.2% had substance abuse disorder; 4% had other diagnoses and 35.7% had no diagnosis. The percentage of cases with DMS IV Axis II antisocial personality disorder diagnosis (APA, 1994) was 54%. Forty-six per cent of the released subjects were incorporated to the Drug Abuse Biochemical Control Program.

Ecological risk factors were assessed with the 5 HCR-20 *R* factors (factors 1, 2, 3 and 5 could not be assessed in all cases): 22% ($n = 116$) had a moderate/severe deficit in feasibility of reinsertion plans; 77% ($n = 116$) were at risk of moderate/severe exposure to destabilisers; 71% ($n = 116$) had moderate/severe deficit of personal support; 74% ($n = 129$) showed moderate/severe probability of non-compliance with therapeutic or rehabilitation regimes; 68% ($n = 116$) were at risk of moderate socio-economic stress, and 12%, of high socio-economic stress.

DRUG ABUSE BIOCHEMICAL CONTROL PROGRAM

As part of the RAPP, the Drug Abuse Biochemical Control Program (DABCP) was designed. Its goal is to help reduce substance abuse recidivism and criminal behaviour associated with substance abuse in those people who, having been institutionalised to serve criminal sentences or security measures and having been drug abusers, are granted conditional release (Folino, Arado, Ferrari, & Marengo, 2002).

The program was established as a pilot project and therefore, it was necessary to select the target population. The program candidate was defined as the person institutionalised for having committed a crime (either punished with a prison term or under a security measure); with a substance abuse history; potentially suitable for conditional release or discharge from a mental health institution; and participating in the RAPP program assessment. DABCP is not the only intervention factor; this is incorporated to other conditions suggested to the Judge by the RAPP Program director (for example, specific outpatient treatment carried out in private or official institutions for drug abusers) and to other conditions independently stipulated by the Judge (e.g., to establish a permanent residence, make efforts to obtain a job, etc).

It is acknowledged that drug monitoring intervention together with other treatment and supervision conditions interfere with the estimate of the relationship of the baseline assessment factors and the outcomes. However, it was considered unethical not to include the monitoring in a program as the one described, given its level of systematisation and preventive aims. It was considered that the ethical aspect had to be given priority and that analytical difficulties arisen from the lack of a control group of abusers without monitoring could be solved in the future by means of a retrospective study about a similar population. On the other hand, it is hoped that monitoring should become a routine intervention in local settings; therefore, it would be part of the general conditions, which all released subjects would be exposed to in the future.

The chemical toxicological analysis was carried out in several matrixes: urine, pericranial hair, axillary and pubic hair. The diversity of samples allows drug detection in different periods. That is to say, substance intake within 72 h can be detected in urine, while previous consumptions can be tested in hair, since the power of concentration and protection of substances in hair is independent of time. Biological samples were obtained observing the conditions stipulated by law. Therefore, each of the subjects gave their informed consent and the samples were protected in accordance with the law. The latest isolation and detection methodologies were used for chemical testing (Gas Chromatography and Mass Spectrometry). Metabolite/drug concentration testing was conducted considering cut-off measures, and negative and positive controls. Possible passive or external contamination was also evaluated.

DRUG ABUSE BIOCHEMICAL CONTROL PROGRAM: RESULTS

Preliminary results of DABCP were obtained with the cases collected from June 2002 to September 2003 (Folino et al., 2005a). The sample included 30 subjects with a substance abuse history, who had been consecutively granted conditional release during the study period. During the baseline assessment, these subjects obtained a peculiar risk profile, with measures significantly higher than the released subjects who were not part of DABCP, both with VRAG (Quinsey et al., 1999) and HCR-20 (Webster et al., 1997; Folino, 2003).

When analysing violent recidivism (with either redetention or rehospitalisation) among the subjects who were part of DABCP and those who were not, the results indicated that the recidivistic rate had been 20% and 4%, respectively, with an odd ratio of 6.00 (IC 1.392;−25.858). This result suggested that being part of the program was associated with a higher risk for recidivism.

The apparent causal relationship resulting from that association was considered counterintuitive. On the other hand, by the deadline of the study, for various reasons, the biochemical testing had only been conducted in part of the sample. For these reasons, it was hypothesised that the highest recidivism risk was due to the severe risk factors presented by those who were part of the program. In other words, it was hypothesised that the group's high risk was manifested despite the program's protecting effects. When comparing the violent recidivism between those subjects who were actually monitored, and those who were part of the program but had not been monitored, it was found that 31.6% of the latter had been redetained or rehospitalised, while none of the former had recidivated. These results supported the hypothesis that the biochemical drug testing monitoring had indeed functioned as a protecting factor. The authors acknowledge that, alternatively, this effect could be due to the fact that those who comply with the chemical control are those who have less probability of recidivating since they are more willing to collaborate and fulfil the release conditions. This should be studied in future research.

The study also showed the importance that risk management mechanisms have – such as the DABCP – in allowing a gradual and supervised process of social reinsertion. On the one hand, the program's availability allowed some substance abusers to have access to a less restrictive option that was previously denied. On the other, the study showed that judges, far from applying a dichotomic concept of risk, make decisions based on the risk assessment conclusions and the availability of management programs or other protecting factors. Finally, the authors rejected the idea that this monitoring system should be enough to prevent drug abuse and its associated criminality. On the contrary, they considered the system as a further tool among those that should be employed in a prevention-based model.

DYNAMIC FACTORS ASSESSMENT IN COMMUNITY

The Risk Assessment Pilot Program includes community assessment, carried out by collaborators from the social work area, with the aim of assessing variations in dynamic risk factors. Based on those assessments, interviews are arranged between the released subject and the Judge and/or the psychiatrist, and adjustments in preventive measures may be implemented. This intervention regarding released offenders is novel because so far such a system had not been coordinated from the Judicial Power. As regards to the offenders acquitted by reason of insanity, in the past, there were social assistance services provided by the Public Guardianship Office, but the services lacked a systematic manner of assessment or outcomes review.

The community assessment phase was designed and evaluated with an interview consisting of three sections. The semi-structured part of the interview was made of the 5 *R* items from the *HCR-20 Versión en Español, Adaptada y Comentada* (Spanish version of the HCR-20) (Folino, 2003). The structured part was developed from a 15-item questionnaire designed to explore the following factors: substance abuse; personal finances; work status; intimate partner relationship; the subject's satisfaction regarding his accommodation and official agencies; and criminal tendency. The Zung's scale (Zung, 1967), as a mood measure, and the *Global Assessment of Relational Functioning Scale* (GARFS scale) (American Psychiatric Association, 1994), as a relational functioning measure were included. Finally, a 0–3-point scale was designed in order to describe the evaluator's conclusion regarding the reliability of the collected information. Violent behaviour measures during community phase were obtained with the *Overt Aggression Scale* (Yudofsky, Silver, Jackson, Endicott, & Willams, 1986) (Spanish version translated for research purposes by the author of the present study).

DYNAMIC FACTORS ASSESSMENT: RESULTS

The dynamic risk factors research was motivated not only by the fact that their influence could be a triggering factor for violence, but also by the fact that they constitute the main target of preventive action. For this research, interviews were carried out with 25 subjects before their release (Folino et al., 2005b)

The results showed important deficiencies in the socio-economic area: released subjects had a very high unemployment rate. On the other hand, most of them informed that they received financial support from relatives or friends. Since most of the conditionally released subjects and their families belong to social sectors with severe structural deficiencies, in general, this financial support can hardly cover the subject's basic needs. Besides, in most cases, this financial help does not compensate for the possible tendency towards erratic and disorganised lifestyle brought about by unemployment.

We also examined the released subject's satisfaction regarding the official agencies with which he is obliged by law. Although almost half of the participants found the relationship with the agency belonging to the Executive Power not very useful or useless, the Judicial Power agency (which is usually regarded as part of the repressive system by the accused or convicts) was perceived as helpful in most cases. Another remarkable finding was that 28% of the participants acknowledged that, sometimes during the community supervision period they felt the temptation to reoffend. The authors believe that it would be naïve and technically erroneous to ignore the distortion caused by defensiveness, but they argue that these data show that, on occasions, an honest and mature interaction between released subjects and Judicial Power agents with the shared aim of maintaining a socially acceptable conduct is possible.

The assessment of the HCR-20 Risk Management Factors (Webster et al., 1997; Folino, 2003) was carried out with an excellent reliability and valuable findings were obtained. The intraclass correlation coefficient for the $R1$, $R2$, $R3$, $R4$ and $R5$ factors were 0.87, 0.96, 0.71, 0.94 and 0.87, respectively, and for the total R score was 0.97 (Folino et al., 2004a). Between the baseline and the community assessment, unfavourable variations were detected on items "Plans lack feasibility" and "Stress". Such variation could be an indication of deterioration of the environmental conditions, or that the data obtained during the baseline assessment was optimistically biased regarding those conditions. An optimistic bias as regards future adjustment and job-finding capacity is usually found among conditional release candidates and some relatives.

After elaborating indices differentiating baseline and community assessment measures, it was found that "Exposure to destabilisers" was the factor significantly associated with recidivism. "Exposure to destabilisers" refers to the situation in which the person is exposed to dangerous conditions, which the subject is vulnerable to and which may trigger violent episodes; more details and examples can be found in Webster et al. (1997). Although "dangerous conditions" are particular to each individual, they usually include the presence of weapons, easy access to substances of abuse and circumstances facilitating their use, lack of professional support and contact with subjects involved in organised crime.

Lastly, aggressive recidivism was also significantly associated with the variables related to drug abuse and the depressive mood indicator. Both factors form a pathological spectrum upon which important preventive action can be carried out from the mental health area.

FINAL COMMENTS

As it occurred in most Latin-American countries, the difficulties in resources administration, among other obstacles, resulted in the deficiencies in the assessment, supervision and assistance services for those who committed a crime in Argentina (Folino, Sarmiento, & Montero Vazquez, 2000). For the last years, some of these aspects have become the main target of several studies (Folino et al., 2001, 2002, 2003, 2004a; Folino & Marchiano, 2002), some improvements have been achieved and further progress is expected.

Here, technical results are encouraging. The impact of RAPP seems to be very important, as it is indicated by the numerous questions received by the program from different provinces in Argentina.[2] There is no doubt that contributions as those described above are only part of the several actions needed to reduce criminal recidivism. A significant decrease of criminal rates could only be achieved with a concomitant reduction of risk factors encouraging the initiation of the criminal career, a task clearly ascribable to primary prevention. Among the local efforts concurring with primary prevention, since the year 2000, the Judicial System of the Province of Buenos Aires have developed some programs that are part of the *Plan Marco de Política Criminal* (Framework Plan of Criminal Politics) (Dameno, 2003). These programs tend to encourage conflict solution in a non-violent manner (e.g., by training primary and secondary school students and neighbourhood leaders) and the creation of community networks to prevent crime, by linking decentralised official agencies with Non-Governmental Organisations.

On the other hand, the work carried out by the RAPP may be described as "secondary prevention", in the sense that the program intervenes once violence has taken place. The program intervenes during the execution of the punishment phase, conducting risk assessment and suggesting management techniques that tend to prevent conditionally released subjects from recidivating. This kind of secondary prevention may be very valuable because it enables to detect subjects with the highest risk for violence and concentrate the limited resources on them. On the other hand, the characteristics of this population make it necessary to plan specific preventive measures quite different from those generally taken in primary prevention. Therefore, the technical model can be directed towards the design and choice of other suitable interventions allowing an ideal investment – result balance. The model also promotes the planning of policies based on evidence. To sum up, with a preventive paradigm as a theoretical framework, a technical model called *Modelo Compuesto* (Composite Model) (Folino, 2004) is currently being applied in Argentina. This model is characterised by the fact that it pragmatically incorporates different types of information about risk and protecting factors arising from actuarial, anamnestic, clinical and risk management studies and from the availability of intervention programs.

NOTES

1. More details, preliminary reports of baseline description and other related information can be consulted in other sources (Folino et al., 2004a, 2004c; Folino & Marchiano, 2002; Folino, Astorga, Sifuentes, Ranze, & Tenaglia, 2003a) and on the web page www.mpba.gov.ar.

2. Also, it is notorious the great number of professionals from different Latin-American countries who turn to the training provided by the Master's Course in Forensic Psychiatry at the National University of La Plata, which works together with the RAPP Program, belonging to the General Prosecutor's Office of the Supreme Court of the Province of Buenos Aires.

ACKNOWLEDGEMENTS

I thank Ms. Mariela G. Merlo and Ms. María Julia Raverta for translating this chapter.

REFERENCES

American Psychiatric Association (APA). (1994). *DSM IV – diagnostic and statistical manual of mental disorders* (4th ed.). Washington, DC: American Psychiatric Association.

Appelbaum, P. S., Robbins, P. C., & Monahan, J. (2000). Violence and delusions: Data from the MacArthur violence risk assessment study. *American Journal of Psychiatry*, *157*(4), 566–572.

Dameno, O. (2003). *El ideal de vivir en paz – Plan marco de política criminal.* [*The ideal of living in peace – Framework plan of criminal politics.*] La Plata: Procuración General de la Suprema Corte de Justicia de la Provincia de Buenos Aires. [General Attorney's office of the supreme court of justice of the province of Buenos Aires.]

Folino, J.O. (2003). *Evaluación de Riesgo de Violencia -HCR - 20- Versión en español, adaptada y comentada.* [Spanish versión of the HCR-20.] La Plata: Interfase Forense.

Folino, J. O. (2004). Nuevos paradigmas en la evaluación de peligrosidad. [New paradigms in the assessment of dangerousness.]. *La Ley; Año, XX*(29), 871–876.

Folino, J. O., Arado, M., Ferrari, L., & Marengo, M. (2002). *Manejo del riesgo de recidiva violenta y el abuso de sustancias [Violent recidivism risk management and substance abuse].* Documento de Trabajo No 7 [Official Report No 7]. La Plata: Programa de Evaluación de Riesgo de Liberados. Procuración General de la Suprema Corte de Justicia de la Provincia de Buenos Aires. [Risk Assessment Pilot Program. General Attorney's Office of the Supreme Court of Justice of the Province of Buenos Aires.]

Folino, J. O., Arado, M. G., Ferrari, L. A., & Marengo, M. (2005a). Prevención de recidiva delictual en abusadores de sustancias. [Criminal recidivism prevention in substance abusers.] *Revista Médica de La Plata.* (in press).

Folino, J. O., Astorga, C., Sifuentes, M., Ranze, S., & Tenaglia, D. (2003a). Confiabilidad de la Hare Psyhcopathy Checklist – Revised En Población Psiquiátrico Forense Argentina. [Reliability of the Hare psychopathy checklist – revised in Argentinean forensic psychiatric population.]. *Alcmeon – Revista Argentina de Clínica Neuropsiquiátrica Año XIV, 11*(1), 5–11.

Folino, J. O., Avalos, A., Urrutia, M. I., Crivos, M., Teves, L., & Marchioni, M. (2001). Investigación Interprovincial sobre Homicidios -Buenos Aires y Córdoba [Interprovincial research about homicides (Buenos Aires and Córdoba).] *Publicación electrónica "Intercambios" de la Carrera en Especialización en Derecho Penal. [Electronic Publication, "Intercambios", Criminal Law Post Graduate Course.]*, http://der.jursoc.unlp.edu.ar/intercambios/index.htm

Folino, J. O., Cáceres, M. S., Campos, M. L., Silveri, M., Ucín, S., & Ascazibar, M. (2005b). Evaluación de factores dinámicos de riesgo de violencia. [Assessment of dynamic risk factors of violence.] *Archivos de psiquiatria.* (in press).

Folino, J. O., Castillo, J. L., Cáceres, M. S., Campos, M. L., Silveri, M., & Ucín, S. (2004a). Confiabilidad de la versión argentina de la HCR-20. [Reliability of the Argentinean versión of the HCR-20.] *Medicina Forense Argentina*, Año *27*(54), 2–5.

Folino, J. O., & Marchiano, S. (2002). Tasa Basal de Recidiva Delictiva. [Crime recidivism base rate.] *Publicación electrónica "Intercambios" de la Carrera en Especialización en Derecho Penal. [Electronic Publication, "Intercambios", Criminal Law Post Graduate Course.]*, http://der.jursoc.unlp.edu.ar/intercambios/index.htm

Folino, J. O., Marengo, C., Marchiano, S., & Ascazibar, M. (2004c). The risk assessment program and the court of penal execution in the province of Buenos Aires, Argentina. *International Journal of Offender Therapy and Comparative Criminology, 48*(1), 49–58.

Folino, J. O., Sarmiento, D. R., & Montero Vazquez, J. (2000). Forensic system in the province of Buenos Aires, Argentina. *International Journal of Law and Psychiatry, 23*, 567–578.

Grann, M., Langstrom, N., Tengstrom, A., & Kullgren, G. (1999). Psychopathy (PCL-R) predicts violent recidivism among criminal offenders with personality disorders in Sweden. *Law-and-Human-Behavior, 23*(2), 205–217.

Hare, R. D. (1990). *The Hare psychopathy checklist – revised.* Toronto: Multi-Health Systems, Inc.

Hare, R. D. (2003). *The Hare psychopathy checklist – revised 2nd Edition Technical Manual.* Toronto: Multi-Health Systems, Inc.

Hare, R. D., Clark, D., Grann, M., & Thornton, D. (2000). Psychopathy and the predictive validity of the PCL-R: An international perspective. *Behavioral Sciences and the Law, 18*(5), 623–645.

Harris, G. T., & Rice, M. E. (1990). An empirical approach to classification and treatment planning for psychiatric inpatients. *Journal of Clinical Psychology, 46*(1), 3–14.

Harris, G. T., Rice, M. E., & Cormier, C. A. (1993a). Violent recidivism of mentally disordered offenders: The development of a statistical prediction instrument. *Criminal Justice and Behavior, 20*, 315–335.

Kropp, P. R., & Hart, S. D. (1997). Assessing risk for violence in wife assaulters: The spousal assault risk assessment guide. In: C. D. Webster & M. A. Jackson (Eds), *Impulsivity: Theory, assessment and treatment.* New York: Guilford.

Monahan, J., & Steadman, H. (1994). *Violence and mental disorder – developments in risk assessment.* Chicago: The University of Chicago Press.

Monahan, J., Steadman, H. J., Appelbaum, P. S., Robbins, P. C., Mulvey, E. P., Silver, E., Roth, L. H., & Grisso, T. (2000). Developing a clinically useful actuarial tool for assessing violence risk. *British Journal of Psychiatry, 176*, 312–319.

Quinsey, V. L., Harris, G. T., Rice, M. E., & Cormier, C. A. (1999). *Violent offenders – appraising and managing risk* (3rd ed.). Washington, DC: American Psychological Association.

Quinsey, V. L., Rice, M. E., & Harris, G. T. (1995). Actuarial prediction of sexual recidivism. *Journal of Interpersonal Violence, 10*, 85–105.

Rice, M. E., & Harris, G. T. (1993). Ontario's maximum security hospital at Penetanguishene: Past, present, and future. *International Journal of Law and Psychiatry, 16*(1–2), 195–215.

Rice, M. E., Harris, G. T., & Cormier, C. A. (1992). An evaluation of a maximum security therapeutic community for psychopaths and other mentally disordered offenders. *Law and Human Behavior, 16*(4), 399–412.

Ross, D. J., Hart, S. D., & Webster, C. D. (1998). *Aggression in psychiatric patients (Using the HCR-20 to assess risk for violence in hospital and in the community).* British Columbia, Canada: Riverview Hospital, Medical and Academic Affairs.

Steadman, H. J., Monahan, J., Appelbaum, P. S., Grisso, T., Mulvey, E. P., Roth, L. H., Robbins, P. C., & Klassen, D. (1994). Designing a new generation of risk assessment research. In: J. Monahan & H. J. Steadman (Eds), *Violence and mental disorder: Developments in risk assessment* (pp. 297–318). Chicago: University of Chicago Press.

Steadman, H. J., Mulvey, E. P., Monahan, J., Robbins, P. C., Appelbaum, P. S., Grisso, T., Roth, L. H., & Silver, E. (1998). Violence by people discharged from acute psychiatric inpatient facilities and by others in the same neighborhoods. *Archives of General Psychiatry, 55*, 393–401.

Steadman, H. J., Silver, E., Monahan, J., Appelbaum, P. S., Robbins, P. C., Mulvey, E. P., Grisso, T., Roth, L. H., & Banks, S. (2000). A classification tree approach to the development of actuarial violence risk assessment tools. *Law and Human Behavior, 24*(1), 83–100.

Tengstrom, A. (2001). Long-term predictive validity of historical factors in two risk assessment instruments in a group of violent offenders with schizophrenia. *Nordic Journal of Psychiatry, 55*(4), 243–249.

Tengstrom, A., Grann, M., Langstrom, N., & Kullgren, G. (2000). Psychopathy (PCL-R) as a predictor of violent recidivism among criminal offenders with schizophrenia. *Law and Human Behavior, 24*(1), 45–58.

Webster, C.D., Eaves, D., Douglas, K.S., & Hart, S.D. (1997). *HCR-20 assessing risk for violence* (version 2). Burnaby, British Columbia: Mental Health, Law and Policy Institute, Simon Fraser University and British Columbia Forensic Psychiatric Services Commission.

Webster, C. D., Harris, G. T., Rice, M. E., Cormier, C., & Quinsey, V. L. (1994). *The violence prediction scheme: Assessing dangerousness in high risk men.* Toronto, Ontario: Centre of Criminology, University of Toronto.

Yudofsky, S. C., Silver, J. M., Jackson, W., Endicott, J., & Williams, D. (1986). The Overt aggression scale for the objective rating of verbal and physical aggression. *American Journal of Psychiatry, 143*, 35–39.

Zung, W. W. K. (1967). Depression in the normal aged. *Psychosomatic, 3*, 287.

PART III:
MITIGATING CIRCUMSTANCES –
TWO CASES FROM THE COURTS

OFFENDER ETHNICITY AND JUVENILE COURT REFERRALS TO SUBSTANCE ABUSE SERVICES

Carolyn S. Breda

ABSTRACT

Courts play a critical role in facilitating access to alcohol, drug, and mental health services for juvenile offenders. This research examines the court's decision to refer offenders to A&D services and whether offender ethnicity affects this rehabilitative response. Results suggest ethnicity has no effect on treatment recommendations independent of its relationship to other variables. Rather, ethnicity modifies the effect offense type has on the treatment referral decision. Specifically, Blacks arrested for A&D offenses are significantly less likely than their White counterparts to be referred to care. Distinctions in drug laws seem to limit access to A&D services for Blacks.

Among the various decisions juvenile courts make is whether to refer a young offender to therapeutic services. This research examines the decision of juvenile courts to facilitate access to treatment for young offenders and whether offenders' ethnicity plays a part in the service referral decision. The significance of the research is multifold. First, it sheds light on the degree to

The Organizational Response to Persons with Mental Illness Involved with the Criminal Justice System
Research in Social Problems and Public Policy, Volume 12, 91–109
ISSN: 0196-1152/doi:10.1016/S0196-1152(05)12005-5

which juvenile courts, historically rooted in therapeutic approaches to delinquency, make clinical interventions available to a particularly at-risk social group. Second, by examining treatment referrals, it examines a court response seldom assessed in prior research, which has largely focused on detention or custody decisions. Third, the research assesses the effect of ethnicity in relation to other characteristics of the offender as well as other decisions courts make on behalf of the offender prior to the final disposition to refer youth to care.

SUBSTANCE USE PROBLEMS AMONG JUVENILE OFFENDERS

In 1997, courts with juvenile jurisdiction disposed of nearly 1.8 million cases nationwide for delinquency alone (U.S. Department of Justice, 2000), representing over one million individual juveniles who came into contact with the court that year. Many of these youth have alcohol, drug, or mental health (ADM) problems. Estimates of co-occurring ADM disorder and delinquency within juvenile justice populations have ranged from 10 to 22% (Harstone & Cocozza, 1984; Otto, Greenstein, Johnson, & Friedman, 1992), to virtually 100% (e.g., McManus, Alessi, Grapentine, & Brickman, 1984; Rogers, Powell, & Strock, 1998), depending on what definitions of *offender* and *disorder* are used (Fagan, 1991; Otto et al., 1992). Clinical diagnosis of substance abuse/dependence disorders as defined by the Diagnostic Statistical Manual of the American Psychiatric Association ranges from 25–50% (Edens & Otto, 1997), although higher rates have been reported. Teplin, Abram, McClelland, Dulcan, & Mericle (2002) report that two-thirds of juvenile detainees have at least one ADM disorder and nearly half have one or more substance abuse disorder.

Arrest data also show that the rate of drug-related offenses by juveniles has increased dramatically – by 169% between 1990 and 1999 (U.S. Department of Justice, 2003). The proportion of total cases (caseloads) that involve drug-related offenses has also risen, 108% between 1993 and 1998 (U.S. Department of Justice, 2001). Moreover, Black juveniles have been involved in drug law violations at nearly twice the rate (29%) than would be expected given their proportion (15%) in the U.S. juvenile population (U.S. Department of Justice, 2001). In short, data suggest a substantial need for ADM services for juveniles.

SERVICE ACCESS THROUGH THE COURTS

Although many offenders need mental health services, juvenile offenders and their needs have generally been ignored (Cocozza, 1992; Knitzer, 1982). Very few jurisdictions provide appropriate treatment services. Thornberry, Tolnay, Flanagan, & Glynn (1991) found that treatment for adolescent substance offenders was available in less than 40% of 3000 public and private juvenile detention, correctional, and shelter facilities (see also Dembo, Williams, & Schmeidler, 1993). Many juvenile offenders who need screening and treatment for ADM problems fail to receive either (Woolard, Gross, Mulvey, & Reppucci, 1992). Breda (2002) reports that only 3–4% of juvenile offenders are referred either to mental health or A&D counseling, a rate far lower than estimates of ADM would suggest.

Several reasons may account for the inattention to offenders' treatment needs, including public stigmatization of those with ADM problems, a belief that offenders with ADM problems may not deserve therapeutic interventions, or an overall dissatisfaction with treatment models of jurisprudence (Otto et al., 1992). Others (McBride, VanderWaal, Terry, & VanBuren, 1999) report that strong support continues for incorporating a rehabilitative philosophy with community protection models of justice. A recent study (Breda, 2001) of juvenile court judges statewide also finds that judges support a *mental health orientation* (MHO); for example, they agree that many offenders have mental health needs (with or without A&D problems), that services can be effective, and that youth's mental health status should affect their case dispositions. However, stronger MHO does not seem to translate into a higher rate of service referrals through the court. Overall, services available through the justice system seem to be entirely inadequate (U.S. Department of Justice, 1998).

ETHNIC BIAS IN COURT OUTCOMES

If referring offenders to needed services is critical, so too is ensuring that all offenders have equal access to services. Evidence suggests that treatment need is at least as great for Black offenders as for Whites (Martin & Grubb, 1990). Glisson (1996) found that about 80% of youth placed in state custody for delinquency had levels of symptomatology that would indicate a need for treatment and that symptomatology did not vary by youths' race. Kessler and colleagues (1994) found no differences specifically in lifetime or past-year substance abuse disorders between Blacks and Whites in the general population. Teplin and colleagues (2002) report lower rates of substance abuse diagnoses among Black than White or Hispanic juvenile detainees, although urinalysis at the time of arrest suggests that the rate of any drug use is somewhat higher for Blacks (68%) than for Whites (61%). Clinician observations have also suggested that the need for clinical intervention is at least as great for Black delinquents as for White delinquents (Lewis, Balla, & Shanok, 1979). In short, the need for ADM services should roughly be comparable for Blacks and Whites unless there are explicit cultural reasons to expect otherwise (Neighbors, Trierweiler, Ford, & Muroff, 2003).

Research about the impact on service referral of ethnicity of youth in various stages of the juvenile justice system is scant. Rogers et al. (1998) found that 9% of Black offenders and 13% of White offenders were referred for clinical evaluation after they were incarcerated in a short-term correctional facility. However, this research was based on a restrictive sample of incarcerated youth, not on the majority of youth who are not placed in custody, and did not control for confounding effects of other variables on the referral decision such as the nature of the juvenile's offense. Glisson (1996) found that service referrals for youth already in state custody were unaffected by race; however, the results were not broken down by whether the reason for custody was delinquency or dependency-neglect. Finally, Breda (2003) found that while offender's ethnicity did not directly affect the court's use of referrals to mental health counseling, it did affect the impact other variables (e.g., offense type) had on mental health referrals. This study did not examine referrals to substance abuse services, however.

While empirical studies of disparity in treatment referrals are scarce, considerable research has been conducted on other court decisions such as detention and adjudication. Results have been mixed and often contradictory, with some studies showing harsher outcomes for Black youth (Dannefer & Schutt, 1982; Frazier & Bishop, 1985; Marshall & Thomas, 1983; McCarthy & Smith, 1986; Thomas & Cage, 1977; Thomson & Zingraff, 1981), some showing harsher outcomes for Whites (Scarpitti & Stephenson, 1971), and others finding no racial differences (Bell & Lang, 1985; Cohen & Kluegel, 1978; Horwitz & Wasserman, 1980; Minor, Hartmann, & Terry, 1991; Niarhos & Routh, 1992). The weight of the evidence on ethnic disparity in juvenile court decision-making seems to show no clear trend (Fagan, Slaughter, & Harstone, 1987; Marshall & Thomas, 1983).

Inconsistent findings may be due to various methodological shortcomings, such as inadequate measures (Bishop & Frazier, 1988); failure to control for salient covariates or to consider multiplicative effects (Bell & Lang, 1985;

Bishop & Frazier, 1988; Cohen & Kluegel, 1978; Myers & Tallarico, 1986); small or restrictive samples (Bishop & Frazier, 1988); lack of comparable data across multiple jurisdictions (Sampson & Laub, 1993); and focus on a single court encounter or a single decision point within an encounter, which cannot detect any cumulative effect of race (Bishop & Frazier, 1988; McCarthy & Smith, 1986; Thornberry & Christenson, 1984). This study overcomes several of these issues by examining a wide range of offenders across multiple jurisdictions using multivariate techniques that allow the assessment of direct, indirect, and moderating effects of ethnicity on treatment referrals through juvenile courts while at the same time adjusts for the lack of independence among subjects (within courts) that can bias results.

THEORETICAL EXPECTATIONS

Previous research on race bias in court outcomes has often adopted a conflict perspective (Chambliss & Seidman, 1971; Leiber, 1994; Quinney, 1970). Hypothetically, Blacks would receive harsher dispositions than Whites because they lack the social, economic, or political resources to resist them (Bell & Lang, 1985; Marshall & Thomas, 1983; Quinney, 1970; Schur, 1971) or they pose a threat to White hegemony, which must be suppressed by the dominant, White group (Frazier, Bishop, & Henretta, 1992).

Alternatively, Martin and Grubb (1990) have suggested that differential experiences by Blacks and Whites may be less a function of overt racism in the system than of more symbolic, cultural differences between groups. For example, data have shown that symptoms that would have been recognized as pathological in White juvenile offenders were either ignored or incorrectly assessed in Black juveniles by predominantly White mental health professionals (Lewis et al., 1979). Such disparities are attributed to ethnocentrism among White professionals whose clinical standards for assessment exclude "the social reality of Blackness" (Martin & Grubb, 1990: p. 264). Others (U.S. Department of Health and Human Services, 2001) suggest that any lack of sensitivity to ethnic differences in symptoms may be attributable to deficient academic and professional training of clinicians, which does not enable them to adjust clinical processes when important cultural factors depart from prototypical expectations (Neighbors et al., 2003). In sum, ethnic disparity in mental health-related decisions, including decisions related to the allocation and provision of services (Brown, 2003) through the courts, may stem from either cross-cultural misunderstanding or racism, subtle or overt.

Based on prior research, it is hypothesized that juvenile courts will be more likely to refer White offenders to A&D services than Blacks. This hypothesis rests on four theoretical assumptions: (1) treatment may represent a valuable and scarce resource that judges (who are predominantly White) may reserve for White offenders; (2) juvenile courts may view mental health services as a lenient, yet still legitimate, sanction they can apply to White offenders; (3) court officials may think that White youth are more suitable candidates for rehabilitation than their Black counterparts; and (4) community-based treatment requires financial resources, which White offenders may be in a better position than Black offenders to obtain.

METHOD

Sample

The sample includes over 36,000 youth between the ages of 5 and 18 who were referred in 1997 to any one of 98 juvenile courts statewide in the Mid-South for a criminal or status offense. The courts preside over urban, suburban, and rural areas throughout the state, and the racial, gender, and offense type distributions among them closely resemble those in the nation (U.S. Department of Justice, 1990).

Only White and Black offenders are included because the number of youth of other ethnic backgrounds was too small to analyze meaningfully. Over a third (36%) of the sample is Black; 64% is White. Unlike many earlier studies, offenders are included regardless of how far they penetrate the system. So, for example, youth who were released upon intake are included as are those who were recommended for judicial review. This avoids a sample selection bias that occurs when court decisions that restrict the range (and alter the composition) of the sample are examined (Frazier & Bishop, 1985).

Measures

Six legal factors are assessed. *Offense* is coded as an A&D offense if any violation involved an alcohol or drug-related offense such as sale, possession, or public drunkenness. *Prior record* indicates whether the youth had a previous encounter with the respective court during the target year. *Police* indicates whether a police officer or someone else (e.g., family member, school official) took the youth to court. *Detention* indicates whether the youth was detained at any time prior to adjudication. *Petition* indicates whether a formal petition was filed against the youth at intake. *Adjudication status* identifies youth who were not recommended for judicial review, those who had judicial review but were found not to be delinquent, and those who were adjudicated delinquent during the review.

Social variables most commonly used in prior research are included, specifically, youth's *age*, *gender*, and *ethnicity* (Marshall & Thomas, 1983). Age includes four categories to approximate developmental groupings – youth < 10 years of age, those 10–12, those 13–15, and youth 16–18 years of age. Youth's *living arrangement* has been less used in studies of court outcomes, though some (Barton, 1976; Thomas & Cage, 1977) suggest it may be relevant for decision making. Here, youth who lived with both biological parents at the time they were taken to court, in a blended household (e.g., with a biological and step parent), with a single parent, with other relatives, or in some other living arrangement (e.g., group home) are compared. A direct measure of social class is unavailable. The database also does not include a measure of offenders' clinical status with regard to substance use, abuse, or dependence, which some research suggests may not be relevant for service-related decisions within the juvenile justice system anyway (e.g., Glisson, 1996; Kelley, 1978).

The dependent variable, *treatment referral*, is a dichotomous variable that identifies youth whom the courts referred or did not refer to community-based A&D services. This service referral disposition can be the only disposition rendered (e.g., as a tool to divert cases from the juvenile justice system to the mental health system) or one among other dispositions rendered such as community service or probation, the latter of which is frequently used to help assure compliance with a treatment referral.

All variables are "dummy" coded so that for each variable there is one missing category or referent group in the analyses to which results for the included categories/groups are compared. For example, ethnicity is coded "1" if an offender is Black; "0" if White. Results that relate to ethnicity will show the difference in the (log) odds of being referred to services for Blacks as compared with Whites, who comprise the missing, or referent group.

Design and Procedure

The design for the analysis is based on the work of Cohen and Kluegel (1978) who offer three criteria for identifying racial bias in court outcomes: (1) race directly affects outcome; (2) race indirectly affects outcome through other factors considered stereotypical in nature; or (3) race moderates the effect of another variable.

The first criterion is straightforward; the second and third may warrant some elaboration. Consider the following premise: youth raised by a single parent are more prone toward criminality than youth raised by both biological parents. Blacks, who are more likely than Whites to live in single-headed households, may experience discriminatory outcomes because of preconceived notions among court officials about youth raised by single parents. Thus, the effect of race is indirect through its relationship to a variable, living arrangement, which can stereotype a particular social group (Cohen & Kluegel, 1978; Schur, 1973). The third criterion is met, for example, when the effect of any variable (e.g., offense type) on the referral decision is found to differ for Black and White offenders. In this case, race is said to moderate the effect of offense type on outcome.

Hierarchical linear modeling (Bryk & Raudenbush, 1992) is used to test for ethnic disparity. This procedure accounts for the lack of independence in nested designs, for example, when multiple offenders are referred to the same court. Nesting tends to reduce the standard errors, thereby making results seem significant when they are not. Two models are tested. First, A&D treatment referral is modeled by youths' social and legal profiles. This allows a direct test of whether offenders' ethnicity affects the chances of referral while simultaneously controlling for other potentially relevant variables. It also provides a basis for determining whether ethnicity indirectly affects the referral decision through an association with living arrangement. Second, interaction terms are included in the model to assess whether ethnicity modifies the effects of other social or legal variables on the courts' decision to recommend A&D services.

The significance of direct, indirect, or moderating effects is based on alpha levels adjusted for the number of variables in each model. This approach accounts for the possibility that, with multiple significance tests (i.e., variables in the model), some variables may appear significant by chance alone. For example, with 20 significance tests, as in the first model, we expect one variable to be significant by chance. The adjusted alpha for each of the two models presented in Table 2 is $p<0.003$ and $p<0.001$, respectively.

RESULTS

Table 1 shows results from a series of cross-tabulations between offender ethnicity and other social and legal variables. Black offenders (2%) seem to

Table 1. Sample Characteristics ($N = 36{,}157$).

Court Referral to A&D Services	Black (35%)	White (65%)
	2%	4%
Social profile		
Gender		
Male	69%	66%
Age (years)		
LT 10	2%	1%
10–12	6%	3%
13–15	33%	25%
16–18	59%	71%
Living arrangement		
Both biological parents	12%	36%
Biological and stepparent	7%	11%
Single-parent	66%	44%
Other relatives	12%	5%
Other	3%	4%
Legal profile		
Prior record	33%	22%
Taken to court by police	77%	63%
Detained	52%	11%
Petitioned	37%	60%
Adjudicated status		
Not referred for judicial hearing	4%	11%
Referred, not adjudicated	69%	37%
Referred, adjudicated	27%	52%
Current A&D offense	9%	14%
Alcohol	2%	7%
Drug	7%	7%

Note: All differences are significant $p < 0.001$.

be less likely than Whites (4%) to be referred to A&D services. However, Blacks also differ from Whites on social and legal variables frequently relevant for court decisions. For example, Blacks tend to be younger than Whites and more likely to live in single-headed households, though the single-headed household is the modal living arrangement for both ethnic groups. Blacks are more likely to have a prior offense record and to be detained than Whites; however, Whites are more likely to be formally petitioned by the court and, among those referred for judicial review, to be adjudicated delinquent. Whites are more likely than Blacks to have been

Table 2. HLM Models of A&D Service Referral by Social and Legal Characteristics of Offenders ($N = 36,157$).

Social Variables	Coefficient (standard error)	p-value	Coefficient (standard error)	p-value
Black	−0.21 (0.13)	0.115	0.40 (0.21)	0.054
Male	0.17 (0.08)	0.037	0.16 (0.09)	0.062
Age (years)				
LT 10	−0.66 (0.39)	0.087	−1.12 (0.57)	0.052
10–12	−1.14 (0.21)	<0.001	−1.15 (0.30)	<0.001
13–15	0.14 (0.08)	0.113	0.17 (0.11)	0.120
Living arrangement				
Biological parent/step-parent	0.14 (0.09)	0.100	0.17 (0.11)	0.109
Single-parent	−0.10 (0.08)	0.253	−0.09 (0.09)	0.325
Relatives	−0.26 (0.11)	0.020	−0.23 (0.16)	0.153
Other living	−0.99 (0.20)	<0.001	−1.00 (0.25)	<0.001
Legal variables				
Any A&D offense	2.98 (0.18)	<0.001	3.18 (0.17)	<0.001
Prior record	0.76 (0.07)	<0.001	0.74 (0.08)	<0.001
Police	−0.16 (0.10)	0.130	−0.19 (0.11)	0.087
Detention	−0.40 (0.16)	0.011	−0.39 (0.21)	0.066
Petition	0.17 (0.13)	0.179	0.24 (0.14)	0.089
Adjudication status				
No adjudication	−0.33 (0.34)	0.329	−0.30 (0.42)	0.478
Adjudicated delinquent	0.50 (0.26)	0.058	0.47 (0.25)	0.062
Interaction terms				
Black*Male			0.19 (0.12)	0.116
Black*LT10			1.14 (0.57)	0.045
Black*10–12			−0.12 (0.47)	0.797
Black*13–15			−0.27 (0.13)	0.043
Black*Biological parent step-parent			−0.33 (0.21)	0.123
Black*1-parent			−0.13 (0.11)	0.255
Black*Relatives			−0.18 (0.20)	0.370
Black*Other-living			−0.09 (0.34)	0.787
Black*A&D offense			−1.00 (0.19)	<0.001
Black*Prior record			0.09 (0.10)	0.360
Black*Police			0.16 (0.15)	0.285
Black*Detention			0.07 (0.20)	0.732
Black*Petition			−0.48 (0.17)	0.005

Table 2. *(Continued)*

Social Variables	Coefficient (standard error)	p-value	Coefficient (standard error)	p-value
Black*No adjudication			−0.07 (0.59)	0.910
Black*Adjudicated delinquent			0.27 (0.19)	0.160
Constant	−4.98 (0.26)		−5.13 (0.27)	
Degrees of freedom	df(16)		df(31)	

Note: The Bonferroni-adjusted α for Model 1 is $p = 0.003$; for Model 2, $p = 0.002$. Estimates are based on a population-average model, unstandardized fixed effects, and robust standard errors.

arrested for an offense related to alcohol, but are as likely as Blacks to have been arrested for a drug offense. While a few differences (e.g., in treatment referral rate) between Blacks and Whites may seem substantively small, all meet χ^2 tests for statistically significant differences at $p < 0.001$, which can be expected with such a large sample.

Table 2 shows the results of the two-step hierarchical linear modeling. Columns 1 and 2 summarize the direct effect of ethnicity on treatment referrals while controlling for other variables; columns 3 and 4 show the moderating effects of ethnicity. Results suggest that ethnicity has no direct effect ($p = 0.115$) on the court's inclination to refer youth to substance abuse services. Also, youth living in single-headed households, which could indirectly affect the chances for Black youth to be referred to A&D services, are as likely to be referred as youth living with both biological parents (the referent group). Youth who live with other relatives, another arrangement more common for Blacks than for Whites, tend to be less likely to be referred for services ($p = 0.02$). However, this effect does not meet the α level adjusted ($p = 0.003$) for multiple tests, nor does it depend on the ethnicity of youth (Black*Relatives), as suggested by the non-significant interaction term presented in column 4 ($p = 0.370$).

Legal circumstances, particularly the nature of the offense and prior offense record, have the strongest effects on the court's decision to provide access to A&D services. Youth arrested for an A&D-related offense are significantly more likely than those with other charges to be referred to care. A prior record with the court also increases the odds of treatment referral.

Thus far, findings do not fulfill Cohen and Kluegel's (1978) first two criteria for racial bias in court decisions. The question remains whether ethnicity modifies any effect other variables have on referral decisions. Columns 3 and 4, particularly the bottom half, show results of modeling interactions between ethnicity and other measures. Only one measure, Black*A&D offense, meets the adjusted alpha level, $p = 0.002$. Black youth arrested for an A&D offense are less likely than their White counterparts to be referred to care. This suggests that the increased chance of treatment referral that having an A&D-related offense generates for all youth is heightened even more for Whites than for Blacks, controlling for other effects in the model.

Fig. 1 graphically illustrates the point. While the figure cannot control for all the covariates in the model, it suggests that 23% of White A&D offenders, compared with just 9% of their Black counterparts, are considered for A&D services through the courts. This finding supports Cohen and Kluegel's (1978) third criterion for ethnic bias in courts' responses to young offenders.

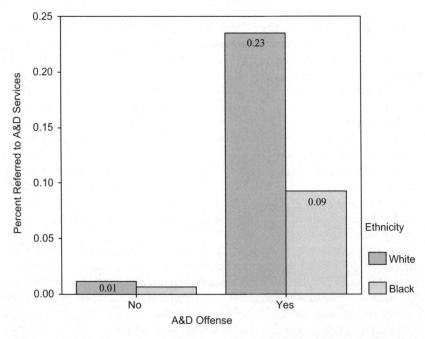

Fig. 1.   Ethnic Differences in Referral to A&D Services among A&D Offenders.

DISCUSSION

This research addresses the important question of ethnic disparity in the juvenile court's decision to make services available to young offenders, many of whom have serious problems related to drugs or alcohol. In its design, the study is able to overcome some of the major limitations of earlier work by using a multivariate model appropriate for nested designs that tests for direct, indirect, and ethnicity-based interaction effects for a large sample of various types of offenders across multiple jurisdictions.

Overall, the 2–4% rate of A&D treatment referral observed suggests that courts seriously underutilize therapeutic options for juveniles, regardless of their ethnicity. Perhaps this reflects an emphasis in juvenile justice over the past 20 years or so on accountability and punishment rather than on rehabilitation; therapeutic approaches may seem too lenient a response in an era of *get tough* public policy (Schwartz, 1989). At the same time, the study shows that offenders charged with an A&D offense are significantly more likely than others to be referred for care. So, while courts may not be responding in numbers proportionate to the need for treatment, they seem to be targeting the most obvious offenders, those with A&D offenses, for counseling. Such a finding may bring added hope to those who call for a public health approach to drug-related offenses (e.g., Alexander, 1996; Longmire, 1993) in the juvenile justice system. Current efforts nationwide to develop juvenile drug court programs for A&D offenders may also represent a shift toward more therapeutic, less punitive approaches to drug-related crime.

As discussed at the outset, conflict perspectives have been used often to predict ethnic differences in court outcomes and findings have often been mixed. Here, a more complex model than available in earlier work, which tests for moderating effects as well as accounts for the correlation inherent in nested designs (e.g., offenders nested within courts), supports the case for ethnic disparity in the specific decision of the court to provide young offenders access to substance abuse services. However, the effect is neither simple nor direct; rather, it is inextricably linked to the impact of other variables – notably, offense type. Black A&D offenders are not given as much access to services as White A&D offenders, controlling for other relevant factors. Some of this disparity is likely attributable to the specific type of A&D offense with which youth are charged. Data (available from the author) showed that Whites were more likely than Blacks to have alcohol-related offenses (e.g., DUI, public intoxication). Whites were also more likely to be charged with possession of controlled substances while

Blacks were more likely to be charged with sale. National data also indicate that Blacks are five times more likely than Whites to be placed in custody for drug trafficking (U.S. Department of Justice, 1999).

Some (Peterson & Hagan, 1984) have suggested that drug laws demonize non-white offenders to the extent that they are, or are perceived to be, "pushers" rather than "users," villains rather than victims. Similar distinctions can be found in laws regarding crack cocaine (associated with Blacks) versus powder cocaine (associated with Whites). While some (e.g., Romer, 1994) advocate a public health response to all A&D offenders including traffickers, present findings suggest that legalistic distinctions related to substances reduces the chances for treatment for Black A&D offenders. Thus, the ethnic disparity observed here may be less a function of overt discrimination by court officials than discrimination in the laws that courts are obliged to uphold. Either way, the more limited use of A&D services for Black A&D offenders does little to break the cycle of drug use for this particularly at-risk group.

The study also sheds another light on a point raised by several scholars (Bishop & Frazier, 1988; Fagan et al., 1987; McCarthy & Smith, 1986; Thornberry & Christenson, 1984) – that the effect of ethnicity on outcome may be a function of its effect on other decisions the court makes before case disposition. In the present study, other decisions made prior to outcome, notably, detention, petitioning, and adjudication status, had little impact on the final decision of whether to refer youth to A&D services. While the decision of whether to detain offenders prior to case disposition seemed to diminish the odds of service referral somewhat, this effect did not attain the adjusted level of statistical significance. The decision (often made at intake to court) of whether to file a formal petition against the youth also had no direct bearing on the A&D referral decision, though filing a petition tended to reduce the odds of service referral for Blacks relative to Whites. Again, however, this interaction effect did not attain the level of statistical significance adjusted for the number of tests conducted. So, while ethnicity may well affect decisions courts make (e.g., detention) prior to final disposition, findings here suggest that such decisions do not influence an outcome when the outcome involves an A&D service referral.

Of course, this study is but one of others that are needed to address more fully the question of service access, and differential access, for the large number of juveniles for whom the court may be the first, best, or last chance for receiving potentially effective services. Perhaps other variables not available to this study can be considered. For example, clinical data on ADM, which are often unavailable to courts before making case dispositions (Breda, 2000), were also unavailable in the database. Nonetheless, individual-level data on the clinical status of offenders would help identify its impact on the referral decision as well as its impact (if any) on the relationship between ethnicity, A&D offense, and service referral observed here. Too, the measure of prior record used here considers previous encounters with the same court within the target year of the study; therefore, it cannot assess whether ethnic differences in more extensive offense histories might help explain the lesser use of service referrals for Black A&D offenders.

Given its limitations, this research suggests that courts do not consider treatment options for Blacks and Whites similarly when offenses are alcohol or drug related. Amidst the large number of offenders with ADM problems, the authority of the court to mandate treatment, the over-representation of Black youth in the juvenile justice system, and the potential efficacy of treatment to help ameliorate the personal and social costs of ADM, it would seem prudent and compassionate to identify service needs, develop more fully the court's capacity to respond to them, while at the same time pro-actively address legal statutes that may constrain the court's capacity to respond equitably.

ACKNOWLEDGMENTS

Carolyn S. Breda, Center for Evaluation and Program Improvement, Peabody College, Vanderbilt University. The author gratefully acknowledges the NIMH for funding the research through grant MH54638-01A2 and the Council of Juvenile and Family Court Judges affiliate who made data available. The research was approved by the Institutional Review Board of the author's institution.

REFERENCES

Alexander, R. (1996). African American youths and drugs: A time to pursue a mental health approach. *Journal of Black Psychology, 22*, 374–387.

Barton, W. (1976). Discretionary decision-making in juvenile justice. *Crime and Delinquency, 22*, 470–480.

Bell, D., Jr., & Lang, K. (1985). The intake dispositions of juvenile offenders. *Journal of Research in Crime and Delinquency, 22*, 309–328.

Bishop, D. M., & Frazier, C. E. (1988). The influence of race in juvenile justice processing. *Journal of Research in Crime and Delinquency, 25*, 242–263.

Breda, C. (2000). The organizational context of courts' treatment referrals for juvenile offenders. In: J. Willis, C. Liberton, K. Kutash & R. Friedman (Eds), *The 12th annual research
conference proceedings, a system of care for children's mental health: Expanding the research base* (pp. 157–162). Tampa, FL: University of South Florida.

Breda, C. (2001). The mental health orientation of juvenile courts. *The Journal of Behavioral
Health Services and Research, 28*, 89–95.

Breda, C. (2002). The impact of external environment on service-related decisions of juvenile
courts. In: C. Newman, C. J. Liberton, K. Kutash & R. Friedman (Eds), *The 14th annual
research conference proceedings, a system of care for children's mental health: Expanding
the research base* (pp. 145–148). Tampa, FL: University of South Florida.

Breda, C. S. (2003). Offender ethnicity and mental health service referrals from juvenile courts.
Criminal Justice and Behavior, 30, 644–667.

Brown, T. (2003). Critical race theory speaks to the sociology of mental health: Mental health
problems produced by racial stratification. *Journal of Health and Social Behavior, 43*,
292–301.

Bryk, A., & Raudenbush, S. (1992). *Hierarchical linear models: Applications and data analysis
methods*. Newbury Park, CA: Sage Publications.

Chambliss, W. J., & Seidman, R. (1971). *Law, order, and power*. Reading, MA: Addison-
Wesley.

Cocozza, J. J. (1992). Introduction. In: J. Cocozza (Ed.), *Responding to the mental health needs
of youth in the juvenile justice system* (pp. 1–6). Seattle, WA: The National Coalition for
the Mentally Ill in the Criminal Justice System.

Cohen, L. E., & Kluegel, J. R. (1978). Determinants of juvenile court dispositions: Ascriptive
and achieved factors in two metropolitan courts. *American Sociological Review, 43*, 162–
176.

Dannefer, D., & Schutt, R. K. (1982). Race and juvenile justice processing in court and police
agencies. *American Journal of Sociology, 87*, 1113–1132.

Dembo, R., Williams, L., & Schmeidler, J. (1993). Addressing the problems of substance abuse
in juvenile corrections. In: J. A. Inciardi (Ed.), *Drug treatment in criminal justice settings*
(pp. 97–126). Newbury Park, CA: Sage Publications.

Edens, J. F., & Otto, R. K. (1997). Prevalence of mental disorders among youth in the juvenile
justice system. *Focal Point: Juvenile Justice and Children's Mental Health, 11*, 1–8.

Fagan, J. (1991). Community-based treatment for mentally disordered juvenile offenders.
Journal of Clinical Child Psychology, 20, 42–50.

Fagan, J., Slaughter, E., & Harstone, E. (1987). Blind justice? The impact of race on the juvenile
justice process. *Crime and Delinquency, 33*, 224–258.

Frazier, C. E., & Bishop, D. M. (1985). The pretrial detention of juveniles and its impact on case
dispositions. *Journal of Criminal Law and Criminology, 76*, 1132–1152.

Frazier, C. E., Bishop, D. M., & Henretta, J. C. (1992). The social context of race differentials
in juvenile justice dispositions. *The Sociological Quarterly, 33*, 447–458.

Glisson, C. (1996). Judicial and service decisions for children entering state custody: The limited
role of mental health. *Social Science Review, 70*, 257–281.

Harstone, E., & Cocozza, J. J. (1984). Providing services for the mentally ill, violent juvenile
offender. In: R. Mathias, P. DeMuro & R. A. Allison (Eds), *Violent juvenile offenders:
An anthology* (pp. 157–175). Newark, NJ: National Council on Crime and Delinquency.

Horwitz, A., & Wasserman, M. (1980). Formal rationality, substantive justice, and discrimination. *Law and Human Behavior, 4*, 103–115.

Kelley, T. M. (1978). Clinical assessment and the detention, disposition, and treatment of emotionally disturbed delinquent youths. *Journal of Criminal Justice, 6,* 315–327.

Kessler, R. C., McGonagle, K. A., Zhao, S., Nelson, C. B., Hughes, M., Eshleman, S., Wittchen, H., & Kendler, K. S. (1994). Lifetime and 12-month prevalence of DSM-III-R psychiatric disorders in the United States. *Archives of General Psychiatry, 51,* 8–19.

Knitzer, J. (1982). *Unclaimed children: The failure of public responsibility to children and adolescents in need of mental health services.* Washington, DC: Children's Defense Fund.

Leiber, M. (1994). A comparison of juvenile court outcomes for Native Americans, African Americans and Whites. *Justice Quarterly, 11,* 257–279.

Lewis, D. O., Balla, D. A., & Shanok, S. S. (1979). Some evidence of race bias in the diagnosis and treatment of the juvenile offender. *American Journal of Orthopsychiatry, 49,* 53–61.

Longmire, D. R. (1993). Re-medicalizing the connection between drugs and crime: Educating for peace rather than war. In: P. B. Kraska (Ed.), *Altered states of mind: Critical observations of the drug war* (pp. 251–265). New York: Garland.

Marshall, I. H., & Thomas, C. W. (1983). Discretionary decision-making and the juvenile court. *Juvenile and Family Court Journal, 34,* 47–59.

Martin, T. W., & Grubb, H. J. (1990). Race bias in diagnosis and treatment of juvenile offenders: Findings and suggestions. *Journal of Contemporary Psychotherapy, 20,* 259–272.

McBride, D., VanderWaal, C., Terry, Y., & VanBuren, H. (1999). *Breaking the cycle of drug use among juvenile offenders.* Final Technical Report for the National Institute of Justice, November.

McCarthy, B. R., & Smith, B. L. (1986). The conceptualization of discrimination in the juvenile justice process: The impact of administrative factors and screening decisions on juvenile court dispositions. *Criminology, 24,* 41–64.

McManus, M., Alessi, N. E., Grapentine, W. L., & Brickman, A. (1984). Psychiatric disturbance in serious delinquents. *Journal of the American Academy of Child Psychiatry, 23,* 602–615.

Minor, K. I., Hartmann, D. J., & Terry, S. (1991). Predictors of juvenile court actions and recidivism. *Crime and Delinquency, 43,* 328–344.

Myers, M. A., & Tallarico, S. M. (1986). The social contexts of racial discrimination in sentencing. *Social Problems, 33,* 236–251.

Neighbors, H., Trierweiler, S., Ford, B., & Muroff, J. (2003). Racial differences in DSM diagnosis using a semi-structured instrument: The importance of clinical judgment in the diagnosis of African Americans. *Journal of Health and Social Behavior, 43,* 237–256.

Niarhos, F. J., & Routh, D. K. (1992). The role of clinical assessment in the juvenile court: Predictors of juvenile dispositions and recidivism. *Journal of Clinical Child Psychology, 21,* 151–159.

Otto, R. K., Greenstein, J. J., Johnson, M. K., & Friedman, R. M. (1992). Prevalence of mental disorders among youth in the juvenile justice system. In: J. Cocozza (Ed.), *Responding to the mental health needs of youth in the juvenile justice system* (pp. 7–48). Seattle, WA: The National Coalition for the Mentally Ill in the Criminal Justice System.

Peterson, R., & Hagan, J. (1984). Changing conceptions of race: Towards an account of anomalous findings of sentencing research. *American Sociological Review, 49,* 56–70.

Quinney, R. (1970). *The social reality of crime.* Boston, MA: Little Brown.

Rogers, K. M., Powell, E., & Strock, M. (1998). The characteristics of youth referred for mental health evaluation in the juvenile justice system. In: J. Willis, C. Liberton, K. Kutash & R. Friedman (Eds), *The 10th annual research conference proceedings, a system of care for children's mental health: Expanding the research base* (pp. 329–334). Tampa, FL: University of South Florida.

Romer, D. (1994). Using mass media to reduce adolescent involvement in drug trafficking. *Pediatrics, 93*, 1073–1077.

Sampson, R. J., & Laub, J. H. (1993). Structural variations in juvenile court processing: Inequality, the underclass, and social control. *Law & Society Review, 27*, 285–311.

Scarpitti, F. R., & Stephenson, R. M. (1971). Juvenile court dispositions: Factors in the decision-making process. *Crime and Delinquency, 17*, 142–151.

Schur, E. M. (1971). *Labeling deviant behaviors.* New York: Harper & Row.

Schur, E. M. (1973). *Radical non-intervention: Rethinking the delinquency problem.* Englewood Cliffs, NJ: Prentice-Hall.

Schwartz, I. (1989). Juvenile crime: The youth corrections agenda for the 1990s. In: C. Russell & C. McCauley (Eds), *Crime and justice in the 1990s* (pp. 45–50). Nashville, TN: Vanderbilt Institute for Public Policy Studies, Vanderbilt University.

Teplin, L. A., Abram, K. M., McClelland, G. M., Dulcan, M. K., & Mericle, A. A. (2002). Psychiatric disorders in youth in juvenile detention. *Archives of General Psychiatry, 59*, 1133–1143.

Thomas, C. W., & Cage, R. J. (1977). The effect of social characteristics on juvenile court dispositions. *The Sociological Quarterly, 18*, 237–252.

Thomson, R. J., & Zingraff, M. T. (1981). Detecting sentencing disparity: Some problems and evidence. *American Journal of Sociology, 86*, 869–880.

Thornberry, T. P., & Christenson, R. L. (1984). Juvenile justice decision-making as a longitudinal process. *Social Forces, 63*, 433–444.

Thornberry, T. P., Tolnay, S. E., Flanagan, T. J., & Glynn, P. (1991). *Children in custody 1987: A comparison of public and private juvenile custody facilities.* Washington, DC: U.S. Department of Justice, Office of Juvenile Justice and Delinquency Prevention.

U.S. Department of Health and Human Services. (2001). *Mental health: Culture, race and ethnicity-a supplement to mental health: A report of the surgeon general.* Rockville, MD: U.S. Department of Health and Human Services, Substance Abuse and Mental Health Services Administration, Center for Mental Health Services.

U.S. Department of Justice, Office of Juvenile Justice and Delinquency Prevention. (1990). *Juvenile court statistics, 1988.* Washington, DC: U.S. Government Printing Office.

U.S. Department of Justice, Office of Juvenile Justice and Delinquency Prevention. (1998). *Mental health disorders and substance abuse problems among juveniles.* Washington, DC: U.S. Government Printing Office.

U.S. Department of Justice, Office of Juvenile Justice and Delinquency Prevention. (1999). *Minorities in the juvenile justice system.* National Report Series: Juvenile Justice Bulletin. Washington, DC: U.S. Government Printing Office.

U.S. Department of Justice, Office of Juvenile Justice and Delinquency Prevention. (2000). *Juvenile court statistics, 1997.* Washington, DC: U.S. Government Printing Office.

U.S. Department of Justice, Office of Juvenile Justice and Delinquency Prevention. (2001). *Drug offense cases in juvenile courts, 1989–1998.* Washington, DC: U.S. Government Printing Office.

U.S. Department of Justice, Office of Juvenile Justice and Delinquency Prevention. (2003). *Drug offense cases in juvenile courts, 1990–1999*. Washington, DC: U.S. Government Printing Office.

Woolard, J., Gross, S., Mulvey, E., & Reppucci, N. D. (1992). Legal issues affecting mentally disordered youth in the juvenile justice system. In: J. Cocozza (Ed.), *Responding to the mental health needs of youth in the juvenile justice system* (pp. 91–106). Seattle, WA: The National Coalition for the Mentally Ill in the Criminal Justice System.

BENEFITS AND RISKS OF USING "DIMINISHED CAPACITY" MITIGATION IN DEATH PENALTY PROCEEDINGS

Beth Bjerregaard, M. Dwayne Smith and Sondra J. Fogel

ABSTRACT

A sample of capital trials in North Carolina was analyzed to determine the impact on death sentencing of introducing mitigators related to diminished capacity on behalf of defendants. The results show that mitigators of this type were frequently submitted to the jury for consideration, and if accepted, the chances of a defendant being sentenced to death were diminished. However, when these mitigators were submitted but not accepted, the defendant's likelihood of receiving a death sentence was substantially escalated. These findings suggest a need for attorneys to carefully weigh the advantages and disadvantages of presenting diminished capacity mitigators in capital trials, and if choosing to do so, the absolute necessity of convincing the jury of their validity.

The Organizational Response to Persons with Mental Illness Involved with the Criminal Justice System

Research in Social Problems and Public Policy, Volume 12, 111–134
ISSN: 0196-1152/doi:10.1016/S0196-1152(05)12006-7
111

BENEFITS AND RISKS OF USING "DIMINISHED CAPACITY" MITIGATION IN DEATH PENALTY PROCEEDINGS

The death penalty has suffered a long and tumultuous history in the United States and has undergone numerous iterations to arrive at its current format. Although the U.S. Supreme Court (hereafter, Court) struck down death penalty statutes across the country in its landmark *Furman v. Georgia* decision in 1972, the Court clearly articulated that it was not the punishment itself, but the application of the statutes, especially their arbitrary and discriminatory enforcement, that was being held unconstitutional. Therefore, immediately following the Court's decision, a number of states rapidly redrafted their death penalty statutes in an attempt to correct the deficiencies objected to by the court.

Mitigation and Contemporary Capital Punishment

In 1976, the Supreme Court upheld the states of Georgia (*Gregg v. Georgia*, 1976), Texas (*Jurek v. Texas*, 1976), and Florida's (*Profitt v. Florida*, 1976) newly enacted death penalty statutes. In the lead case, the Court approved a number of key factors incorporated into the Georgia statute that were supposed to guide the sentencing process and, in so doing, significantly reduced its arbitrary and capricious aspects. Included in the newly revised statutes was the requirement that the defendant be provided the opportunity to present to the jury any information that might mitigate his or her responsibility for the crime, thereby potentially lessening the punishment. Juries were then required to balance these mitigating factors against statutory aggravating factors (aspects of the case that made it subject to capital punishment) to arrive at an appropriate punishment. The Court felt that this new sentencing scheme would focus the jury's attention on the unique characteristics of both the crime itself and the characteristics of the defendant, therefore guiding sentencing discretion. To further emphasize this point, the Court ruled on the same day in two other cases that mandatory death penalty laws were unconstitutional because they did not allow a jury to consider the unique aspects of each case that make for individual sentencing decisions (*Roberts v. Louisiana*, 1976; *Woodson v. North Carolina*, 1976).

While most states ultimately adopted sentencing schemes either identical or very similar to those of Georgia, two states chose to take a different approach, and had their schemes upheld by the Court. Both Texas and Oregon chose to guide jury discretion by requiring the jury to answer a series of special questions, with the answers dictating the recommended punishment. In both states, however, juries were required to hear mitigating circumstances presented by the defendant in formulating their sentencing decisions.

Although the Court made it clear that defendants must be allowed to present mitigating evidence, the exact scope of this requirement was left unclear. In 1978, the Court addressed this issue in *Lockett v. Ohio*, ruling that in order to ensure individualized sentencing, defendants must have the ability to present any mitigating evidence that is relevant to the defendant's character, record, or circumstances of the offense. This decision allowed many different types of evidence to be introduced at the sentencing phase of capital trials. Subsequently, scholars have separated mitigators into three broad categories: (1) those that reduce culpability; (2) those related to the defendant's lack of future dangerousness or the potential for rehabilitation; and (3) those that serve to demonstrate the defendant's general good character (Acker & Lanier, 1994; Garvey, 1998). In order to accommodate the wide variety of mitigating factors that can be introduced, most statutes simply incorporated a statutory open-ended mitigating factor, which operates as a so-called "catchall" category. For example, North Carolina, the state from which the sample for this study is derived, includes a statutory mitigator that allows the jury to consider "any other circumstance arising from the evidence which the jury deems to have mitigating value,"[1] as well as allowing the defendant to argue any evidence that can be supported by a preponderance of the evidence.

In subsequent cases regarding mitigation, the Court ruled that jurors could not be required to unanimously agree on the existence of a mitigating factor before it could be considered (*McKoy v. North Carolina*, 1990). Also, the Court specified that jurors should not draw any distinctions between the relative weights given to statutory and non-statutory mitigating factors in reaching their sentencing decisions (*Hitchcock v. Dugger*, 1987). All told, the present situation is one where, theoretically, capital defendants have the opportunity to bring to jury members' attention a wide variety of information that could influence their sentencing decisions.

Mitigation Involving Diminished Capacity

While the new laws placed virtually no limits on the introduction of relevant mitigating evidence, defense attorneys quickly learned that the introduction of certain types of mitigating evidence presented unique challenges. One area where this is particularly salient is in the presentation of evidence involving the defendant's mental state at the time of the crime. In some cases, the claims of the defendant can involve long-standing mental or emotional disturbances subject to specific psychiatric diagnoses. In other cases, the claims involve mental impairments that derive from shorter term, situational conditions. Drug and alcohol abuse is frequently cited in the latter claims, as well outbursts of behavior that are otherwise uncharacteristic of the defendant.

There is ample evidence that mental illness is a relevant factor among a large proportion of capital defendants, as several studies have found psychological disorders to be disproportionately prevalent among death row inmates (Cunningham & Vigen, 2002; National Mental Health Association, 2001; Slobogin, 2004; Stetler, 1999). For instance, Robinson and Stephens (1992) studied death penalty cases from 1973 to 1991 and found that approximately one-third of the defendants were characterized as psychologically disturbed while 26% were found to be mentally retarded. Likewise, slightly less than one-third of these persons evidenced low IQ scores. Similarly, Perlin (1996) found that as many as half of the inmates in his study exhibited signs of serious mental illness, and that some 10–20% were mentally retarded. In a study of 15 adult inmates selected because of the imminence of their sentences, Lewis, Pincus, Feldman, Jackson, and Bard (1986) found that all of the members of their sample had corroborated histories of head injuries and nine were found to have had severe psychiatric disorders during childhood. Also, a Lewis et al. (1988) study of 14 juveniles on death row found that 9 of the juveniles had serious neurological abnormalities, 7 were psychotic, and 12 had IQs of less than 90.

Apart from specific mental or psychological disabilities, alcohol and drug abuse appears to be a common component in the frequently chaotic backgrounds of capital defendants. As but one indicator of this fact, narratives from the 441 cases of North Carolina capital defendants that constitute the sample for the present study (to be discussed below) reveal that drug and/or alcohol use was involved in the dynamics of 54% of those murders.

Traditionally, the U.S. criminal justice system has afforded special consideration and leniency to criminals suffering from mental disabilities (Sondheimer, 1990). The general belief is that defendants with mental or emotional problems (assumably, both long and short term) are less culpable or morally blameworthy than defendants without such problems. If the defendant lacked the inability to make a free and rationale choice to commit the crime, or lacked the ability to control their behavior, state and federal courts have recognized that the deterrent and/or retributive doctrines underlying the application of the death penalty will not be served (e.g., *Atkins v. Virginia*, 2002; *Penry v. Lynaugh*, 1989; *Thompson v. Oklahoma*, 1988).

These beliefs have been clearly embraced by state legislatures, most of whom have explicitly incorporated the notion of reduced culpability via mental or emotional disorders into their list of statutory mitigating factors.[2] In fact, most states model their statutory mitigators after the popular McNaghten insanity defense by including both volitional (lacks the substantial capacity to conform his conduct to the requirements of the law) and cognitive (lacks the substantial capacity to appreciate the criminality of his conduct) mitigators in their statutory schemes (Acker & Lanier, 1994).

However, as mentioned earlier, presenting this type of mitigation evidence can pose a number of challenges for defense teams. In some cases, defendants indicate that their crimes were committed while they were in such a stupor and/or rage that they simply do not recall any details about their behavior. If trying to establish the fact of long-standing problems, defense attorneys may find themselves working with clients who are reluctant to reveal sensitive information, with families that dissuade defendants from sharing embarrassing aspects of their lives, and with defendants who lack the judgment and social competence to effectively assist the defense in communicating factors that may be relevant to the defense (Bjerregaard, Smith, & Fogel, 2005; McPherson, 1995; Tomes, 1997). Saddled with difficulties of these natures, defense attorneys often face a formidable challenge of presenting whatever information they have to jurors in a persuasive, comprehensible manner that will sway them toward recommending a life sentence.

There is even more reason for concern in situations where the mitigating factor is presented in a manner that closely mirrors an insanity defense. For example, the North Carolina statutory mitigating factor of "lacks the capacity of the defendant to appreciate the criminality of his conduct or to conform his conduct to the requirements of law was impaired" is very similar in substance and wording to the insanity defense utilized by the state.[3] In such instances, if the defendant has already unsuccessfully presented an insanity defense, there is a real danger that this evidence may be ignored or discounted at the sentencing phase on the basis that it was already argued and dismissed (McPherson, 1995). Although mental illness and insanity are distinct legal concepts, the difference may be difficult for jurors to grasp and incorporate into their decision making. Perhaps the largest risk in presenting this type of mitigation lies in the possibility that jurors may interpret such factors as evidence of future dangerousness. This is very much a risk in situations where future dangerousness is an explicit issue at sentencing and even when it is not. These issues are particularly relevant in Texas and Oregon because the issue of future dangerousness is a part of the sentencing assessment. In addition, several states designate future dangerousness as a specific statutory aggravator (Connell, 2003). Similarly, several states utilize the defendant's lack of future dangerousness as a statutory mitigator.[4] However, there is evidence that jurors will often consider this issue as a "non-statutory" aggravating factor (Sondheimer, 1990), and take it into account in their deliberations even if it is not submitted.

Justice Sandra Day O'Connor clearly recognized this risk in the *Penry v. Lynaugh* (1989, p. 324) decision where she proclaimed that Penry's mental retardation and history of abuse presented a "two-edged sword." While such evidence may operate to diminish culpability, O'Connor believed that it may also function to alert the jury that this individual may be dangerous in the future and influence their decision accordingly. Attorneys arguing that their clients' mental illness renders them incapable of conforming to the requirements of the law may in effect also be arguing that their client will continue to pose a threat to the community unless appropriately treated or eliminated (Sondheimer, 1990). If this occurs, jurors are in fact taking information that was introduced to mitigate the punishment and utilizing it to aggravate the punishment (Berkman, 1989; Crocker, 1997; Eisenberg & Wells, 1993; Haney, 1998; Sevilla, 1999). Haney, Sontag, and Costanzo (1994, p. 164) refer to this phenomenon as "converted mitigation." Therefore, several writers have suggested that mental health mitigators may inadvertently function to *increase* the probability of receiving a death sentence (Berkman, 1989; Eisenberg, Garvey, & Wells, 1998; Slobogin, 2004; Sundby, 1997).

Contributing to this phenomenon is the fact that as soon as defendants introduce evidence of mental disability, they open the door for the state to have their mental capacities assessed. This can be especially risky in states such as Texas and Oregon that focus on future dangerousness in guiding sentencing decisions. In *Barefoot v. Estelle* (1983), the Court upheld the practice of allowing state psychiatrists to give their expert opinions concerning the future dangerousness of the defendant. Typically, jurors have been found to believe that the testimony of state expert witnesses is less biased than experts for the defense, and are therefore likely to give more credence to testimony from state experts (Sundby, 1997).

Even when not countered by state witnesses, the use of expert witnesses can have a detrimental effect for the defense. As mentioned above, there is evidence to suggest that jurors view experts with a certain degree of skepticism, especially those for the defense, who they may view as "hired guns." In general, jurors are doubtful that doctors, who typically spend little time with the defendant, are able to testify with authority as to both the existence of and the impact of the defendant's mental disorder (Sundby, 1997).

The risk of converted mitigation occurring may be especially high in situations where the murders are judged to be especially heinous or brutal. The aggravating factor of "heinous and/or cruel," one frequently included in states' lists of aggravators, invites or even requires jurors to assess the defendant's mental state and attitude (Crocker, 1997). While psychiatric evidence may help to explain the heinous nature of the offense, it may also reveal that the defendant is not amenable to rehabilitation. There is also evidence that in particularly vile offenses, jurors are less likely to fully consider mitigation evidence of any type (Bowers & Steiner, 1998).

In addition to the practical implications involved with the inappropriate use of mental illness as a potential aggravator, there are several legal implications. As Slobogin (2004) points out, the use of mental illness as an aggravating factor in death sentencing implicates due process rights of defendants. The *Lockett v. Ohio* (1978) decision certainly indicated that due process required jurors to consider such evidence as mitigating factors. Similarly, Slobogin suggests that such situations may also violate equal protection of the law, as the empirical evidence does not support the conclusion that mentally ill offenders are more violent than non-mentally ill offenders. At the very minimum, we know that predictions of future violence are often invalid (Connell, 2003).

Last, and perhaps the most relevant at the present time, recent decisions by the Court imply that executing offenders who are mentally impaired at the time of their offense may violate the Eight Amendment (in particular, *Atkins v. Virginia*, 2002). This would seem to reflect a developing consensus that executing such individuals does not serve to further the legitimate goals of punishment.

The Present Study

The foregoing discussion suggests that defense attorneys with clients who were mentally ill at the time of the offense may be placed in the unfortunate position of deciding whether to present evidence that may mitigate their defendants' culpability and therefore reduce his or her sentence, or to exclude such evidence due to the possibility that it may be utilized to justify a death sentence. The purpose of this study is to empirically examine capital cases from North Carolina to assess the impact of mental health mitigators on jury sentencing decisions. Specifically, this research addresses the following questions:

(1) How frequently do defendants present mitigation defenses based on di-
    minished capacity, and how are these factors related to the sentences
    recommended by juries?
(2) If *prima facie* evidence suggests that these factors are associated with
    sentencing decisions, do these associations hold when controlling for a
    variety of case-specific factors?
(3) Does the impact of these mitigators vary depending on the heinousness
    of the offense?

METHOD

Source of Data for Cases

The analysis is based on information from reviews of capital murder trials in
North Carolina. These cases were determined from *LexisNexis* searches of
the North Carolina Supreme Court and the Court of Appeals cases. In these
trials, the defendants were convicted of, or pled guilty to, 1st degree murder,
the state sought the death penalty, the trial progressed to a sentencing phase
whereby the jury heard evidence concerning aggravating and mitigating
factors, and the jury issued a binding recommendation for a sentence. In
making a sentencing recommendation, North Carolina capital juries have
only two options, a death sentence or a sentence of life in prison. Included in
the data are cases where the sentencing phase was conducted, but the jury
members declared that they could not reach the required unanimous decision regarding a sentence (in essence, a deadlocked jury), resulting in the
default sentence of life in prison.

Reviews of capital trials were derived from public records documents that
accompany decisions regarding appeals of capital murder convictions rendered by the North Carolina Supreme Court and the North Carolina Court
of Appeals. These materials include defendant and state briefs, as well as a
form completed by the jury that records their responses to aggravating and
mitigating factors, and concludes with the jury's sentencing recommendation. Historically, these materials have been published in hard copy form
and placed in two university law libraries in North Carolina, while other
locations have microfilm copies. Beginning with decisions returned from
cases appealed in 1999, hard copies have not been made available, but
materials are accessible via an electronic data file (http://www.ncappellate-
courts.org). This information was supplemented with newspaper accounts
of the trial where such coverage was available through *LexisNexis* or

Newsbank, another electronic databank that includes varying years of stories from eight North Carolina newspapers with metropolitan area coverage.

The unit of analysis for this research is the jury recommendation for a life or death sentence. The data include situations where the same defendant received sentences for multiple victims (each treated as a separate case), and where multiple defendants were charged with the death of one victim (again, each treated as a separate case). Although the full dataset covers the period of 1979–2000, the cases relevant for this analysis are those occurring subsequent to the *McKoy v. North Carolina* (1990) ruling by the Court whereby the manner in which juries respond to mitigation was altered. Specifically, that ruling mandated that juries do not have to agree unanimously in their finding of a mitigator for it to have relevance in reaching a sentencing decision. This departed from the earlier practice of requiring juries to agree unanimously in their finding of a mitigator. Thus, the meaning of a mitigator being accepted was altered from earlier years, and theoretically freed any individual juror to vote against the death penalty on the basis of a mitigator that he/she believed relevant to that decision, regardless of the beliefs of the other jurors.

The first post-*McKoy* trial was held in April 1990, and our data consist of 441 sentences returned in capital cases since that time through 2000, the latest year for which North Carolina Supreme or Appeals Court decisions have been issued for the substantial majority of appeals filed. Of these cases, 374 are original trials while 67 are retrials following a vacating of the defendant's conviction or a remand of his/her death sentence. Not included in these 441 cases are those involving two types of situations emerging from jury deliberations in the penalty phase of the trial. In the first, the jury did not find an aggravating factor. In the second, the jury found an aggravating circumstance to exist, but judged that it did not merit the death penalty. Jury deliberations cease in both these situations; mitigation is not considered and the sentencing decision defaults to life imprisonment.

Because there is no centralized source of information regarding capital murder trials in North Carolina, it is impossible to determine the precise number of all capital murder trials conducted during the period covered in the data. However, appeals of death sentences are automatically referred to the state Supreme Court. Also, a large proportion of defendants receiving a life sentence appeal their 1st degree murder convictions to the state Court of Appeals. If the Court of Appeals decision is not in their favor, defendants may appeal to the Supreme Court, but the court has the option of declining to hear the case. Given that the substantial majority of capital cases are appealed to at least one of these courts, we estimate that the available data includes approximately 75% of all capital sentencing recommendations made by juries during the period of the study.[5]

Variables

Sentencing Decisions
The final question posed to North Carolina jurors in completing an "Issues and Recommendation as to Punishment" form is what sentence they recommend for the defendant – death or life in prison. These responses constituted the dependent variable of the analysis, which is coded one for death and zero for life.

Mitigators
These responses constitute the dependent variable. In the penalty phase of the North Carolina capital murder trials, jurors are asked to indicate on the "Issues and Recommendation as to Punishment" form their responses to submitted mitigating circumstances by answering the following question: "Do you find from the evidence the existence of one of more of the following mitigating circumstances?" Defendants who wish to have psychological or emotional impairments ("diminished capacity") taken into account may submit one or both of two statutory mitigators. As cited in the North Carolina statutes (see the appendix for a full list of statutory aggravators and mitigators), these mitigators are:

"The capital felony was committed while the defendant was under the influence of mental or emotional disturbance" (labeled "Mental or Emotional Disturbance" in the analyses); and "The capacity of the defendant to appreciate the criminality of his conduct or to conform his conduct to the requirements of the law was impaired" (labeled "Capacity Impaired" in the analyses).

Jurors deliberate on each mitigator presented, then record their decisions by answering "yes" or "no" on the "Issues and Recommendation as to Punishment" form. For both these mitigators, a code of one indicates that the jury accepted the mitigator, while a code of zero designates that the jury rejected the mitigator.

Control Variables
We determined the overall impact of our targeted mitigating factors by controlling for other factors that had a demonstrated association with the sentencing recommendation. Utilizing a large number of case-specific variables that capture both legal and extra-legal variables that could

influence sentencing outcomes, a backwards stepwise entry was employed to determine a set of control variables,[6] excluding the two mitigators that are the focus of the analysis. A final model of six significant control variables was derived.[7] These were used to construct an equation that examined the net effects of the two diminished capacity variables. For each of the control variables, a code of one indicates the presence of the factor being examined and a code of zero represents the absence of that factor. The control variables, with their labels shown in parentheses, were:

(1) Whether the case was a retrial (Retrial).
(2) Acceptance of the aggravating circumstance "the capital felony was especially heinous, atrocious, or cruel" (Heinous).
(3) Acceptance of the aggravating circumstance "the murder for which the defendant stands convicted was part of a course of conduct in which the defendant engaged and which included the commission by the defendant of other crimes of violence against another person or persons" (Course of Violent Conduct).
(4) Acceptance of mitigating factor "the defendant has no significant history of prior criminal activity" (No Criminal History).
(5) Age of the defendant (Defendant's Age).
(6) Acceptance of mitigating factor "the defendant was an accomplice in or accessory to the capital felony committed by another person and his participation was relatively minor" (Minor Participation).

FINDINGS

The discussion of findings that follows is organized to address the specific research questions that were explored in the analyses.

How frequently do defendants present mitigation defenses based on diminished capacity and how are these factors related to the sentences recommended by the juries?

As shown in Table 1, the answer to the first part of this question is that diminished capacity mitigators were submitted to juries in a healthy majority of the 441 cases. The Mental or Emotional Disturbance mitigator was submitted in 303 (68.6%) of the cases; when submitted, the success rate was quite high, with the juries accepting it in 70.6% of cases. The Capacity

Table 1. Distribution of Mental Health Mitigators Considered by Juries
($N = 441$).

	Not Submitted	Submitted but Not Accepted	Accepted	Success Rate if Submitted
Under the influence of mental or emotional disturbance	138 31.3%	89 20.1%	214 48.5%	70.6%
Capacity to appreciate criminality impaired	139 31.5%	171 38.8%	131 29.7%	43.4%
Both mental or emotional disturbance and capacity impaired	172[a] 39.0%	165[b] 37.4%	104[c] 23.6%	38.7%

[a]Neither mitigator was submitted or only one was submitted.
[b]Both mitigators were submitted, but one was not accepted.
[c]Both mitigators were submitted and both were accepted.

Impaired mitigator was submitted in a nearly identical number of cases (302; 68.5%). However, with an acceptance rate of 43.4%, juries were less likely to accept it as a mitigating element of the crime.

Also revealed in Table 1 is the considerable overlap in submitting these two variables together. In 269 (61%) of the cases, juries were asked to consider the impact of both mitigators. In a majority of those cases, the jury accepted one, but not the other mitigator; typically, this involved accepting the Mental or Emotional Disturbance mitigator while rejecting the Capacity Impaired mitigator. In a minority of cases (23.6%), both mitigators were accepted, representing a success rate of 38.7% for co-submission.

The results shown in Table 2 estimate the impact of submitting these mitigators on the juries' recommendation of a death sentence. The results suggest that while having either of these mitigators accepted by the jury reduces the chances a defendant will receive a death sentence, the Capacity Impaired mitigator had a much stronger influence. Defendants who had this mitigator accepted were five times less likely to receive a death sentence.[8] However, the results demonstrate that defendants who submit these mitigators, but fail to convince the jury of their existence, suffer a substantially escalated risk of receiving a death sentence. As shown in the odds ratio column, defendants who submit to the jury that they were under the influence of a mental or emotional disturbance, but who do not have this mitigator accepted, are five

Table 2. Impact of Diminished Capacity Mitigation on Sentencing Decisions ($N = 441$).

	Death Sentence	Odds Ratio
	$(0 = 0.66)$	
Mental or emotional disturbance**		
Not submitted	59.4%	
Submitted but not accepted	88.8%	5.09
Accepted	61.7%	0.66
Capacity impaired**		
Not submitted	63.3%	
Submitted but not accepted	88.9%	7.32
Accepted	40.5%	0.20
Both disturbance and capacity**		
Submitted but not accepted	87.9%	11.11
Accepted	39.4%	0.09

**$p < 0.01$.

times more likely to receive a death sentence than those who did have it accepted. Similarly, those defendants who fail to convince the jury that their capacity was impaired are over seven times more likely to receive a death sentence than those who had this mitigator accepted.

The impact of these mitigators is even more pronounced when they are submitted together. Referring to the odds ratio column, defendants who submitted both to the jury, but had one or the other rejected, were at 11 times greater risk of receiving the death penalty than those defendants who had both mitigators rejected.

The findings presented in Tables 1 and 2 suggest that succeeding in convincing a jury that one's reasoning capacities were deficient at the time of the offense modestly reduced the likelihood of receiving a death sentence. However, submitting these mitigators, but failing to convince a jury of their validity, carried the cost of significantly increasing a defendant's chances of receiving a death sentence. Pursuing diminished capacity as a mitigation strategy is indeed a gamble in which the risks are quite high.

Do these effects hold when controlling for a variety of other factors associated with sentencing outcomes?

In order to test whether the effects observed at the bivariate level would hold after controlling for a variety of case-specific factors, logistic regression analysis was utilized because the dependent variable is dichotomous. As described in the Method section, a set of six variables were determined to be predictive of sentencing outcomes, and these were utilized as controls to further examine the influence of the diminished capacity variables. We note here that because of their preponderance among cases with the diminished capacity mitigators included, we focus our analyses on the 269 cases in which both mitigators were submitted. Of these cases, three had missing data on at least one of the control variables, so the analyses derive from the 266 remaining cases.

Table 3 includes two sets of analyses. The results shown in the first three columns examine the individual impact of the diminished capacity mitigators while controlling for other relevant variables. The second set of columns examines the influence of having both statutory mitigators accepted. A perusal of Table 3, where the logistic regression results are presented, reveals that the two diminished capacity mitigators are statistically significant predictors of sentencing outcomes, even when controlling for the effects of other variables known to have a similar influence.

The analysis on the total sample demonstrates that defendants who are involved in a retrial are significantly more likely to receive a death sentence than those who are involved in their initial trials. Concentrating on the "probability" column, the first analysis demonstrates that the jury accepting that the offense was heinous increases the probability of a defendant being sentenced to death by 28% compared to those who had it rejected.[9] Likewise, defendants who committed their offense during a course of violent conduct were 17% more likely to receive a death sentence.

Similarly, several mitigating factors emerged as significant predictors. Defendants with no significant history of prior criminal activity were 24% less likely to receive a death sentence. Defendants whose age at the time of the offense was deemed mitigating were 41% less likely to receive a death sentence. Likewise, situations where the defendant was an accomplice and a minor participant and/or was acting under duress when the homicide was committed were 52% less likely to be sentenced to death.

The first analysis also demonstrates that the jury accepting the Mental or Emotional Disturbance mitigator decreased the probability of a defendant being sentenced to death by 30% compared to those defendants who had it rejected. Likewise, those defendants who had the Capacity Impaired mitigator accepted were 40% less likely to receive a death sentence. Overall, these eight variables together improved our ability to predict death sentencing by 14.3% and explained 54% of the variance in death sentences, figures that are relatively high in the death sentencing literature.

Table 3.   The Influence of Mental Health Mitigators Controlling for Case Characteristics ($n = 266$).

	B	Odds Ratio	Probability	B	Odds Ratio	Probability
Retrial	1.59**	4.92	0.25	1.60**	4.95	0.37
Heinous	2.01**	7.47	0.28	1.92**	6.84	0.42
Course of violent conduct	0.95**	2.59	0.17	0.97**	2.63	0.24
No criminal history	−0.99**	0.37	−0.24	−1.00**	0.37	−0.20
Defendant's age	−1.77**	0.17	−0.41	−1.47*	0.23	−0.27
Minor participation	−2.51**	0.08	−0.52	−2.87**	0.06	−0.36
Mental or emotional disturbance	−1.24*	0.29	−0.30			
Capacity impaired	−1.71**	0.18	−0.40			
Both mental or emotional disturbance and capacity impaired				−2.15**	0.12	−0.48
Improvement in case classification	14.3%			15.8%		
Nagelkerke R^2	0.54**			0.53**		

*$p < 0.05$
**$p < 0.01$.

However, these findings also demonstrate the risk involved in presenting such evidence and failing to convince the jury of its mitigating value. Since the analysis compares those who succeed in presenting this type of mitigation with those who fail, the findings indicate that even after controlling for a variety of case characteristics, failing to convince a jury of diminished capacity had a very detrimental impact on juries' sentencing decisions. For example, the odds ratio for the mitigator of Mental or Emotional Disturbance is 0.29. This indicates that defendants who successfully present this mitigator are 3.5 times less likely to receive a death sentence than those who fail to convince the jury (see note 10 for how this statistic is derived). Conversely, this also means that defendants who introduce evidence of this mitigator but fail to convince the jury are almost 3.5 times as likely to receive a death sentence. Similarly, defendants who unsuccessfully argued the Capacity Impaired mitigator were 5.5 times more likely to receive a death sentence. While these findings do not support the contention that juries are inappropriately considering evidence of mental incapacity as aggravators (see the discussion above of converted mitigation), it appears that a jury rejecting claims about diminished capacity significantly increased a defendant's probability of receiving a death sentence.

The second set of findings in Table 3 examines the impact of submitting both of these mitigators. The results are substantively similar, with each of the aggravators included increasing the probability of a death sentence while the mitigators decrease that probability. If a defendant successfully argues both diminished capacity mitigators, he or she reduces the risk of receiving a death sentence almost in half. In contrast, defendants who submit both mitigators, but fail to convince the jury of either, are eight times more likely to be sentenced to death. Again, these findings demonstrate that successful presentation of such evidence is extremely beneficial to defendants. However, they also highlight the risk to defendants in failing to substantiate such claims.

Does the impact of these mitigators vary depending on the heinousness of the offense?

Previous research suggests that the risk of converted mitigation – i.e., acceptance of a mitigator *increasing* the likelihood of a death sentence – is greatest among those cases where the offense is considered especially cruel and/or heinous. In order to test this proposition, separate analyses were run for those defendants where the jury deemed the offense heinous and atrocious versus those defendants for whom this aggravator was not found.

The first three columns in Table 4 show results for cases where the offenses were judged to be heinous via the jury's accepting the "cruel and heinous" aggravator. Interestingly, the only variables to emerge as significant predictors of sentencing in this equation were the diminished capacity variables. Contrary to predictions of converted mitigation, both Mental or Emotional Disturbance and Capacity Impaired, if accepted, are shown to significantly reduce defendants' chances of receiving a death sentence, even when the offense was heinous. In fact, these variables actually have a stronger influence in this model than in the previous model shown in Table 3, where it is shown that accepting the Mental or Emotional Disturbance mitigator reduced the probability of a death sentence by 66% if the offense was heinous versus 30% for all cases.

Table 4.   Examining the Influence of Heinous and Atrocious Offense.

	Heinous Offense ($n = 111$)			Non-heinous Offense ($n = 155$)		
	B	Odds Ratio	Probability	B	Odds Ratio	Probability
Retrial	0.02	1.02	0.00	2.43**	11.39	0.38
Course of Violent Conduct	0.75	2.12	0.07	0.91*	2.49	0.20
No Criminal History	−1.16	0.31	−0.20	−1.04*	0.35	−0.25
Defendant's Age	−1.93	0.15	−0.39	−1.25	0.29	−0.29
Defendant was accomplice and participation was minor	−3.01	0.05	−0.63	−9.75	0.00	−0.56
Under influence of Mental/ Emotional Disturbance	−3.19*	0.04	−0.66	−0.45	0.64	−0.11
Capacity to appreciate conduct	−1.55*	0.21	−0.29	−2.08**	0.13	−0.42
Improvement in case classification	4.5%			24.5%		
Nagelkerke R^2	0.38**			0.55**		

*$p < 0.05$
**$p < 0.01$.

The second set of columns in Table 4 examines cases where the offenses were not deemed heinous. For the non-heinous homicides, the fact that the case was a retrial significantly increased the likelihood of getting a death sentence. The aggravator of the murder occurring during a course of violent conduct likewise increased the chance that a defendant would be sentenced to death. Interestingly, the only mitigating factor to achieve statistical significance was Capacity Impaired. If jurors believed that this had mitigating value, the probability of receiving a death sentence was significantly reduced (42%). However, the risk of failing to convince jurors of one's claim is also demonstrated; defendants who presented evidence of this mitigator but failed to convince the jury were 7.7 times more likely to be sentenced to death.

Even under conditions of statistical control, the potential impact of the reduced capacity mitigators remains substantial. In short, the results demonstrate the importance of being able to convince a jury that diminished capacity mitigators should be taken into account when making an appeal to juries to spare the defendant's life. Notably, even in cases where the capital murder was judged to be especially cruel and heinous, juries appear to be willing to factor in these situational elements of the crime when making sentencing decisions.

DISCUSSION AND CONCLUSIONS

Our analyses of North Carolina capital sentencing decisions show that diminished capacity mitigators were frequently submitted to the jury for consideration. The results of the analyses indicate that if these mitigators were accepted, the chances of a defendant being sentenced to death were definitely reduced. However, when these mitigators were submitted but not accepted, the defendant's likelihood of receiving a death sentence was substantially escalated.

The results do not support the contention that jurors may have treated these statutory mitigators as *de facto* non-statutory aggravators. When accepted, both mitigators operated as one would expect to reduce the probability of a death sentence. However, the results also emphasize the risk of submitting this type of claim as a mitigating circumstance. In situations where defendants introduced evidence of these mitigators, but failed to convince the jury of their mitigating value, the jurors appear to have been even more swayed toward recommending a death sentence.

These results signal a need to carefully weigh the advantages and disadvantages of presenting such testimony and if choosing to do so, the absolute necessity of convincing the jury of its validity. Clearly, this presents a dilemma for defense attorneys in capital cases. In some cases, failure to present such evidence may be later judged to constitute a reversible error and may subject the attorney to charges of ineffective assistance of counsel. On the other hand, it may be in the defendant's best interests in some situations not to emphasize certain factors, because of damaging testimony that can ensue from the prosecution's rebuttal. To make matters more complicated for defenses, trial judges in North Carolina can compel a defense to submit a statutory mitigator if they believe it is supported by the evidence, even if the defense wishes not to (see Bjerregaard et al., 2005).

The risks involved in presenting impaired capacity mitigators underscores the need to adequately prepare for sentencing hearings and to develop strategic approaches to the presentation of mitigation evidence. One recent development that aids in this area is the use of mitigation specialists.[10] These experts can now be funded by the courts and can assist the defense in a number of ways by helping attorneys collect and assemble background information on their defendants as well as develop effective strategies for presenting such evidence (Bjerregaard et al., 2005; Schroeder, 2003). Mitigation specialists are trained to both recognize the importance of certain characteristics as well as to sensitively collect such information (Tomes, 1997). Importantly, they can explain to family members and others the importance of such information and attempt to overcome potential problems such as embarrassment or simply a lack of understanding the importance of such information. When appropriate, they can also assist attorneys in preparing family members and others for testimony in the penalty phase of the trial.

As Connell (2003, p. 334) notes, it is imperative for the defense to help jurors understand how the defendant could have engaged in such behavior. Likewise, Stetler (1999, p. 17) stresses that experts must help "the jury to understand the human context, to see the impact of disability on the choices the capital client could make in everyday life, and to track the origin of the disabilities to biological, environmental, psychological and social influences which the client never chose." It is equally important to emphasize any redeeming qualities of the defendant, and to assist jurors to "see the defendant in a more multidimensional light" (Connell, 2003, p. 334). Schroeder (2003, p. 426) refers to this as the "life history approach," emphasizing the importance of a team approach to gathering, assessing, and preparing such data.

When mitigation evidence is introduced that has the potential to be utilized against the defendant (e.g., mental illness, drug abuse), the defense should be careful to develop a strategy that counteracts the potentially damaging aspects of this information. Countervailing evidence such as previous efforts to seek treatment and/or a supportive family may help to emphasize the mitigating value of this type of evidence. Similarly, highlighting the defendant's ability to do well in a structured environment (e.g., prison) would be particularly relevant in these situations, and has been held by the Court to be appropriate evidence at the sentencing stage (*Skipper v. South Carolina*, 1986).

It is also important to integrate such mitigation defenses into both the guilt and penalty stages of the trial process. This is especially important in situations where defendants fail to present a diminished capacity defense at the guilt stage. Such defendants are at a clear disadvantage when they must argue the mitigation of such evidence a short time later before the same jury that convicted them. Therefore, it is crucial that the defense begin to collect information and strategize as early as possible in the process. The results discussed here suggest that if diminished capacity claims are to be part of that strategy, the likelihood of failure must be seen as potentially quite damaging.

At some level, the results are promising because they suggest that the system appears to be working in the way in which it was designed to function. It is important to note that none of the extra-legal factors examined (see note 8) emerged as significant predictors of the defendant's sentence. Instead, the factors found to predict that sentencing outcomes were aggravating and mitigating factors highlighted during the sentencing phase of the process, along with whether the case was a retrial. All of these could be construed as legal factors that would be expected to guide and influence the jury's decision.

That said, we recognize that there may be an important control variable that is too vague to take into account, and that is simply the *quality of the presentation* made by the defense counsel or by the prosecution. In essence, the defense and prosecution must compete to "sell" their versions of events, as well as their interpretations of the blameworthiness and character of the defendant, to the jury. The results of this competition may, at times, obscure the legal facts of a case when jurors convene to make their decisions. We can offer no ready solution to this common problem, but we subscribe to the "death is different" doctrine articulated in *Furman v. Georgia* (1972) when it comes to capital cases. Therefore, our results may ultimately serve to underscore the absolute necessity of competent, experienced counsel in capital cases involving defendants whose crimes can be linked to their mental or emotional conditions at the time of the offense.

NOTES

1. North Carolina General Statutes §15A-2000 (2004).
2. For example, the Model Penal Code includes "extreme mental or emotional disturbance" and the presence of "mental disease or defect" among its lists of mitigating factors. Model Penal Code §210.6(4)(b)(1980).
3. North Carolina utilizes the M'Naghten rule which holds that a defendant is legally insane if at the time of the offense he was laboring under such a defect of reason from disease or deficiency of mind as to be incapable of knowing the nature and quality of his act or, if he did know this, of distinguishing between right and wrong in relation to the act (N.C. Gen. Stat. §14–17, VI-C (2004)). The statutory mitigator that is most similar is worded "The capacity of the defendant to appreciate the criminality of his conduct or to conform his conduct to the requirements of law was impaired." See also, *State v. Claytor*, 574 N.E. 472, 480–482 (Ohio, 1991) where the Court rejected the appellant's argument that special jury instructions were

necessary because of the similarity between insanity and the mitigating factors being presented.

4. For example, see Wash. Rev. Code Ann. 10.95.070 (8).

5. We have identified 149 eligible cases that are not included in the dataset. The reasons for their omission include (1) defendants' sentences not being appealed (e.g., the individual pleads guilty and is sentenced to life, or is retried from a death sentence and receives life), and therefore trial documents not being available through *LexisNexis*; (2) the conviction and/or sentence was appealed, but the "Issues and Recommendation as to Punishment" form was, for whatever reason, not included in the file; and (3) in a small number of cases, case materials were not available because hard copies were missing from both libraries or not yet posted in electronic form. The missing cases disproportionately comprise cases where defendants received life sentences, leading to an overrepresentation of death penalty cases in the working dataset. However, a comparison between life sentence cases included and not included in the dataset revealed no substantive differences that may have altered the findings of the analysis.

6. At the initial iteration the following variables were included in the analysis: defendant and victim's gender and race, type of attorney, whether trial was a retrial, stranger homicide, victim shot, total number of victims murdered and injured, whether the defendant was the triggerman, the total number of aggravator and mitigators submitted, in addition to the statutory aggravators and mitigators.

7. This final model was checked for multicollinearity. The V.I.F. scores ranged from 1.04 to 1.34, indicating that multicollinearity was not a problem.

8. Taking the inverse of the odds ratio indicates the impact of the zero category of the independent variable on the dependent variable. Therefore, in this example $1/0.20 = 5$.

9. Probabilities calculated using the following formula (see Peterson, 1985):

(A) $L_0 = \ln[P/1 - P]$
(B) $L_1 = L_0 + B$
(C) $[\exp(L_1)/1 + \exp(L_1)] - [\exp(L_0)/1 + \exp(L_0)]$.

10. Mitigation experts can be qualified social workers and sociologists in addition to psychiatrists and psychologists.

REFERENCES

Acker, J. R., & Lanier, C. S. (1994). In fairness and mercy: Statutory mitigating factors in capital punishment laws. *Criminal Law Bulletin, 30*, 299–345.

Atkins v. Virginia (2002). 536 U.S. 304.

Barefoot v. Estelle (1983). 463 U.S. 880.

Berkman, E. F. (1989). Mental illness as an aggravating circumstance in capital sentencing. *Columbia Law Review, 89*, 291–309.

Bjerregaard, B., Smith, M. D., & Fogel, S. J. (2005). Issues in the use of aggravating and mitigating circumstances during the sentencing phase of capital murder trials. In: R. Muraskin (Ed.), *Key correctional issues* (pp. 285–310). Upper Saddle River, NJ: Pearson.

Bowers, W. J., & Steiner, B. D. (1998). Choosing life or death: Sentencing dynamics in capital cases. In: J. R. Acker, R. M. Bohm & C. S. Lanier (Eds), *America's experiment with capital punishment: Reflections on the past, present, and future of the ultimate penal sanction* (pp. 309–349). Durham, NC: Carolina Academic Press.

Connell, M. A. (2003). A psychobiographical approach to the evaluation for sentence mitigation. *Journal of Psychiatry & Law, 31,* 319–354.

Crocker, P. L. (1997). Concepts of culpability and deathworthiness: Differentiating between guilt and punishment in death penalty cases. *Fordham Law Review, 66,* 21–86.

Cunningham, M. D., & Vigen, M. P. (2002). Death row inmate characteristics, adjustment, and confinement: A critical review of the literature. *Behavioral Sciences and the Law, 20,* 191–210.

Eisenberg, T., & Wells, M. T. (1993). Deadly confusion: Juror instructions in capital cases. *Cornell Law Review, 79,* 1–17.

Eisenberg, T., Garvey, S. P., & Wells, M. T. (1998). But was he sorry? The role of remorse in capital sentencing. *Cornell Law Review, 83,* 1599–1637.

Furman v. Georgia (1972). 408 U.S. 238.

Garvey, S. P. (1998). Aggravation and mitigation in capital cases: What do jurors think? *Columbia Law Review, 98,* 1538–1576.

Gregg v. Georgia (1976). 428 U.S. 153.

Haney, C. (1998). Mitigation and the study of lives: On the roots of violent criminality and the nature of capital justice. In: J. R. Acker, R. M. Bohm & C. S. Lanier (Eds), *America's experiment with capital punishment: Reflections on the past, present, and future of the ultimate penal sanction* (pp. 351–384). Durham, NC: Carolina Academic Press.

Haney, C., Sontag, L., & Costanzo, S. (1994). Deciding to take a life: Capital juries, sentencing instructions, and the jurisprudence of death. *Journal of Social Issues, 50,* 149–176.

Hitchcock v. Dugger (1987). 481 U.S. 393.

Jurek v. Texas (1976). 428 U.S. 262.

Lewis, D. O., Pincus, J. H., Bard, B., Richardson, E., Prichep, L. S., Feldman, M. Y., & Yeager, C. (1988). Neuropsychiatric, psychoeducational, and family characteristics of 14 juveniles condemned to death in the United States. *American Journal of Psychiatry, 145,* 585–589.

Lewis, D. O., Pincus, J. H., Feldman, M., Jackson, L., & Bard, B. (1986). Psychiatric, neurological and psychoeducational characteristics of 15 death row inmates in the United States. *American Journal of Psychiatry, 143,* 838–845.

Lockett v. Ohio (1978). 438 U.S. 586.

McKoy v. North Carolina (1990). 494 U.S. 433.

McPherson, S. (1995). Psychosocial investigation in death penalty mitigation: Procedures, pitfalls and impact. In: G. Davies & S. Lloyd-Bostock (Eds), *Psychology, law and criminal justice: International developments in research and practice* (pp. 286–295). Oxford, England: Walter De Gruyter.

National Mental Health Association (2001). Policy position: Death penalty and people with mental illness. http://www.mha-mi.org/policy44.html.

Penry v. Lynaugh (1989). 492 U.S. 302.

Perlin, M. L. (1996). Professionalism, mental disability, and the death penalty: The executioner's face is always well-hidden: The role of counsel and the courts in determining who dies. *New York Law School Law Review, 41,* 201–236.

Peterson, T. (1985). A comment on presenting results from logit and probit models. *American Sociological Review, 50,* 130–131.

Profitt v. Florida (1976). 428 U.S. 242.

Roberts v. Louisiana (1976). 428 U.S. 325.

Robinson, D. A., & Stephens, O. H. (1992). Patterns of mitigating factors in juvenile death penalty cases. *Criminal Law Bulletin, 28,* 246–275.

Schroeder, J. (2003). Forging a new practice area: Social work's role in death penalty mitigation investigations. *Families in Society, 84,* 423–432.

Sevilla, C. (1999). Antisocial personality disorder: Justification for the death penalty? *Journal of Contemporary Legal Issues, 10,* 247–262.

Skipper v. South Carolina (1986). 476 U.S. 1.

Slobogin, C. (2004). Mental illness and the death penalty. http://www.boalt.org/CCLR/v1/v1slobogintext.htm.

Sondheimer, J. N. (1990). A continuing source of aggravation: The improper consideration of mitigation factors in death penalty sentencing. *Hastings Law Journal, 41,* 409–446.

Stetler, R. (1999). Capital cases. *Champion Magazine.* Http://www.criminaljustice.org/public.nsf/0/1f190a60788274dd8525674b00597b54?OpenDocument.

Sundby, S. E. (1997). The jury as critic: An empirical look at how capital juries perceive expert and law testimony. *Virginia Law Review, 83,* 1109–1188.

Thompson v. Oklahoma (1988). 487 U.S. 815.

Tomes, J. P. (1997). Damned if you do, damned if you don't: The use of mitigation experts in death penalty litigation. *American Journal of Criminal Law, 24,* 359–399.

Woodson v. North Carolina (1976). 428 U.S. 280.

APPENDIX. NORTH CAROLINA CAPITAL PUNISHMENT (§15A-2000)

Aggravating Circumstances

1. The capital felony was committed by a person lawfully incarcerated.

2. The defendant had been previously convicted of another capital felony or had been previously adjudicated delinquent in a juvenile proceeding for committing an offense that would be a capital felony if committed by an adult.

3. The defendant had been previously convicted of a felony involving the use or threat of violence to the person or had been previously adjudicated delinquent in a juvenile proceeding for committing an offense that would be a Class A, B1, B2, C, D, or E felony involving the use or threat of violence to the person if the offense had been committed by an adult.

4. The capital felony was committed for the purpose of avoiding or preventing a lawful arrest or affecting an escape from custody.

5. The capital felony was committed while the defendant was engaged, or was an aider or abettor, in the commission of, or an attempt to commit, or flight after committing or attempting to commit, any homicide, robbery, rape or a sex offense, arson, burglary, kidnapping, or aircraft

piracy or the unlawful throwing, placing, or discharging of a destructive
device or bomb.
6. The capital felony was committed for pecuniary gain.
7. The capital felony was committed to disrupt or hinder the lawful exercise of any governmental function or the enforcement of laws.
8. The capital felony was committed against a law-enforcement officer,
   employee of the Department of Correction, jailer, fireman, judge or
   justice, former judge or justice, prosecutor or former prosecutor, juror
   or former juror, or witness or former witness against the defendant,
   while engaged in the performance of his official duties or because of the
   exercise of his official duty.
9. The capital felony was especially heinous, atrocious, or cruel.
10. The defendant knowingly created a great risk of death to more than one
    person by means of a weapon or device which would normally be haz-
    ardous to the lives of more than one person.
11. The murder for which the defendant stands convicted was part of a
    course of conduct in which the defendant engaged and which included
    the commission by the defendant of other crimes of violence against
    another person or persons.

Statutory Mitigating Circumstances

1. The defendant has no significant history of prior criminal activity.
2. The capital felony was committed while the defendant was under the
   influence of mental or emotional disturbance.
3. The victim was a voluntary participant in the defendant's homicidal
   conduct or consented to the homicidal act.
4. The defendant was an accomplice in or accessory to the capital felony
   committed by another person and his participation was relatively minor.
5. The defendant acted under duress or under the domination of another
   person.
6. The capacity of the defendant to appreciate the criminality of his conduct
   or to conform his conduct to the requirements of law was impaired.
7. The age of the defendant at the time of the crime.
8. The defendant aided in the apprehension of another capital felon or
   testified truthfully on behalf of the prosecution in another prosecution of
   a felony.
9. Any other circumstance arising from the evidence which the jury deems
   to have mitigating value.

PART IV:
PRISONS – TWO CASES ON IDENTIFICATION AND TREATMENT OF MENTALLY ILL OFFENDERS BEHIND BARS

SCREENING FOR SERIOUS MENTAL ILLNESS AMONG CRIMINAL OFFENDERS

James A. Swartz and Arthur J. Lurigio

ABSTRACT

Resource constraints at all levels of the criminal justice system as well as the lack of a widely accepted, validated screening scale have made it difficult to screen adequately for serious mental illnesses (SMI) in offender populations. This study examined the use of the K6 scale, a recently developed and validated screening tool for SMI, using a sample of past-year arrestees. Among the main findings were that 18% of the sample screened positive for SMI. In contrast, commonly used screening questions misidentified a large proportion of arrestees with SMI. Based on these findings, we recommend the use of K6 scale to more accurately identify offenders with SMI.

Large- and small-scale epidemiological studies have shown that disproportionate numbers of offenders, compared with persons in the general population, have serious mental illnesses (SMI) such as schizophrenia, bipolar disorder, and major depressive disorder (Abram & Teplin, 1991; Abram, Teplin, & McClelland, 2003; Bureau of Justice Statistics (BJS), 1999;

The Organizational Response to Persons with Mental Illness Involved with the Criminal Justice System
Research in Social Problems and Public Policy, Volume 12, 137–161
ISSN: 0196-1152/doi:10.1016/S0196-1152(05)12007-9

Diamond, Wang, Holzer, Thomas, & des Anges, 2001; Human Rights Watch (HRW), 2003). The influx of large numbers of individuals with mental illnesses into the criminal justice system – precipitated, in part, by the closing of state psychiatric hospitals – resulted in a shifting of inpatient psychiatric treatment to criminal justice settings (Lamb, 1998; Lamb & Weinberger, 1998; Torrey, 1995). Presently, the three largest providers of psychiatric treatment services are urban jails: the Los Angeles County Jail, the Cook County Jail (CCJ) in Chicago, and the jail at Riker's Island in New York (Insel, 2003).

These continuing trends highlight the need for appropriate and effective mental health treatment services in criminal justice settings. Federal courts have consistently ruled that jails and prisons are legally obligated to provide mental health services (Diamond et al., 2001; Veysey & Bichler-Robertson, 2002). Without treatment, offenders with SMI often have trouble adapting to the daily routines and obeying the rules of prisons and jails (HRW, 2003; Torrey, 1995). Furthermore, inmates and detainees with mental illnesses are at increased risk for suicide, disciplinary infractions, and victimization (Dicataldo, Green, & Profit, 1995; HRW, 2003). In addition, mentally ill persons on community supervision can have problems adjusting to their sentences. For example, mentally ill probationers might have trouble complying with their probation orders (e.g., finding employment, reporting to officers) and are at an increased risk for re-arrest for a technical violation or a new offense (Solomon & Draine, 1999). Thus, from an organizational standpoint, treatment of mental illnesses is not only a legal and clinical requirement; it can also improve offender management and reduce recidivism.

Despite the clear legal and clinical obligations to provide mental health services, many mentally ill offenders are unidentified and untreated while under the authority of the criminal justice system (HRW, 2003; National Commission on Correctional Health Care (NCCHC), 2002; Steadman & Veysey, 1997). Moreover, as noted by Lurigio and Swartz (2000), because linkages between the criminal justice and mental health systems are often tenuous, the mentally ill involved in these systems often "fall through the cracks" and become both chronic patients and arrestees (see also Lamb, Weinborger, & Gross, 2004).

Multiple factors are related to the failure to provide adequate mental health treatment to correctional populations (Lurigio & Swartz, 2000). An important problem is the failure to properly screen and assess offenders for mental health services. In many criminal justice settings, screening is not standardized, resulting in invalid and unreliable diagnostic information

(HRW, 2003; Steadman & Veysey, 1997). For example, in a study of female detainees, Teplin, Abram, & McLelland (1997) found that only 25% of those meeting criteria for SMI received treatment within a week of admission. In particular, detainees with major depression went undiagnosed and untreated. Surveys of state prisons and probation departments have revealed similar shortcomings in screening and assessment practices (Hornung, Anno, Greifinger, & Gadre, 2002; HRW, 2003; Lurigio et al., 2003; Skeem, Encandela, & Louden, et al., 2003; Steadman & Veysey, 1997).

THE NEED FOR A VALIDATED SCREENING TOOL

A primary barrier to implementing standardized screening for mental illness in criminal justice settings has been the lack of a brief and validated screening tool (Swartz, 2001). Concurrent with the "war on drugs" the criminal justice system has placed considerable emphasis on developing screening and assessment tools for drug use but not on comparable instruments for detecting mental illness (e.g., see Peters et al., 2000). Consequently, many criminal justice agencies develop their own psychiatric screening tools, which are rarely subjected to rigorous reliability and validity studies, and are often based solely on face validity.

Typical are the screening procedures and instruments presently used in a large midwestern jail where the authors have conducted previous studies. New detainees at the jail are screened for mental illness by correctional staff who ask a short series of questions about previous psychiatric hospitalizations, outpatient psychiatric treatment, current use of psychiatric medication, and recent thoughts of suicide. The content covered by the questions is consistent with recommended screening practices for jails and prisons (American Psychiatric Association (APA), 1989; Steadman & Veysey, 1997) and might be effective in identifying *some* individuals who require further assessment and treatment. Nonetheless, many psychiatrically ill detainees with no previous hospitalizations, no prescriptions for medication, and who do not have or admit to suicidal thoughts are likely to be overlooked for services given this screening protocol (Teplin, 1990; Teplin, Abram, & McLelland, 1997; Teplin & Swartz, 1989).

The unique conditions of criminal justice settings impose constraints on the kind of screening instrument best suited for these contexts. Two such constraints are the high volume of screenings that must be conducted in a short time and the fact that the correctional staff who conduct the screenings often have no clinical or diagnostic expertise or training. Considering these issues, Hepburn (1994) recommended that screening instruments for substance use disorders in criminal justice settings have standardized and replicable scoring criteria appropriate for use and interpretation by lay interviewers. He also recommended that instruments be brief and easy to administer without extensive training.

Screening for psychiatric illnesses in a criminal justice context is subject to the same limitations and burdens as screening for substance abuse; thus, the ideal psychiatric screener would have the same structural properties as those Hepburn recommended for a substance abuse screener. A screener for psychiatric disorders should be brief in order to accommodate a high volume of screenings and it should be easy to administer and score so that valid results can be obtained by non-clinical, correctional staff.

Unlike substance use disorders, however, there is no parallel for defining the optimal content of a screening instrument for psychiatric disorders. First, there are many more DSM-IV Axis I non-substance use disorders than substance use disorders. Although it is possible to briefly screen for all drugs of abuse or simply for any substance abuse or dependence disorder, it is not possible to concisely screen for every Axis I psychiatric disorder. Second, even if it were possible to screen for every DSM-IV Axis I disorder, not everyone with such a disorder needs treatment. There is a continuum of clinical severity and treatment need; some persons with SMI are able to function adequately without clinical intervention or with only minimal treatment (Regier, Kaelber, Rae, Farmer, Knauper, Kessler, & Norquist, 1998).

The challenge is to ascertain which psychiatric disorders to screen for and to define when a disorder is severe enough to warrant further assessment or clinical intervention. Failure to consider clinical severity during screening and assessment could lead to "net-widening," that is, the identification of individuals who, while technically meeting the DSM criteria for a psychiatric disorder, need no clinical services or at least no intensive clinical services. Over-identification would tax the capacity of a system that is already resource poor by wasting resources on individuals who need no services (see Manderscheid, Graresande, & Goldstrom, 2004).

CANDIDATE SCREENING INSTRUMENTS

Two approaches have been taken to make standardized screening for psychiatric disorders more manageable. The first determines if an individual meets the diagnostic criteria for a limited number of diagnoses likely to be clinically severe and to require treatment intervention. The restricted subset of all DSM-IV diagnoses typically includes those already enumerated as constituting SMI: non-affective psychotic disorders or (equivalently) schizophrenia-spectrum disorders, bipolar disorder, and major depressive disorder. Similar to the longer assessment instruments for psychiatric diagnosis such as the Composite International Diagnostic Interview (CIDI; Robins et al., 1988) from which they were derived, these instruments are modular. Each module consists of a sequence of questions for diagnosing a specific disorder or class of disorders. Among the tools that adopt a diagnostic approach to screening are the Composite International Diagnostic Interview -Short Form (CIDI-SF; Kessler, Andrews, Mroczek, Ustun, & Wittchen, 1998), the Mini-Neuropsychiatric Interview (MINI; Sheehan et al., 1998) and the Referral Decision Scale (RDS; Teplin & Swartz, 1989). Administration time for these relatively brief instruments can be further shortened by omitting modules that screen for disorders that are of no interest to clinicians or researchers.

Despite their administrative flexibility, there are problems of over- and under-identification with this class of instruments that limit their usefulness, particularly in resource-constrained criminal justice settings where accuracy is crucial. The diagnostic approach to screening equates need for clinical intervention with diagnosis. Those who meet the diagnostic criteria for one or more disorders are referred for further assessment and possibly treatment. Those who do not meet the criteria for any disorders are not referred for a fuller assessment.

The potential drawback of such techniques is that they miss persons who have a severe disorder that is not contained in the screening tool (e.g., post-traumatic stress disorder, generalized anxiety disorder) but that, nevertheless, require clinical intervention (i.e., false negatives). Such individuals might receive no treatment while detained or under supervision despite the clinical severity of their conditions. When released, they are at an increased risk for problems associated with untreated SMI (e.g., re-arrest, homelessness, violence, substance abuse). Moreover, despite the administrative flexibility of selecting the diagnoses that are included in the screening, the necessity of obtaining valid DSM-IV diagnoses adds a level of complexity to the instruments through the use of skip patterns and question probes. Given the lack of clinical interviewing skills of many criminal justice correctional staff, the inclusion of even a small number of skip patterns and probes can sharply reduce the validity of the instrument.

The problems related to screening for psychiatric treatment using a diagnostic approach have recently led to a second approach that de-emphasizes diagnosis and focuses on symptom severity and level of impairment (Kessler et al., 2002). Although not a new idea (see Murphy, 2002), this approach has recently gained currency because large-scale epidemiological surveys such as the Epidemiological Catchment Area (ECA) study and the more recent National Comorbidity Survey (NCS) have found surprisingly high prevalence rates of psychiatric disorders (Kessler et al., 1994; Regier et al., 1990). In both studies, between 20 and 30% of the general population met the DSM-IV criteria for at least one past-year Axis 1 disorder. As it seemed unlikely this large proportion of the general population required mental health treatment services, the findings of these surveys were of limited use for guiding federal and state treatment resource allocations. These findings also suggested that screening for symptom severity and level of functional impairment is a better way of discriminating the need for psychiatric treatment (see Regier et al., 1998; Slade & Andrews, 2002). The tools related to this approach are particularly relevant for criminal justice settings. Some of their advantages such as, briefer, simpler, screening instruments without skip patterns and probes, and the identification of persons with the most severe psychiatric disorders regardless of diagnosis make them simpler to administer. Such screening tools can be used by lay interviewers to identify individuals with the most severe psychiatric disorders thereby conserving resources for those most in need of services.

Among the class of instruments that take this approach to screening are the recently developed K6/K10 scales (Kessler et al., 2002), which, for the reasons mentioned above, appear to be especially promising for use with criminal justice populations. Beginning with a large pool of items derived from an extensive battery of existing psychological instruments, Kessler and colleagues (Kessler et al., 2002) used analytic procedures based on item-response theory to distill a subset of 10 questions (the K10) and a completely overlapping subset of six questions (the K6). These questions identified with maximum sensitivity, individuals meeting the following two criteria: a past-year diagnosis of any DSM-IV Axis I psychiatric disorder, and a Global Assessment of Functioning (GAF) score below 60 (i.e., moderate to severe impairment in functioning; see American Psychiatric Association (2002) and also Endicott, Spitzer, Reiss, & Cohen, 1976).

Further calibration of the K6/K10 scales was done to develop cut-scores identifying individuals above the 90th percentile in symptom severity, consistent with estimates that 6–10% of the general population need psychiatric treatment services at any given time (Kessler et al., 2002). In validity studies, the K6 scale has performed as well as the K10 in identifying individuals with SMI (Kessler et al., 2003) and has become the more widely used instrument.

The K6 is now included in national surveys such as the National Survey on Drug Use and Health (NSDUH) and the National Health Interview Survey (NHIS). Despite its widespread adoption for general population studies, the K6 is yet to be validated for and used with criminal justice populations.

In the current study, we demonstrate the use of the K6 scale with a sample of adults reporting an arrest in the past year and compare the classification results obtained using the K6 screener with those obtained using a common, but unvalidated, set of screening questions (e.g., receipt of past psychiatric treatment services, use of prescribed psychiatric medications). Specifically, we compare the diagnostic accuracy of the unvalidated set of questions with the K6 classification results and examine the characteristics of participants who are misclassified in order to understand why they are incorrectly identified by standard criteria. We also examine the characteristics of offenders who screen positive on the K6 scale for an SMI, compared with those who screen negative. We conclude by considering the potential organizational impact of incorporating the K6 scale into routine screening for SMI in criminal justice settings.

METHODS

Overview

Data analyzed for this study were derived from interviews conducted for the 2002 NSDUH. Additional details on the 2002 NSDUH sampling design, protocol, questionnaire, and public data set construction are available from the United States Department of Health and Human Services (DHHS), Substance Abuse and Mental Health Services (2004). Formerly known as the National Household Survey on Drug Abuse (NHSDA), the recently renamed NSDUH survey has been conducted annually since 1991. Its main purpose is to assess the levels of substance use and misuse among non-institutionalized residents of the United States, 12 years of age and older.

NSDUH participants are selected using a multi-stage, area probability sampling design. The sampling frame includes residents of non-institutional settings such as college dormitories and civilians living on military installations but excludes those residing in institutional settings such as prisons and hospitals. To improve the validity of the responses, NSDUH participants use audio computer-assisted self-interviewing (ACASI) software to self-administer questionnaire sections that include questions about private or stigmatized behaviors (e.g., drug use, mental health treatment), while interviewers administer other, less-sensitive parts of the questionnaire (e.g., household information). The 2002 NSDUH survey had an interview response rate of 79% (DHHS, 2004).

Participants

The 2002 NSDUH sample in the public use data set consists of completed questionnaire results from 36,369 adults, 18 years of age and older. Because the focus of this study was on screening for SMI among criminal justice populations, we selected the NSDUH participants (about 5% of the total unweighted sample) who reported an arrest in the preceding year. This yielded an analytic sample size of 1,684, that was comprised of 1,215 males (72%) and 469 females (28%). Demographically (see Table 2), the majority of sampled participants were white (62%), young (75% between the ages of 18 and 25), single (75%), had a high school education or less (74%), and were employed full time (53%).

Measures

SMI

We used the K6 scale, which is embedded in the mental health section of the 2002 NSDUH questionnaire, as our gold-standard measure of SMI. Participants responded to the K6 items by indicating the extent to which they experienced each of six symptoms of general psychological distress in the month they felt the most anxious, depressed, or nervous, in the past year. Item scores are based on 5-point Likert scales that range from 0 ("none of the time") to 4 ("all of the time"), yielding a summed total score that ranges from 0 to 24. In validation studies using general population samples, the K6 has demonstrated excellent validity (area under the receiver operating characteristic curve of about 0.86) and internal consistency (Chronbach's $\alpha = 0.89$) when measured against clinician-administered semi-structured interview instruments such as the structured clinical interview for DSM-IV ((SCID); First, Spitzer, Gibbon, & Williams, 1997; Kessler et al., 2003). General population studies in other countries have also supported the diagnostic accuracy of the K6 (e.g., Andrews & Slade, 2001; Furukawa, Kessler, Slade, & Andrews, 2002). In our study, participant were assessed to having an SMI if they scored 13 or above on the K6, the optimal cut-score based on general population studies (Kessler et al., 2003).

Standard Practice SMI Scales

We selected items from the NSDUH questionnaire to represent commonly asked SMI screening questions in criminal justice settings (for e.g., see HRW, 2003; Lurigio et al., 2003; Swartz & Lurigio, 1999; Teplin & Swartz, 1989). The selected items included four questions about treatment services received in the past year for a mental health problem either in an inpatient or outpatient setting, taking prescribed medication for any mental health problem in the past year, or currently feeling the need for treatment for a mental health problem. We also selected six items that represent symptoms common to each of the three types of disorders that are often taken to comprise SMI (see Johnson, 1997): major depressive disorder (e.g., felt depressed for two or more weeks in the past year), mania (e.g., felt "hyper" for four or more days in the past year; took medication to prevent a manic episode in the past year), and schizophrenia (e.g., heard voices that did not exist; felt a force that was trying to take over your mind; felt that others were plotting to harm you in the past year).

Based on these 10 items, we created two representations of commonly asked screening questions: one that included only the four treatment questions and the other that included the four treatment questions plus the six SMI symptom questions. For both scales, participants were assessed as likely to have an SMI if they responded positively to any item; the procedure followed by the midwestern jail whose procedures we are familiar with and which are likely representative of the screening practices followed by other criminal justice institutions.

Demographics and Substance Dependence Covariates

Bivariate descriptive analyses and the logistic regression models included sample demographic characteristics as well as substance dependence and abuse and criminal justice variables. Demographic variables included: gender, race/ethnicity, age group, educational level, employment status, overall health status, and marital status. Criminal justice variables included whether a participant had been on probation or parole in the past year and the types of crimes for which they had been arrested. Participants were determined as having a substance use disorder if their responses to the series of drug use questions in the 2002 NSDUH questionnaire indicated they met the DSM-IV criteria for past-year abuse or dependence on any of the following substances: alcohol, marijuana, cocaine, heroin, hallucinogens, stimulants, inhalants, tranquilizers, and analgesics.

Analyses

After downloading the 2002 NSDUH public use data file and control statements from the Interuniversity Consortium for Political and Social Research (ICPSR) web site, we created a local version of the data set by selecting participants who reported a past-year arrest as described above. All analyses were conducted using Statistical Package for the Social Sciences (SPSS) statistical software (SPSS Inc., 2003). To reduce the possibility of an inflated Type-I error attributable to running multiple statistical tests, we adopted a more conservative α level of $p < 0.01$ instead of the conventional $p < 0.05$ for assessing statistical significance (Tabachnick & Fidell, 2001).

FINDINGS

About 18% (17.8%, $n = 300$) of the 1,684 participants with a past-year arrest in the 2002 NSDUH sample had a K6 score of 13 or higher, indicating that in the past year they had experienced symptoms of severe psychological distress consistent with the presence of an SMI. The developers of the K6 have noted the final set of included items all demonstrated equally high diagnostic sensitivity (Kessler et al., 2002). To determine if this held true for the arrestee sample, we examined the individual K6 item scores of the 300 participants who scored above the threshold for an SMI on the K6. For this analysis, we collapsed item responses into two categories according to whether a participant reported experiencing a symptom "most of the time" or "all of the time" versus less often than that.

Table 1 shows the results of this analysis, disaggregated by gender. The data indicate that all the K6 items were consistently elevated among both men and women who scored above the threshold for an SMI. None of the χ^2 tests comparing the individual K6 items between men and women participants were statistically significant, although men had a tendency to report being "fidgety and restless" more often than women whereas women tended to express feelings of worthlessness and "everything being an effort" more often than men. The mean K6 scores for both men (16.8) and women (17.3) who screened positive for an SMI were one standard deviation above the threshold score of 13 and were also not significantly different from each other. Moreover, in findings not shown in Table 1, all K6 items were significantly different ($p < 0.001$) for respondents scoring above threshold for SMI, compared with respondents scoring below threshold. Taken together, these findings suggest that all the items comprising the K6 work equally well

Table 1. K6 Item Results by Gender for Participants with a Serious Mental Illness.

K6 Item	Males ($N = 178$)	Females ($N = 122$)	Total ($N = 300$)
	% SD	% SD	% SD
(1) Nervousness	55.6	65.6	59.7
(2) Hopelessness	74.2	73.8	74.0
(3) Restless or fidgety	69.7	55.7	64.0
(4) So depressed nothing could cheer up	65.7	68.9	67.0
(5) Everything was an effort	61.2	71.3	65.3
(6) Worthlessness	66.9	78.7	71.7
Mean K6 Score (0–24 possible)	16.8 (3.0)	17.3 (3.4)	17.0 (3.1)

Note: All figures are based on unweighted data for the 300 adult participants in the 2002 National Survey on Drug Use and Health, aged 18 and older, who reported a past-year arrest and who scored 13 or above on the K6 scale. All figures are percentages unless otherwise indicated. The percentages reflect the proportion of respondents who indicated they experienced a symptom "most of the time" or "all of the time" in their worst month of functioning in the past year. Statistical comparisons of K6 item responses were done using χ^2 tests while the total mean score comparison was done using a *t*-test. None of the comparisons were significant at the $p < 0.01$ level.
SD = standard deviation.

for detecting SMI among arrestees for both genders. In other analyses not shown, we found the same pattern of item and scale consistency across racial/ethnic and age groups (see also Kessler et al., 2002).

Table 2 presents the results of bivariate statistical comparisons of participants with and without an SMI on demographics and, for the past year, the presence of a substance use disorder, substance abuse and mental health treatment received, and criminal justice status. Among the demographic variables shown in Table 2, respondents with an SMI compared with those without an SMI were more likely to be women (40% versus 25%), and more likely to report their general health as being fair or poor in the past year (16% versus 8.5%). Respondents with an SMI were also more likely to report having a past-year substance use disorder that met the DSM-IV criteria for dependence or abuse (63% versus 49%), and to have been more likely to have received both drug (23% versus 15%) and mental health treatment (39% versus 12%) in the past year.

The final set of figures shown in Table 2 present criminal justice characteristics by SMI status. The 2002 NSDUH questionnaire allows

Table 2. Demographics, Substance Use Disorder, and Criminal Justice Status by Serious Mental Illness Classification.

	No Serious Mental Illness	Serious Mental Illness	Totals	Significance
	($N = 1,384$)	($N = 300$)	($N = 1,684$)	
Gender	%	%	%	
Female	25.1	40.7	27.9	***
Ethnicity				
White	61.8	62.7	62.0	
African American/ Black	18.0	19.0	18.2	
Hispanic	13.2	12.3	13.1	
Other	3.9	6.0	6.8	
Age group				
18–25	75.4	74.3	75.2	
26–34	11.8	12.0	11.8	
35+	12.8	13.7	12.9	
Marital status				
Single (never married)	76.2	74.0	75.8	***
Divorced	10.0	12.0	10.3	
Married	13.8	14.0	13.8	
Education (highest grade)				
Less than high school	31.1	34.3	31.7	***
High school graduate/ GED	43.5	35.7	42.1	
Some college	20.1	23.7	20.7	
College graduate	5.3	6.3	5.5	
Employment status				
Full time	54.6	45.7	53.0	
Part time	14.8	16.3	15.1	
Unemployed	12.7	16.0	13.3	
(Other, including not in labor force)	17.9	22.0	18.6	
Overall health past year				
Excellent	25.1	14.3	23.2	***
Good	37.8	34.0	37.1	
Very good	28.7	35.7	29.9	
Fair	7.5	12.0	8.3	
Poor	1.0	4.0	1.4	

Table 2. (*Continued*)

	No Serious Mental Illness	Serious Mental Illness	Totals	Significance
	(*N* = 1,384)	(*N* = 300)	(*N* = 1,684)	
Co-occurring past-year substance use disorder[a]	48.8	63.0	51.4	***
Received any drug treatment past year	15.2	23.3	16.7	**
Received any mental health treatment past year	12.3	39.1	17.1	***
Past-year arrest for[b]				***
Violent crime	19.9	31.0	21.9	
Property crime	16.5	22.3	17.6	
Drug crime	35.8	31.3	35.0	
Other crime	48.7	46.3	48.3	
Mean number of arrests past year	1.4 (0.9)	1.5 (1.0)	1.4 (1.0)	
On probation past year	36.3	34.3	36.0	
On parole past year	10.0	12.7	10.5	

Note: All figures are based on the unweighted data from the 1,684 adult participants in the 2002 National Survey on Drug Use and Health, ages 16 and older, who reported a past-year arrest. All figures are percentages unless otherwise indicated. Tests of significance for percentages are based on Pearson's χ^2 and on *t*-tests of independent samples with non-equal variances for means.
SD = standard deviation.
**$p < 0.01$;
***$p < 0.001$.
[a]Past-year substance use disorder is based on DSM-IV criteria for abuse and dependance on one or more of the following classes of substances: alcohol, marijuana, cocaine, heroin, hallucinogens, stimulants, inhalants, tranquilizers, and analgesics.
[b]Violent crime offenses include assault, aggravated assault, robbery, homicide, and arson. Property crimes include: motor vehicle theft, larcent, burglary, and fraud. Drug crimes include: drug sale or possession and drunkenness. Other crimes include sex offenses, prostitution, DUI, and others.

participants to indicate the specific types of crimes for which they have been arrested, if any, in the past year and allows for recording multiple types of offenses. Among the types of crimes for which participants could report a past-year arrest, those with an SMI (31%) were significantly more likely ($p < 0.001$) to report an arrest for a violent offense than those without an SMI (19.9%). We examined the types of violent offenses and found that this difference was largely attributable to those with an SMI reporting an arrest for an assault or an aggravated assault (data not shown in Table 2). This finding is consistent with studies that report a tendency for persons with mental illnesses to be more violence prone than non-mentally ill persons (Lurigio & Swartz, 2000; Tiihonen, Isohanni, Rasanen, Koiranen, & Moring, 1997; Wallace, Mullen, & Burgess, 2004). There were no other statistically significant differences among the remaining charge categories or other criminal justice characteristics shown in Table 2; all respondents reported an average of about 1.5 arrests in the past year, a little over a third reported being on probation in the past year, and 10% reported being on parole.

The data in Table 3 compare the SMI results with the two approximations of standard sets of screening questions. The first set includes questions about past-year treatment for a mental illness. The second set also includes the treatment questions as well, and adds questions about symptoms related to depression, mania, and paranoia. The data in Table 3 show that neither set of screening questions performs especially well when compared with the K6 classification results. Although both sets of instruments have an overall percentage agreement above 70% with the K6 results, this figure is somewhat inflated because a high proportion of the participants screened negative for an SMI (82%), and because overall percentage agreement does not control for chance results. Thus, simply guessing that no person had an SMI would yield an overall percentage agreement of 82%. This is also partially the reason that both standard sets of questions have relatively high negative predictive values, reflecting that a large proportion of those identified as not needing treatment actually do not need treatment.

Although misclassification errors occur in both directions, the number of false positives obtained using either set of questions is especially large. In the case of the set of screening questions that include mental health treatment only, the sensitivity of 0.51 means that only about half of those with an SMI (per the K6) are identified as such. Moreover, the low-positive predictive value of 0.40 means that only 40% of those identified as having an SMI actually require further assessment. That is, a full psychiatric assessment of these individuals would indicate that they do not need treatment. Therefore, when measured against the K6, asking only about past-year mental health treatment services results in many misclassification errors.

Table 3. A Comparison of K6 and Standard Screening Question Results.

Standard Screen-Treatment Questions Only				
Standard Indicator Results		K6 Results		
		SMI	No SMI	Total
	SMI	153	226	379
	No SMI	146	1,152	1,296
		299	1,376	1,677
Sensitivity		0.51		
Specificity		0.84		
Positive predictive value		0.40		
Negative predictive value		0.89		
Percentage agreement		0.78		
Likelihood ratio (Positive)		3.12		
Likelihood ratio (Negative)		0.58		

Standard Screen-Treatment and Symptom Questions

Standard Indicator Results		K6 Results		
		SMI	No SMI	Total
	SMI	213	351	564
	No SMI	86	1,028	1,114
		299	1,379	1,678
Sensitivity		0.71		
Specificity		0.75		
Positive predictive value		0.38		
Negative predictive value		0.92		
Percentage agreement		0.74		
Likelihood ratio (Positive)		2.80		
Likelihood ratio (Negative)		0.39		

Note: All figures are based on the unweighted data from the 1,684 adult participants in the 2002 National Survey on Drug Use and Health, ages 18 and older, who reported a past-year arrest. N's vary between analysis due to missing cases.

The addition of symptom questions to the past-year treatment questions improves sensitivity to 0.73 meaning that 73% of the cases with an SMI are correctly identified (right column of figures in Table 3). However, the positive predictive value of the classification results obtained using treatment and symptom questions remains low (0.38) and is slightly worse than the positive predictive value with the first set of questions (0.40). This pattern of

Table 4. Binary Logistic Regression Models of Incorrectly Identified Cases Using Standard Screening Questions.

	Standard Screen – Treatment and Symptom Questions			
	False negative		False positive	
	OR	(95% CI)	OR	(95% CI)
Gender (Males)				
Females	2.38	(1.44–3.24)**	0.97	(0.72–1.32)
Ethnicity (Whites)				
African-American	1.20	(0.66–2.18)	1.00	(0.69–1.44)
Hispanic	0.45	(0.17–1.18)	0.89	(0.59–1.34)
Other	0.53	(0.34–2.21)	0.97	(0.57–1.65)
Age Group (18–25)				
26–35 years old	0.90	(0.41–1.97)	0.72	(0.48–1.15)
36 + years	0.10	(0.10–0.78)	0.61	(0.37–.99)
Marital Status (Single)				
Divorced, Separated	0.47	(0.11–2.09)	1.21	(0.73–2.00)
Married	1.43	(0.64–3.19)	1.03	(0.67–1.60)
Educational Level (High school)				
High school GED	0.53	(0.30–0.94)	0.91	(0.66–1.24)
Some college	0.88	(0.47–1.66)	0.85	(0.56–1.24)
College graduate	0.50	(0.26–2.47)	0.66	(0.34–1.28)
Employment Status (Full time)				
Part time	1.22	(0.63–2.33)	0.71	(0.47–1.06)
Unemployed	2.30	(1.22–4.29)**	0.83	(0.55–1.27)
(Other, including not in labor force)	0.86	(0.42–1.78)	1.04	(0.74–1.48)
Substance use disorder (No abuse or dependence)	1.57	(0.95–2.38)	1.23	(0.94–1.62)

Variable		AOR	(95% CI)
Received any inpatient mental health treatment past year (No treatment)	NE	2.45	(1.19–5.04)
Received any outpatient mental health treatment past year (No treatment)	NE	0.45	(0.31–.74)**
Prescribed medication for mental health problems past year (No medication)	NE	0.28	(0.19–.41)***
Needed but did not get treatment for mental health problems past year (Did not need treatment)	NE	0.49	(0.33–71)***
Depressed 2 weeks or longer past year (Not depressed 2 weeks or longer)	NE	1.23	(0.81–1.31)
Symptoms of mania past year (No symptoms)	NE	2.90	(2.03–4.22)***
Symptoms of psychosis past year (No symptoms)	NE	1.98	(1.29–3.02)**
Likelihood ration omnibus test of model significance	χ^2 (15) ■ 45.93***	χ^2	(22) ■ 255.78***

Note: All figures are based on unweighted data from 1,684 adult participants in the 2002 National Survey on Drug Use and Health, aged 18 and older, who reported a past-year arrest (brackets) = Reference category.
**$p < 0.01$;
***$p < 0.001$.

results means that the addition of symptom questions provides a partial correction for the high false-negative rate when only past-year treatment experiences are assessed, but does not correct the high false-positive rate; a large proportion of individuals are identified as needing further assessment when their K6 results suggest they do not. Therefore, although including questions about a few targeted symptoms correctly identifies more individuals with an SMI who likely require clinical intervention, many individuals who do not need treatment are misclassified as such.

We conducted follow-up analyses of the classification comparisons to identify which cases were being incorrectly identified by the standard series of screening questions. We used two binary logistic regression models: one comparing cases that were false negatives with those that were correctly identified, and one comparing false-positive cases with those that were correctly identified. We restricted these analyses to the set of standard screening questions that included treatment history and symptoms because this slightly longer set of questions performed better than the set that contained only treatment history questions. The results of these analyses are shown in Table 4. In these analyses, odds ratios greater than 1 indicate a higher chance of being in the false-negative or false-positive group whereas odds ratios less than 1 indicate a lower chance (i.e., a better chance of being correctly identified).

Using the standard set of questions, among respondents with an SMI, women and those who were unemployed were twice as likely to be in the false-negative group (i.e., to not have been detected as having an SMI) compared with men and those who were employed. Women with an SMI, who express more feelings of worthlessness and effortfulness than men with an SMI, are perhaps under-identified because these symptoms *per se* do not usually result in treatment and would not be captured when only one or two questions are being asked to diagnose depression. Those unemployed and with an SMI might not have as ready access to treatment or the ability to pay for treatment because of a lack of insurance, compared with those who are employed.

Although they might have needed treatment, such individuals might not have had access to treatment and would have responded "no" when asked on the standard question set if they had received psychiatric treatment in the past year. This explanation is negated by the fact that these individuals would also have had to say "no" when asked if they needed treatment. Treatment and symptom questions could not be evaluated for the false-negative cases because the scoring of the standard question set meant that all false negatives had a score of 0 on all the screening questions and were therefore perfectly predicted by the items comprising the screening scales.

None of the demographic covariates was significant for the false-positive cases. However, persons reporting symptoms of mania were three times as likely and those reporting symptoms of a psychotic disorder such as schizophrenia were twice as likely to be misidentified as having an SMI when they did not. Respondents who reported receiving any inpatient mental health treatment in the past year were more than twice as likely to be in the false-positive category but just below ($p < 0.05$) our more restrictive level of statistical significance ($p < 0.01$). Conversely, respondents who received outpatient treatment or psychiatric medication, or who felt they needed psychiatric treatment were less likely to be in the false-positive group, suggesting that these factors are more accurate (but still inadequate) indicators of SMI than are the symptom questions.

DISCUSSION

The current study supports the use of the K6 with criminal justice populations. The K6 scale is simple to administer and score, and is particularly appropriate for use in settings in which staff members have little mental health training. The completion time of a few minutes places a low burden on respondents and those conducting the screenings. The study also found the items comprising the K6 as equally sensitive diagnostically and consistent across gender, ethnicity, and age groups for a sample of individuals with recent criminal justice involvement. The SMI prevalence rate of 18% obtained using the K6 scale with the NSDUH arrestee sample is consistent with an estimated composite prevalence rate of about 16% (i.e., 1 in 7) for inmates in correctional settings (BJS, 1999; Fazel & Danesh, 2002). It is also consistent with the rate of 16%, which we obtained administering the K6 to arrestees being held for a bond court hearing (Swartz, Lurigio, & Loose, 2003). However, caution must be taken in comparing K6-derived estimates of the prevalence of SMI with estimates from other studies that assess for the prevalences of varying but restricted groups of diagnoses rather than for symptoms of generalized psychological distress that are common across many diagnoses.

Our research showed that screening for psychiatric disorders using approximations of relatively standard sets of questions that focus on treatment history and on a few specific symptoms of SMI, was inaccurate despite the intuitive appeal of this approach. In particular, using treatment history as the only basis for referring for a fuller assessment appears to lead to many misclassification errors in both directions. We believe that the false-negative errors are attributable to the fact that many individuals with SMI are not getting treatment in the community because treatment is unavailable or unaffordable; they do not feel they need treatment; or they are concerned about the stigma of being labeled mentally ill. Therefore, using treatment history as the basis for a screen for SMI essentially compounds the problems of inadequate treatment access and utilization in community settings (e.g., WHO World Mental Health Survey Consortium, 2004). On the other hand, some people who have been previously treated in the community might no longer be in need of continued psychiatric services because they have successfully ended their previous treatment and do not require an intensive, inpatient, clinical intervention – although they may need continued medication management or access to outpatient psychiatric services.

Adding a few questions to cover prominent symptoms associated with SMI improves diagnostic accuracy somewhat, but is especially prone to high false-positive rates. This finding is consistent with validation studies of the Referral Decision Scale (RDS), a scale developed for offenders and comprised of items representing DSM-III-R symptoms of depression, mania, and schizophrenia. These studies found unacceptably high false-positive rates for the RDS (Hart, Roesch, Corrado, & Fox, 1993; Veysey, Steadman, Morrisey, Johnson, & Beckster, 1998). A common source of the false-positive rates on the RDS and on the standard set of screening questions are items that assess the paranoid symptoms that accompany some types of schizophrenia. Many offenders live in dangerous, gang-infested environments where, in fact, others do plot to harm them. Indicating as much on a questionnaire in these circumstances indicates good reality-testing and not paranoia; a distinction that is difficult to make in the context of conducting a brief screening.

We acknowledge a number of the more important limitations of our study. Our sample consisted of individuals who had been arrested in the past year. This sample might not generalize to individuals in prisons or jails or on probation; nonetheless, over a third of our sample had been on probation in the previous year. The K6 threshold for SMI that we used in our study is based on general population studies and might not generalize to offender populations. If there is an error in this regard, it would be in the direction of the threshold being too low, resulting in the identification of too many offenders as needing a fuller psychiatric assessment. These offenders would be in the top 10% of persons in the general population with severe psychiatric problems, but not in the top 10% of the offender population, which likely has a higher proportion of individuals with severe psychiatric disorders. Formal validation and calibration studies of the K6 with offender populations would clarify these issues. In addition, because the NSDUH data are based entirely on self-reported information without verification, there may be errors of over- or under-reporting, the extent of which cannot be determined from the available data.

The aforementioned HRW report (2003) that describes the generally poor conditions for the mentally ill in American prisons is replete with examples of inmates whose psychiatric disorders are misdiagnosed as malingering and who, as a result, are treated poorly by staff and other inmates. Failure to adopt sound and valid screening practices for SMI at all levels of the criminal justice system can be the first misstep in a series of missteps that leads to undetected and untreated psychiatric disorders. These in turn can lead to a poorer adjustment to prison or jail conditions, greater rates of rule violations and disciplinary infractions and, ultimately, a greater chance of criminal and treatment recidivism. Untreated psychiatric conditions, particularly in the presence of co-occurring substance use disorders, also increase the risk for violent behavior (Swartz et al., 1998).

We cannot say whether accurate screening will, on balance, result in fewer or more cases being identified as needing psychiatric services. It is possible that more people will be identified and thus, the potential benefits of improved screening must be weighed against the additional financial and staffing burdens associated with treating a larger number of people with SMI. As the HRW report (2003) aptly notes: "...because they are already overworked, 'prison mental health staff aren't looking for business, for more customers.'" (p. 101). Yet, we would argue that the short-term gains of providing minimal psychiatric services to as few offenders as possible are offset by the long-term disruptions, law suits, unsafe conditions, and higher recidivism rates. Nonetheless, we realize that the argument of the long-term versus the short-term benefits of adequately screening for SMI is difficult to sell when budget decisions are often made on short-term projections and when fiscal and staff resources are already stretched thin.

In conclusion, the need to provide better screening for mental illness in criminal justice populations is well established given the high prevalence of psychiatric problems and the high rates of under-identification of mentally ill offenders. The criminal justice context, however, poses certain challenges to effective screening, owing to the high volume of screenings that must be done by staff that often have little clinical training and the need to efficiently utilize scarce treatment resources. The potential benefits of accurate screening for SMI, however, are many and include: optimal use of treatment resources, a safer institutional milieu, and lower recidivism rates. Among instruments in current use, the K6 scale appears to be a good candidate screening instrument because of its solid grounding in item response theory, its brevity and ease of administration, and its demonstrated validity and reliability in large-scale population studies. We recommend that criminal justice organizations consider incorporating the K6 questions into their screening instruments but continue to ask questions about prior psychiatric treatment and medication history in the event that such treatment or medication successfully managed the psychiatric disorder and should be continued.

ACKNOWLEDGEMENTS

We gratefully acknowledge support for this research from the Robert Wood Johnson Foundation's Substance Abuse Policy Research Program under grant 049629 and from the National Institute on Drug Abuse under grant R01 DA013943-02.

REFERENCES

Abram, K. M., & Teplin, L. A. (1991). Co-occurring disorders among mentally ill jail detainees: Implications for public policy. *American Psychologist, 46*(10), 1036–1045.

Abram, K. M., Teplin, L. A., & McClelland, G. M. (2003). Comorbidity of severe psychiatric disorders and substance use disorders among women in jail. *The American Journal of Psychiatry, 160*(5), 1007–1010.

American Psychiatric Association (APA). (1989). *Psychiatric services in jails and prisons. Report of the task force on psychiatric services in jails and prisons.* Washington, DC: American Psychiatric Association.

American Psychiatric Association (APA). (2002). *Diagnostic and statistical manual of mental disorders, text-revision.* Washington, DC: American Psychiatric Association.

Andrews, G., & Slade, T. (2001). Interpreting scores on the Kessler psychological distress scale (K10). *Australian and New Zealand Journal of Public Health, 25*(6), 494–497.

Bureau of Justice Statistics (BJS). (1999). *Mental health and treatment of inmates and probationers* (U.S. DOJ Publication No. NCJ 174463). Washington, DC: U.S. Government Printing Office.

Diamond, P. M., Wang, E. W., Holzer III, C. E., Thomas, C., & des Anges, C. (2001). The prevalence of mental illness in prison. *Administration and Policy in Mental Health, 29*(1), 21–40.

Dicataldo, F., Greer, A., & Profit, W. E. (1995). Screening prison inmates for mental disorder: An examination of the relationship between mental disorder and prison adjustment. *Bulletin of the American Academy of Psychiatry and the Law, 23*(4), 573–585.

Endicott, J., Spitzer, R. L., Reiss, J., & Cohen, J. (1976). The Global Assessment Scale: A procedure for measuring overall severity of psychiatric disorders. *Archives of General Psychiatry, 33,* 766–771.

Fazel, S., & Danesh, J. (2002). Serious mental disorder in 23000 prisoners: A systematic review of 62 studies. *Lancet, 359*(9306), 545–550.

First, M. B., Spitzer, R. L., Gibbon, M., & Williams, J. B. W. (1997). *Structured clinical interview for DSM-IV axis I disorders, research version, non-patient edition (SCID-I/ NP).* New York: Biometrics Research, New York State Psychiatric Institute.

Furukawa, T. A., Kessler, R. C., Slade, T., & Andrews, G. (2002). The performance of the K6 and K10 screening scales for psychological distress in the Australian national survey of mental health and well-being. *Psychological Medicine, 33,* 357–362.

Hart, S. D., Roesch, R., Corrado, R. R., & Cox, D. N. (1993). The Referral Decision Scale: A validation study. *Law and Human Behavior, 17,* 611–623.

Hepburn, J. R. (1994). Classifying drug offenders for treatment. In: D. L. MacKenzie & C. D. Uchida (Eds), *Drugs and crime: Evaluating public policy initiatives* (pp. 172–187). Newbury Park, CA: Sage.

Hornung, C. A., Anno, B. J., Greifinger, R. B., & Gadre, S. (2002). Health care for soon-to-be-released inmates: A survey of state prison systems. In: , *The health status of soon-to-be-released inmates: A report to Congress,* (Vol. 2, pp. 1–11). Chicago: National Commission on Correctional Health Care.

Human Rights Watch (HRW) (2003). *Ill equipped: U.S. prisons and offenders with mental illnesses.* Retrieved October 22, 2003 from http://www.hrw.org/reports/2003/usa1003/index.htm.

Insel, T. R. (2003). *Introductory presentation.* Presented at beyond the clinic walls: Expanding mental health, drug and alcohol services research outside the specialty care system, a conference co-sponsored by the National Institute of Mental Health and the National Institute on Alcoholism and Alcohol Abuse, Washington, DC.

Johnson, D. L. (1997). Overview of severe mental illness. *Clinical Psychology Review, 17*(3), 247–257.

Kessler, R. C., Andrews, G., Colpe, L. J., Hiripi, E., Mroczek, D. K., & Normand, S. L. T. (2002). Short screening scales to monitor population prevalences and trends in nonspecific psychological distress. *Psychological Medicine, 32,* 959–976.

Kessler, R. C., Andrews, G., Mroczek, D., Ustun, T. B., & Wittchen, H. U. (1998). The World Health Organization Composite International Diagnostic Interview Short-Form (CIDI-SF). *International Journal of Methods in Psychiatric Research, 7,* 171–185.

Kessler, R. C., Barker, P. R., Colpe, L. J., Epstein, J. F., Gfroerer, J. C., & Hirpi, E. (2003). Screening for serious mental illness in the general population. *Archives of General Psychiatry, 60*(2), 184–189.

Kessler, R. C., McGonagle, K. A., Zhao, S., Nelson, C. B., Hughes, M., Eshleman, S., Wittchen, H. U., & Kendler, K. S. (1994). Lifetime and 12-month prevalence of DSM-III-R psychiatric disorders in the United States: Results from the national comorbidity study. *Archives of General Psychiatry, 51,* 8–19.

Lamb, H. R. (1998). Deinstitutionalization at the beginning of the new millennium. *Harvard Review of Psychiatry, 6,* 1–9.

Lamb, H. R., & Weinberger, L. E. (1998). Persons with severe mental illness in jails and prisons: A review. *Psychiatric Services, 49*(4), 483–492.

Lamb, H. R., Weinberger, L. E., & Gross, B. H. (2004). Mentally ill in the criminal justice system: Some perspectives. *Psychiatric Quarterly, 75*(2), 107–126.

Lurigio, A. J., Cho, Y. I., Swartz, J. A., Johnson, T. P., Graf, I., & Pickup, L. (2003). Standardized assessment of substance-related, other psychiatric, and comorbid disorders among probationers. *International Journal of Offender Therapy and Comparative Criminology, 47*(6), 630–653.

Lurigio, A. J., & Swartz, J. A. (2000). Changing the contours of the criminal justice system to meet the needs of persons with serious mental illness. In: W. Reed & L. Winterfield (Eds), *Policies, processes, and decisions of the criminal justice system.* Washington, DC: National Institute of Justice.

Manderscheid, R. W., Gravesande, A., & Goldstrom, I. D. (2004). Growth of mental health services in state adult correctional facilities, 1988 to 2000. *Psychiatric Services, 55*(8), 869–872.

Murphy, J. M. (2002). Symptom scales and diagnostic schedules in adult psychiatry. In: M. T. Tsuang & M. Tohen (Eds), *Textbook in psychiatric epidemiology,* (2nd ed.) (pp. 273–332). New York: Wiley.

National Commission on Correctional Health Care (NCCHC) (2002). *The health status of soon-to-be-released inmates: A report to Congress* (Vols. 1 and 2). Chicago: Author.

Peters, R. H., Greenbaum, P. E., Steinberg, M. L., Carter, C. R., Ortiz, M. M., Fry, B. C., & Valle, S. K. (2000). Effectiveness of screening instruments in detecting substance use disorders among prisoners. *Journal of Substance Abuse Treatment, 18*(4), 349–358.

Regier, D. A., Kaelber, C. T., Rae, D. S., Farmer, M. E., Knauper, B., Kessler, R. C., & Norquist, G. S. (1998). Limitations of diagnostic criteria and assessment instruments for mental disorders. *Archives of General Psychiatry, 55*(2), 109–115.

Regier, D. A., Farmer, M. E., Rae, D. A., Locke, B. Z., Keith, S. J., Judd, L. L., & Goodwin, F. K. (1990). Comorbidity of mental disorders with alcohol and other drug abuse: Results from the Epidemiological Catchment Area (ECA) Study. *Journal of the American Medical Association, 264*(19), 2511–2518.

Robins, L. N., Wing, J., Wittchen, H. U., Helzer, J. E., Babor, T. F., Burke, J., Farmer, A., Jablenski, A., Pickens, R., Regier, D. A., et al. (1988). The Composite International Diagnostic Interview. *Archives of General Psychiatry, 45,* 1069–1077.

Sheehan, D. V., Lecrubier, Y., Sheehan, K. H., Amorim, P., Janavs, J., Weiller, E., Hergueta, T., Baker, R., & Dunbar, G. (1998). The Mini-International Neuropsychiatric Interview (MINI): The development and validation of a structured diagnostic psychiatric interview for the DSM-IV and ICD-10. *Journal of Clinical Psychiatry, 59,* 22–33.

Skeem, J. L., Encandela, J., & Louden, J. E. (2003). Perspectives on probation and mandated mental health treatment in specialized and traditional probation departments. *Behavioral Science and the Law, 21*(4), 429–458.

Slade, T. B., & Andrews, G. (2002). Empirical impact of DSM-IV diagnostic criterion for clinical significance. *The Journal of Nervous and Mental Disease, 190*(5), 334–337.

Solomon, P., & Draine, J. (1999). Using clinical and criminal involvement factors to explain homelessness among clients of a psychiatric probation and parole service. *Psychiatric Quarterly, 70*(1), 75–87.

SPSS, Inc. (2002). *Statistical package for the social sciences* (Version 11.0). (Computer software). Chicago: Author.

Steadman, H. J., & Veysey, B. M. (1997). *Providing services for jail inmates with mental disorders* (Research in Brief, U.S. DOJ Publication No. NCJ 162207). Washington, DC: U.S. Department of Justice, National Institute of Justice.

Swartz, J. A. (2001). Considering psychiatric comorbidities among addicted offenders: A new strategy for client-treatment matching. *Offender Substance Abuse Report, 1*(5), 65–66, 70–73.

Swartz, J. A., & Lurigio, A. J. (1999). Psychiatric illness and comorbidity among adult male detainees in drug treatment. *Psychiatric Services, 50*(12), 1628–1630.

Swartz, J. A., Lurigio, A. J., & Loose, P. (2003, November). *Screening for severe psychological distress among arrestees.* Paper presented at the meeting of the American Society for Criminology, Denver, CO.

Swartz, M. S., Swanson, J. W., Hiday, V. A., Borum, R., Wagner, H. R., & Burns, B. J. (1998). Violence and severe mental illness: The effects of substance abuse and nonadherence to medication. *American Journal of Psychiatry, 155*(2), 226–231.

Tabachnick, B. G., & Fidell, L. S. (2001). *Multivariate statistics* (4th ed.). Needham Heights, MA: Allyn & Bacon.

Teplin, L. A. (1990). Detecting disorder: The treatment of mental illness among jail detainees. *Journal of Consulting and Clinical Psychology, 58*(2), 233–236.

Teplin, L. A., Abram, K. M., & McLelland, G. M. (1997). Mentally disordered women in jail: Who receives services? *American Journal of Public Health, 87*(4), 604–609.

Teplin, L. A., & Swartz, J. A. (1989). Screening for severe mental disorder in jails: The development of the Referral Decision Scale. *Law and Human Behavior, 13*(1), 1–18.

Tiihonen, J., Isohanni, M., Rasanen, P., Koiranen, M., & Moring, J. (1997). Specific major mental disorders and criminality: A 26-year prospective study of the 1966 northern Finland birth cohort. *American Journal of Psychiatry, 154*(6), 840–845.

Torrey, E. F. (1995). Jails and prisons: America's new mental hospitals. *American Journal of Public Health, 85*(12), 1611–1613.

United States Department of Health and Human Services [DHHS], Substance Abuse and Mental Health Services Administration, Office of Applied Studies. (2004). *National Survey on Drug Use and Health 2002* (Computer file). 2nd ICPSR version. Research Triangle Park, NC: Research Triangle Institute (producer). Ann Arbor, MI: Inter-university Consortium for Political and Social Research (distributor).

Veysey, B. M., & Bichler-Robertson, G. (April 2002). Providing psychiatric services in correctional settings. In: , *The health status of soon-to-be-released inmates: A report to Congress,* (Vol. 2, pp. 157–165). Chicago: National Commission on Correctional Health Care.

Veysey, B. M., Steadman, H. J., Morrisey, J. P., Johnson, M., & Beckstead, J. W. (1998). Using the Referral Decision Scale to screen mentally ill jail detainees: Validity and implementation issues. *Law and Human Behavior, 22*(2), 205–215.

Wallace, C., Mullen, P. E., & Burgess, P. (2004). Criminal offending in schizophrenia over a 25-year period marked by deinstitutionalization and increasing prevalence of comorbid substance use disorders. *American Journal of Psychiatry, 161*(4), 716–727.

WHO World Mental Health Survey Consortium. (2004). Prevalence, severity, and unmet need for treatment of mental disorders in the World Health Organization world mental health surveys. *Journal of the American Medical Association, 291*(21), 2581–2590.

THE IMPACT OF A RESIDENTIAL TREATMENT UNIT ON THE PRISON ADJUSTMENT OF MENTALLY DISORDERED INMATES

Christine Gagliardi

ABSTRACT

Medical and legal records of 64 inmates receiving mental health services at a maximum-security prison located in the Northeast United States were examined to look at whether prison adjustment is impacted by housing in a mental health residential treatment unit. Inmates in the residential treatment unit, the "treatment group" had a significant decrease in hospitalizations and disciplinary reports while housed in the residential treatment unit. Inmates with a mental health history housed in the general population, the "control group," did not show a decrease in these behaviors during a similar time period. Results find that inmates referred to the residential treatment unit seem to have high numbers of hospitalizations and segregations while housed in the general population, which level off and become similar to the control group upon entry to the residential treatment unit. Implications for future research evaluating the impact of the residential treatment unit on the behavior of the inmate after he has left the unit are discussed.

The Organizational Response to Persons with Mental Illness Involved with the Criminal Justice System

Research in Social Problems and Public Policy, Volume 12, 163–178
ISSN: 0196-1152/doi:10.1016/S0196-1152(05)12008-0

INTRODUCTION

It is estimated that mentally disordered individuals make up 16% of the male and 24% of the female prison inmate population (Ditton, 1999). These inmates differ from other criminal offenders (Lamb & Weinberger, 1998). They are more likely to be under the influence of drugs or alcohol during the offense, serve longer sentences and are more likely to have been unemployed and homeless prior to incarceration (Ditton, 1999). Mentally disordered offenders may also have difficulty adjusting to the environment of the correctional facility. This can lead to a number of behaviors that disrupt the required order of the institution. Correctional mental health services can assist in improving prison adjustment and reducing problems. This chapter evaluates one type of service that can work in alleviating disruptive behaviors among mentally disordered inmates: a residential mental health rehabilitation unit.

SIGNIFICANCE TO THE ORGANIZATIONAL, INSTITUTIONAL AND POLICY RESPONSE TO OFFENDERS WITH MENTAL ILLNESS

Correctional institutions benefit from the services provided by mental health treatment in that these services can help inmates adjust to the prison environment, and therefore, reduce problematic behaviors. In the late 1950s, Clemmer defined the concept of prisonization to refer to an inmate's transformation during incarceration (Clemmer, 1958). Clemmer argued that inmates assimilate into the prison culture by learning and adapting to the norms and values of the total institution. All individuals entering into a correctional institution must learn the behavioral expectations in order to fully adjust to the social environment. Due to psychiatric symptoms and the stigma of mental illness within the prison walls, this process of socialization and adjustment may be more difficult for inmates with a mental disorder. Adjustment problems can lead to behaviors detrimental to the required social order in prisons.

A number of research studies have found mentally disordered inmates to have higher rates of disciplinary problems than other inmates. A study of released prison inmates found that those with a mental disorder (as defined by prior hospitalization) had higher rates of infractions, even when controlling for prior criminal history, age and institutional security level

(Adams, 1983). Similarly, Adams' (1986) study of a New York prison found higher rates of disciplinary infractions among inmates referred to a mental health unit than those housed in the general population. Within those referred to the mental health unit, higher infraction rates were found among inmates with a mental disorder diagnosis (Adams, 1986).

Disruptive behaviors resulting in disciplinary infractions cause a number of problems for correctional institutions. These behaviors disturb the order and structure of the institution, take time away from the duties of correctional officers and are costly. Disciplinary infractions require additional labor inside the prison to assist in disciplinary hearings and punishments. There are also a number of additional fees required for the paperwork involved in reporting a disciplinary offense. In a study of prisons in Washington, Lovell and Jemelka (1996) found that the average disciplinary infraction costs $569 (with a range of $66–$12,500). The authors estimated that discipline problems resulting in infractions cost the state $900,765 annually (Lovell & Jemelka, 1996).

The correctional institution has limited methods for dealing with disciplinary problems. One way disruptive behavior is sanctioned in by taking away inmate privileges, such as visits or telephone calls. Being sent to solitary confinement, or segregation, is another way in which inmates with disciplinary problems are punished. Segregation had been found to have a number of psychological effects on inmates, especially those with mental disorders. The enclosed environment, along with the reduction of any social support can have a direct effect on the mentally disordered inmate. Segregation can escalate a mental illness, leading to increased disciplinary problems and hospitalizations (Rold, 1992).

Incidents of self-harm could also be related to a pattern of poor adjustment among mentally disordered inmates. Studies have found that individuals with high disciplinary infraction rates also have more self-harm incidents. Adams (1986) found self-harm to be one of the behaviors contributing to high rates of disciplinary infractions among mentally disordered inmates in his study of New York State inmates referred to a mental health unit. A study comparing self-mutilators to non-mutilators in Virginia found that self-mutilators had more severe disciplinary reports (Jones, 1986). Incidents of self-harm are also costly on the institution, since the incidents also require hospital care.

Inmates who are identified as having a mental disorder and engage in numerous disruptive behaviors are sometimes sent to a psychiatric hospital for evaluation, especially if the behaviors seem to be related to the illness. Often, a small group of inmates make up a large portion of hospital stays. In a study of inmates in a Maryland medium security correctional institution, Swetz et al. (1989) found that of the 12% who had been hospitalized in a psychiatric facility during incarceration, 50% had more than one and 25% had more than three hospitalizations. The importance of reducing hospitalizations is apparent: at the time of the study, the Maryland Department of Corrections had only 150 psychiatric beds available, of which 30 were for those with chronic mental illnesses (Swetz et al., 1989). Due to the high costs of hospital care, there are only a limited number of resources available for all inmates in a correctional institution. It is important to find other methods of reducing hospitalizations to ensure that all inmates in need of care receive it.

Given the high rates of disciplinary reports, incidents of self-harm and hospitalizations among mentally disordered inmates, correctional institutions would benefit from programs developed to reduce poor adjustment behaviors. Previous studies have looked at how mental health residential treatment units have worked to reduce disciplinary infractions and improve social interaction (Lovell et al., 2001a, b; O'Connor, Lovell, & Brown, 2002). This study will extend these studies by looking at segregation and self-harm incidents as well as disciplinary infractions. It will also look at how prison adjustment among inmates housed in the mental health rehabilitation unit compares to similar inmates housed in the general population.

METHOD

This study will attempt to look at the impact of a residential treatment unit on the adjustment of mentally disordered inmates in a maximum-security prison located in the Northeast. The adjustment to prison of mentally disordered inmates housed in the residential treatment unit will be compared to other inmates housed in the general population who also belong to open mental health cases. Prison adjustment will be measured by rates of self-harm incidents, hospitalizations, segregation trips, and disciplinary reports. The study will explore the impact of housing in a mental health residential treatment unit on the adjustment of mentally disordered prison inmates as compared to similar inmates housed in the general population.

The Mental Health Residential Treatment Unit

The mental health residential treatment unit is a housing unit for inmates with mental disorder, who have difficulties adjusting to and living in the general population in prison. A number of different mental health professionals are employed at the unit to assist in inmates' adjustment. A licensed social worker, a licensed mental health counselor, a psychologist, an occupational therapist, and an occupational therapist assistant work in the unit with the inmates. The goal of the unit is to provide services to meet the needs of individual inmates and improve the skills needed for the proper adjustment to prison, as well as rehabilitation upon release. Either a mental health director or psychiatrist refers inmates to the unit. Inmates with a psychiatric disorder that impairs functioning, but does not require hospitalization or impinge on program participation meet the selection criteria, as long as the inmate does not have a medical condition that requires special care.

Inmates housed in the residential treatment unit spend a great deal of time together in housing and programs. They are required to participate in 10 groups, which take place on Monday through Friday. Those who are employed or in school are required to participate in five groups. There are a number of different groups the inmates can participate varying from anger management, coping, and symptom management to health awareness and current events.

Sampling Design

Subjects were taken from the population of inmates with an open mental health case (defined as receiving mental health services at the time of data collection) housed in a maximum-security prison located in the Northeast. The subjects were placed either in the treatment or control group, depending on where they were currently housed in the correctional facility at the time of data collection. A total of 42 inmates were living in the residential treatment unit around the time of data collection and make up the "treatment group." In order to look at the effectiveness of the change in reducing problematic behaviors resulting from poor adjustment, a "control group" was also identified. The control group is made up of inmates housed in the general population with an open mental health case. The control group is composed of 53 inmates housed in the general population at the time of data collection with an open mental health case at the correctional facility.

Variables and Measures

The following four variables were used to measure prison adjustment: hospitalization, self-harm incidents, segregation trips, and disciplinary reports.

Archival research examining medical records and counting the number of hospital evaluations, determined hospitalization and incidents of self-harm. Trips to segregation were determined by counting the number of times the inmate had been placed in segregation for disciplinary problems according to the segregation log found in the inmate's legal records. Disciplinary reports were also found in a log in the inmate's legal record.

Hospitalization, self-harm incidents, segregation trips, and disciplinary reports were calculated into three sets of variables measuring adjustment before and during treatment, as well as the rate of change. Due to differences in the amount of time incarcerated, each of these variables was computed into an annual rate. The annual rate was computed by dividing the number of incidents by the number of months incarcerated and multiplying by 12. This rate allowed the researcher to compare the adjustment behaviors of inmates who have been incarcerated for various amounts of time. The measurement is consistent with research looking at inmate behaviors, such as Malbi and Barber's (1983) study of disciplinary problems and housing security level.

To ensure that inmates in the control group were being studied during a time period similar to that of the treatment group, a cutoff point of treatment was determined by looking at the earliest point of entry for those housed in the residential treatment unit. The earliest date in which inmates in the treatment group were housed in the residential treatment unit was December 1998. For this reason, prior to treatment rates for inmates in the control group were calculated by counting the number of incidents prior to December 1998, dividing that number by the number of months incarcerated prior to December 1998 and multiplying by 12. The same process was used to compute prior to treatment rates for inmates in the residential treatment unit, only the cutoff date was the date the inmate was moved from the general population to the residential treatment unit. Rates during treatment were computed in the same fashion, only using the number of incidents and months incarcerated following either December 1998 (for the control group) or entry into the residential treatment unit (for the treatment group). Finally, a rate of change was computed for each variable by subtracting the rates during treatment from those before treatment.

It is important to note that missing data did result in before and during treatment rate calculations for the control group. This computation greatly affected the sample size of the control group. A large number of the inmates in the control group had not been incarcerated before the cutoff date. For this reason, these inmates were excluded from the analysis. Only 22 inmates of the original control group were included in the modified control group due to differences in time of incarceration.

Hypotheses

The primary focus of this study was to evaluate the role of a mental health residential treatment unit in reducing problematic behaviors that result from poor prison adjustment among mentally disordered inmates. The first hypothesis to be tested is: *Inmates housed in the residential treatment unit will display less behaviors related to poor adjustment while housed in the residential treatment unit than while housed in the general population.*

A number of different factors could play a role in the adjustment of mentally disordered inmates other than housing in the residential treatment unit. Changes within the prison environment (different employees or policies), for example, may contribute to the behaviors of prison inmates. For these reasons, it is important to look at how the inmates housed in the residential treatment unit compare to similar inmates in the general population who were not housed in the residential treatment unit. Since the inmates in the control group did not receive treatment, their behavior should remain stable over the time period. The second hypothesis is: *There will be no difference in the amounts of behaviors indicating poor adjustment in the control group during the entire time period studied.*

Adjustment to prison may improve with time whether the inmate is housed in special housing or not. Therefore, inmates in the control group may experience a change in behaviors during the studied time period and disprove the second hypothesis. If this is the case, it is expected that inmates housed in the residential treatment unit will change more than the control group during the studied time period. The final hypothesis is: *Inmates in the residential treatment unit will have a higher rate of change than the control group for each of the measures of prison adjustment during the studied time period.*

FINDINGS

Table A.1 in the appendix describes the age, criminal history, and number of months incarcerated for the sample studied. Criminal history is defined as the number of times incarcerated, with one indicating that the inmate has been incarcerated for the first time. The average age among inmates in the treatment group ranged from 19 to 66, with an average age of 41 years. This is significantly higher than the control group, which ranged from 21 to 62, with an average age of 37 years ($t = 1.98$, df $= 93$, $p = 0.05$). The modified control group has an age distribution closer to the treatment group, ranging from 24 to 56, with an average age of 43 years (see Table A.1).

Inmates selected for housing in the residential treatment unit are, on average, serving their third incarceration (ranging from one to ten) and have been incarcerated for almost 6 years (ranging from 6 months to over 26 years). Inmates in the control group are, on average, serving a little more than their third incarceration, although they tend to have slightly more variation in criminal history (ranging from one to 18 incarcerations). The average amount of time incarcerated ranged from 6 months to around 25 years for inmates in the control group, with the average inmate having spent a little more than 7 years incarcerated so far. There were no significant differences in criminal history or amount of time incarcerated between the treatment and control group. The modified control group is slightly different from the control group. The modified control group has been incarcerated more and has been incarcerated for a longer period of time (see Table A.1).

Table A.2 in the appendix describes the distribution of current offense and mental disorder for the treatment group, control group, and modified control group. There was no significant difference between the current offense of inmates in the treatment and control group. Over half of the inmates in the residential treatment unit were incarcerated for murder or manslaughter (33%) or a sexual offense (31%). Inmates in the control group tended to commit more murder or manslaughter (36%) and other offense (19%). Fewer inmates in the control group were incarcerated for a sex offense (17%). Inmates in the modified control group were more likely to have been incarcerated for murder or manslaughter (45%) than the control group (see Table A.2). Almost half (47%) of the inmates in the treatment group had a mood disorder and about a third (33%) had a thought disorder. Although differences in the mental disorders of the treatment and control group were not found to be significant, inmates in the control group were more likely to have a mood disorder (70%). The difference in disorder is larger when considering the modified control group, which had slightly more mood (73%) and personality (14%) disorders than the control group (see Table A.2). The difference between the control group and modified control group with regard to diagnosis was not found to be significant.

Prison Adjustment among Inmates Housed in the Residential Treatment Unit

Inmates in the treatment group had an average of 1.38 hospitalizations, 0.21 self-harm incidents, 13.76 disciplinary reports, and 3.74 trips to segregation during the entire time period studied. Table A.3 in the appendix shows the average yearly rates of each of the prison adjustment behaviors for inmates in the treatment group both before (while housed in the general population) and during (while housed in the residential treatment unit) treatment. There was a decrease in the yearly hospitalization rates, disciplinary report rates and segregation rates among those inmates in the treatment group after entry into the residential treatment unit. The average yearly hospitalization rate decreased from 0.34 to 0.02. This change was found to be statistically significant ($t = 3.406$, df $= 41$, $p < 0.01$). A statistically significant change was also found regarding the decrease in the average yearly disciplinary report rate from 2.93 to 1.25 ($t = 2.186$, df $= 41$, $p < 0.05$). The average rate of segregation trips slightly decreased from 0.79 before treatment to 0.77 after entry into the residential treatment unit. The average self-harm rate slightly increased after entry into the residential treatment unit (see Table A.3).

Prison Adjustment among Mentally Disordered Inmates Housed in the General Population

During the time period studied, inmates in the modified control group had an average of 0.09 hospitalizations, 0.14 incidents of self-harm, 27.64 disciplinary reports, and 5.78 trips to segregation. As observed in Table A.3, none of the average yearly rates in adjustment behaviors significantly changed among inmates in the modified control group. There was a slight decrease in the average hospitalization rate from 0.01 to 0. The average disciplinary report rate fell from 1.64 to 1.41. There were no incidents of self-harm before treatment in the control group, but a small number of self-harm incidents did occur during the treatment time period. The inmates in the modified control group also had more segregation trips during the treatment time period. The average yearly segregation rate increased from 0.29 to 0.45 (see Table A.3).

Changes in Prison Adjustment between the Treatment and Modified Control Group

In order to evaluate the difference in change between the treatment and modified control group, *t*-tests were conducted to look at differences between the treatment and modified control groups both before and during treatment. *T*-tests were also conducted to look at differences in the actual rate of change between the two groups.

Table A.4 in the appendix shows the average yearly rates of each of the measures of prison adjustment prior to treatment for both the treatment and modified control group. The treatment group had higher average yearly rates before treatment for all of the measures of adjustment. A significant difference was found between the treatment and modified control group in regards to average yearly hospitalization rates and segregation trips prior to treatment. The average yearly hospitalization rate before treatment for the treatment group was 0.34, compared to 0.02 of the modified control group ($t = 3.698$, df $= 41.35$, $p < 0.01$). The modified control group had an average of 0.29 segregation trips before the treatment time period, compared to an average yearly segregation rate of 0.79 found among inmates in the treatment group before entry into the residential treatment unit ($t = 3.131$, df $= 49.59$, $p < 0.01$). A trend was found between the modified control group and the treatment group regarding the average yearly disciplinary report rate and average yearly self-harm rate before treatment. The treatment group had more than one disciplinary report per year than the modified control group before treatment. While the treatment group had an average yearly self-harm rate of 0.05, the modified control group did not have any incidents of self-harm before the treatment time period (see Table A.4).

The modified control group and the treatment group were not found to have any significantly different average yearly rates on any of the behavioral measures of prison adjustment during the treatment time period (see Table A.4). During treatment, the treatment group had slightly higher average yearly hospitalization rates, segregation rates and self-harm rates than the modified control group. While inmates in the modified control group had no hospitalizations after the treatment time period began, inmate in the treatment group had an average of 0.02 hospitalizations per year. The average yearly segregation rate during treatment for inmates in the modified control group was found to be 0.45, compared to 0.77 in the treatment group. Inmates in the treatment group had an average yearly self-harm rate of 0.10 following the treatment, while the modified control group had an average of 0.03. The modified control group did have a higher rate of disciplinary reports during the treatment time period. Inmates in the treatment group had an average of 1.25 disciplinary reports per year during the treatment time period, compared to an average of 1.41 among inmates in the modified control group (see Table A.4).

Table A.5 in the appendix describes the average rates of change for each of the measures of prison adjustment during the entire time period studied. The treatment group was found to have changed more than the modified control group on all measures of prison adjustment except segregations. For hospitalizations and disciplinary reports, the treatment group had a greater change than the modified control group, and this change was a decrease in these behaviors. The modified control group had a greater change than the treatment group in segregations, but this change was an increase compared to a decrease in the treatment group. Although the treatment group changed more than the modified control group in regards to self-harm incidents, the change was an increase over the time period. There was a significant difference in the rate of hospitalization change during the studied time period between the treatment and modified control group. On average, the treatment group had 0.31 less hospitalizations per year after entry into the residential treatment unit, compared to a decrease in 0.01 hospitalizations per year for the modified control group ($t = 3.311$, df $= 41.321$, $p < 0.01$). A trend was observed in the disciplinary report rate of change between the two groups. Inmates in the treatment group were found to decrease an average of 1.67 disciplinary reports per year while housed in the residential treatment unit, while inmates in the modified control group only decreased on an average of 0.23 disciplinary reports per year after the start of the treatment time period (see Table A.5).

DISCUSSION AND CONCLUSIONS

This study examined the role of a mental health residential treatment unit on the adjustment of mentally disordered inmates incarcerated at a maximum-security prison in the Northeast United States. It was found that the mentally disordered inmate behaved in a manner reflecting better prison adjustment after he was moved from the general population to the residential treatment unit. Hospitalizations and disciplinary reports significantly decreased after the change in housing, and a slight decrease was found in segregations. The decrease in disciplinary reports is consistent with the findings of the evaluations of similar programs (Lovell et al., 2001a). Although the modified control group did have slight decrease in disciplinary reports and hospitalizations, none of the changes were found to be significant.

The change in behaviors found among inmates housed in the residential treatment unit could possibly be understood when looking at the differences in behaviors between the modified control group and the treatment group before the introduction of treatment. Mentally disordered inmates referred and accepted to the residential treatment unit had higher rates of all of the measures of adjustment while they were housed in the general population than those in the modified control group before the treatment time period.

The rate of hospitalization and segregation also seemed to be different between the two groups in relation to change. Inmates in the residential treatment unit had a significantly higher change in hospitalizations. While segregation trips increased for the modified control group, there was a decrease in this sanction among members of the treatment group. Segregation and hospitalizations may possibly be related in the experiences of the mentally disordered inmate. As discussed by Rold (1992), segregation could escalate a mental illness, requiring hospitalization. Further research is required to examine the possible relationship between segregation trips, hospitalizations, and the adjustment of the mentally disordered inmate. Reductions in segregation trips could possibly lead to a reduction of symptomatic and/or disruptive behaviors in this special population.

In looking at the rates of hospitalization, the treatment group had higher rates before the treatment because the modified control group had only 0.01 hospitalizations per year. This difference may reflect the criteria used in the selection and referral process of the residential treatment unit. Mentally disordered inmates who engage in disruptive behavior related to their illness may be first evaluated at a psychiatric hospital, and then referred to the residential treatment unit if their symptoms become stabilized.

A final interesting finding that emerged from this study concerns incidents of self-harm. Although there were no significant findings for self-harm incidents, both the treatment and modified control group tended to have an increase in these behaviors over time. Future research needs to look at the possible relationship between self-harm and length of incarceration, as well as any other factors that may predict increases in self-harm incidents.

It is important to note that there were a number of limitations to this study. Inmates selected into the residential treatment unit had to be referred to the unit, meet the criteria and want to leave the general population for the residential treatment unit. Therefore, it is impossible to use a pure experimental design with random sampling. Inmates in the treatment group may differ from the control group with regard to factors other than the treatment, for example, inmates may be referred to the residential treatment unit because they have more severe psychiatric symptoms or disciplinary problems.

A second limitation is that there may be differences in how behavior is reacted to while housed in the residential treatment unit as opposed to the general population. The general population and residential treatment unit have different staff members with different goals and ideologies about corrections. Negative behaviors may be looked at more leniently in the therapeutic environment of the residential treatment unit than in the general population. Inmates in the residential treatment unit may receive less disciplinary reports, for example, due to decisions by employees in the unit to not report the behavior. There may also be differences in how medications are managed between the two groups that may play a role in behavioral change.

Finally, the results are limited by the small sample size of the two groups and the limited variability found in some of the variables being tested to measure prison adjustment. Little variability was found in the total number of hospitalizations and incidents of self-harm for the treatment and modified control group. The range of hospitalizations for inmates in the residential treatment unit for their entire stay is eight and the range of self-harm incidents is three. The range is even smaller for inmates in the modified control group. None of the inmates in the modified control group had more than one hospitalization or self-harm incident during the time period studied.

Given the limitations of sample size and variation, this study has found that the residential treatment unit may have an impact on the reduction of negative behaviors resulting from poor adjustment. Hospitalizations seemed to have the best reduction after entry into the unit. This provides evidence that the residential treatment unit may work best for inmates, whose behavior is a direct result of psychiatric symptoms. The residential treatment unit seems to be a good place for mentally disordered inmates to return to after hospitalization. The supportive environment of the unit may provide the inmate with an opportunity to work on prison adjustment while preventing psychiatric symptoms detrimental to the required order.

Future research needs to look at whether this change in behavior continues once the inmate returns to the general population, as well as to society on release. The skills and support provided in the residential treatment unit seem to improve psychiatric symptoms, allowing the inmate more opportunity to adjust to prison. This adjustment not only reduces problems within the correctional institution, but also allows the inmate the opportunity to focus on receiving treatment needed for release into the community and rehabilitation.

ACKNOWLEDGEMENTS

I would like to thank Dr. Stephanie Hartwell and Dr. Russell Schutt for all of their assistance during this study.

REFERENCES

Adams, K. (1983). Former mental patients in a prison and parole system: A study of socially disruptive behavior. *Criminal Justice and Behavior, 10*(3), 358–384.

Adams, K. (1986). The disciplinary experiences of mentally disordered inmates. *Criminal Justice and Behavior, 13*(3), 297–316.

Clemmer, D. (1958). *The prison community*. New York: Rinehart and Company.

Ditton, P. M. (1999). *Mental health and treatment of inmates and probationers*. Washington, DC: U.S. Department of Justice.

Jones, A. (1986). Self-mutilation in prison: A comparison of mutilators and nonmutilators. *Criminal Justice and Behavior, 13*(3), 286–296.

Lamb, R. H., & Weinberger, L. E. (1998). Persons with severe mental illness in jails and prisons: A review. *Psychiatric Services, 49*(4), 483–492.

Lovell, D., & Jemelka, R. (1996). When inmates misbehave: The costs of discipline. *Prison Journal, 76*(2), 165–183.

Lovell, D., Allen, D., Johnson, C., & Jemelka, R. (2001a). Evaluating the effectiveness of residential treatment for prisoners with mental illness. *Criminal Justice and Behavior, 28*(1), 83–104.

Lovell, D., Johnson, C., Jemelka, R., Harris, V., & Allen, D. (2001b). Living in prison after residential mental health treatment: A program follow-up. *The Prison Journal, 81*(4), 473–490.

Malbi, J., & Barber, S. (1983). The effect of inmate security level on incident report rates at a medium security federal correctional institution. *Journal of Offender Counseling, Services & Rehabilitation, 8*(1/2), 37–45.

O'Connor, F. W., Lovell, D., & Brown, L. (2002). Implementing residential treatment for prison inmates with mental illness. *Archives of Psychiatric Nursing, 14*(5), 232–238.

Rold, W. J. (1992). Consideration of mental health factors in inmate discipline. *Journal of Prison and Jail Health, 11*(1), 41–49.

Swetz, A., Salive, M. E., Stough, T., & Bruwer, T. F. (1989). The prevalence of mental illness in a state correctional institution for men. *Journal of Prison & Jail Health, 8*(1), 3–15.

APPENDIX

Table A.1. Age, Criminal History, and Number of Months Incarcerated by Group.

		RTU	Control	Modified Control Group
Age	Mean	41.02	37.06*	42.86
	SD	9.66	9.70	7.43
	N	42	53	22
Criminal history	Mean	2.93	3.40	3.77
	SD	2.58	2.96	3.85
	N	42	53	22
Number of months incarcerated	Mean	69.15	87.68	173.14
	SD	55.44	86.86	73.14
	N	42	53	22

$*p = 0.05.$

Table A.2. Current Offense and Mental Disorder by Group.

		RTU (%)	RTU N	Control (%)	Control N	Modified Control Group (%)	Modified Control Group N
Current offense	Murder/manslaughter	33	14	36	19	46	10
	Sex offense	31	13	17	9	18	4
	Assault/robbery	29	12	28	15	27	6
	Other offense	7	3	19	10	9	2
	Total	100	42	100	53	100	22
Mental disorder	Mood disorder	47	20	70	37	73	16
	Thought disorder	33	14	11	6	9	2
	Personality disorder	10	4	9	5	14	3
	Other disorder	10	4	9	5	5	1
	Total	100	42	99[a]	53	101[a]	22

[a]Percents do not equal 100 due to rounding error.

Table A.3. Average Yearly Rates of Prison Adjustment by Time Period.

		Hospitalizations	Self-harm	Disciplinary Reports	Segregation
Treatment group	Rates before treatment	0.34	0.05	2.92	0.79
	Rates during treatment	0.02	0.10	1.25	0.77
	t	3.406***	−0.579	2.186*	0.084**
Modified control group	Rates before treatment	0.01	0.00	1.64	0.29
	Rates during treatment	0.00	0.03	1.41	0.45
	t	1.411	−1.821	0.553	−1.421

*$p < 0.05$.
**$p < 0.01$.
***$p < 0.001$.

Table A.4.   Average Yearly Rates of Prison Adjustment by Group.

		Hospitalizations	Self-harm	Disciplinary Reports	Segregation
Rates before treatment	Treatment group	0.34	0.05	2.92	0.79
	Modified control group	0.01	0.00	1.64	0.29
	t	3.698***	1.785	1.808*	3.131**
Rates during treatment	Treatment Group	0.02	0.10	1.25	0.77
	Modified control group	0.00	0.03	1.41	0.45
	t	0.721	0.555	1.41	1.371

*$p<0.05$.
**$p<0.01$.
***$p<0.001$.

Table A.5.   Average Rates of Change in Prison Adjustment.

	Hospitalizations	Self-harm Incidents	Disciplinary Reports	Segregation Trips
Treatment group	0.31	−0.05	1.67	0.02
Modified control group	0.01	−0.03	0.23	−0.17
T	3.311***	−0.155	1.666*	0.696**

*$p<0.05$.
**$p<0.01$.
***$p<0.001$.

PART V:
ASSESSING OUTCOMES – TWO STUDIES EXAMINING OUTCOMES OF EX-OFFENDERS WITH MENTAL ILLNESS

BEYOND RECIDIVISM: IDENTIFYING ADDITIONAL MEASURES OF SUCCESS FOR SPECIAL OFFENDERS PROGRAMS

Anne Marie Coté and Kimberly A. Mahaffy

ABSTRACT

Recidivism is often used to measure the success of the criminal justice initiatives. We explore alternate measures of success that were identified for special offenders through the development of program theory. Using content analysis of 50 closed files from the Special Offenders Services program in Lancaster County, PA, we found that most offenders completed the program without re-offending, maintained their medication, participated in counseling, fulfilled their court cost obligations, and had few housing transitions. However, there were differences between parolees and probationers in terms of their outcomes. We recommend that special offender programs use uniform data-recording procedures.

Recidivism is commonly used to measure the success of probation and parole. However, the unique needs of offenders with developmental disabilities and mental illness require additional measures of successful program

The Organizational Response to Persons with Mental Illness Involved with the Criminal Justice System

Research in Social Problems and Public Policy, Volume 12, 181–196

Copyright © 2005 by Elsevier Ltd.

ISSN: 0196-1152/doi:10.1016/S0196-1152(05)12009-2

completion. The purpose of this paper is to define and examine additional measures of success that were developed using program theory. Specifically, we discuss measures that we, the authors, identified with staff from the Lancaster County (PA) Special Offenders Services (SOS) program.[1] We argue that relying on recidivism alone fails to adequately assess the impact that such programs have on offenders with mental illness or developmental disabilities. Further, incorporating additional measures in an evaluation of special offender programs has greater methodological validity. The remainder of this paper describes the program theory developed with the staff of the Special Offenders Services program. We discuss how the indicators were measured and provide descriptive statistics to illustrate alternate definitions of success. We also explore correlates of these alternate definitions of success. Finally, we make recommendations for evaluators and probation departments based on our experiences.

PROGRAM THEORY FOR SPECIAL OFFENDERS SERVICES

Offenders with mental illness and developmental disabilities constitute a unique segment of the population. According to Harlow (1998), approximately 37% of jail inmates have a physical or mental disability. Others estimate that between 8% and 16% of jail and prison inmates have a mental illness (Ditton, 1999). Approximately one-third of the total number of inmates surveyed said that they either have a mental condition or have received mental health services at some point of time (Ditton, 1999, pp. 2–3). Offenders who are mentally retarded range from 2 to 10% (http://www.thearc.org/faqs/crimqa.html).

The offenders with developmental disabilities or mental illness necessitate additional services to reduce the risk of re-offending, improve their emotional well-being, and enhance the likelihood that they will achieve independence (Council of State Governments, 2002). A number of communities have established services to assist offenders with developmental disabilities and mental illness (Linhorst, McCutchen, & Bennett, 2003). The Lancaster County (PA) SOS program has been described elsewhere (White & Wood, 1986; Wood & White, 1992). More recently, the program has been expanded to serve offenders with developmental disabilities and mental illness. The majority of these offenders have been diagnosed with a mental illness. Juvenile offenders have been referred for standard supervision with Juvenile Probation and Parole Services since 2003. The program staff consists of a team of four probation and parole officers as well as additional case managers from the County Mental Health and Mental Retardation (MH/MR) office who monitor offenders with developmental disabilities and mental illness to ensure that they comply with the court's sentencing recommendations and receive services that enhance their quality of life.

In 2003, staff associated with the Lancaster County (PA) SOS requested a study to establish baseline data with regard to their program's effectiveness and to recommend data collection strategies for future research. At the onset, we encouraged the staff to define what successful completion of the program meant to them. At the individual level, success may vary. For example, an offender who has inconsistently taken his/her medication prior to sentencing might be defined as successful if he or she persists in taking the medication throughout the supervision period. In addition, a probationer who completes the program with only a technical violation may be defined as successful because a technical violation (e.g., missing a counseling session and failing to report it to the probation officer) is not as severe as committing a new offense. A previously hospitalized offender who obtains independent housing during the supervision period may also be described as a success. These are a few examples of how successful completion of probation or parole may differ for this population of ex-offenders. We incorporated these outcomes in addition to recidivism to establish measures of success for the SOS program.

To determine whether a program is successful, Weiss (1998) argues that "it is useful to know not only what the program is expected to achieve, but also how it expects to achieve it" (p. 55). In addition to assessing whether a program has met its outcomes, an evaluation based on program theory identifies paths to these outcomes. The program theory elaborates the mechanisms by which change occurs in the program participants (Weiss, 1998). In other words, what responses are expected from the participants to create change and lead to the expected outcomes?

Readers may be more familiar with logic models devised to evaluate criminal justice programs (see http://www.jrsa.org/jjec/resources/logic-model.html) or substantive theories related to reducing criminal behavior such as Braithwaite's (2000) theory of reintegrative shaming. Program theory is a subset of analytic frameworks known as logic models and "... [it] is a set of hypotheses upon which people build their program plans" (Weiss, 1998, p. 55). Although program theory articulates the "causal links between program inputs and expected program outcomes" (Weiss, 1998, p. 55), these hypotheses are not necessarily devised to test a particular substantive theory developed within an academic discipline. Rather, the program theory provides an analytic framework for understanding how and why certain outcomes were achieved.

There are four components of program theory: program inputs, program activities, interim outcomes, and desired end results (Weiss, 1998). Program inputs refer to resources and program activities that represent the ways in which the program is implemented (Weiss, 1998). Interim outcomes are the mediating steps that the activities create on the way to the desired end result (Weiss, 1998). The goal of the program theory is to explain the causal links between program inputs and expected outcomes as the stakeholders perceive them. The theory does not need to be endorsed by all stakeholders nor does the theory need to be right (Weiss, 1998, p. 55). In fact, an impact evaluation can be used to test the theory.

Fig. 1 illustrates the factors that the SOS staff identified as critical for special offenders. These factors are participation in counseling, violation of conditions of probation or parole by the offender, the court's assessment of fines and costs, and meetings with case managers and probation officers. The desired end result is that the offenders will successfully complete the

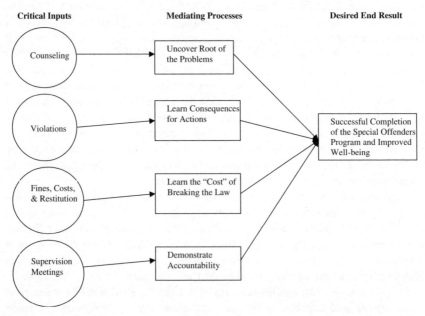

Fig. 1. Program Theory for the Special Offenders Service Program of Lancaster County, PA.

program, no longer participate in criminal activity, and improve their lives. There are several mediating factors that link program inputs to the desired result. These mediating factors represent the changes the individual must undergo as a result of the critical inputs.

Ideally, people who go through counseling get to the root of the issues that contribute to their actions. Recognizing these issues may empower the individual to change. Violations and the enforcement of sanctions teach probationers and parolees about the consequences of their actions. Hopefully, as a result, the offenders are more law-abiding in their decision-making. Also, fines and costs teach individuals about the "cost" of violating the law, and, in turn, deter them from further criminal activity. Lastly, regular meetings with case managers establish accountability. This accountability can also act as a deterrent from additional crimes. To the extent that the organization's practices and the individual's responses enable the ex-offender to become economically independent, acquire a "permanent" residence with minimal supervision, maintain one's medication, and deter criminal activity, then the program has achieved its desired end result. With an articulated program theory, we were better equipped to assess the interactions between the organization and the individual.[2]

DATA AND ANALYTIC STRATEGY

To establish baseline data, the Lancaster County SOS program granted the first author access to case files that were closed between 2000 and 2002.[3] Some cases had been open as early as 1989, the date of sentencing, and included 13 years of information. The probation officer assigned to the case was responsible for maintaining the files. These files included information on sentencing, diagnoses, demographic information, counseling type and attendance, housing, fines and costs, income, medication, number and type of violations, date of offenses or violations, if any, and disposition at the end of the probation or parole supervision. In total, there were 50 analyzable case files. To maintain confidentiality, we created a coding sheet for manifest coding of the files so that we could enter the data in Statistical Package for the Social Sciences (SPSS) later.

As the case files were reviewed, we found that we were unable to obtain measures of the mediating processes and some of the critical inputs. For example, we did not have access to the case managers' files from the County MH/MR office. We do not know how consistently the ex-offender attended those meetings nor do we know the nature of the interactions between the case manager and the ex-offender. Further, the probation officers' case files did not always record information on whether the ex-offenders learned the consequences of their actions or the costs associated with breaking the law. This lack of information provided us with an opportunity to recommend that the program collect the data that specifically address the theoretical framework for program operations. Additional recommendations are located in the conclusion section.

MEASURES

Outcomes

In addition to using traditional measures of recidivism (number and type of violations, time to next offense and completion of probationary period without violation), we included indicators of medication maintenance, financial self-sufficiency, consistency of attendance at counseling services, and residential stability. We coded the closed cases as: completed the program, died, in jail, probation revoked, no longer eligible for the program, and incomplete information; completion of probationary period without a violation (0 = no, 1 = yes); type of violation (technical, new offense, or both);[4] time to next offense was determined by the date of sentence and date of next offense (the data were censored for those who did not re-offend); fines and costs were measured as paid in full, court remitted, no information, other, and still paying; consistency of attendance at counseling or day programming for each type (never attended, attended less than 50% of the time, attended between 50 and 75% of the time, attended 80–100% of the time, and other); housing status when the case was closed: independent living, personal care with 24 hour staff, community rehabilitation residence, hospital, with family members, group home, or other living situation; number of housing transitions during SOS supervision; income source: wages, social security insurance, social security disability insurance, public welfare (cash assistance, food stamps, medical assistance), a combination of these sources, and other sources of income. For offenders who required medication, we coded whether they maintained their medication as no, yes, or no record of maintenance of medication.

Demographic and Background Characteristics

We recorded the ex-offender's sex (1 = male, 0 = female); race (white, Black, and Hispanic); age; parole status (1 = probationer, 0 = parolee);[5]

housing status at the time the offender was referred to the program (independent living, personal care with 24 hour staff, community rehabilitation residence, hospital, with family members, group home, or other living situation); and diagnosis (up to six different presenting diagnoses were coded as mental retardation, personality disorder, bipolar disorder, psychotic disorder, depression, schizophrenia/affective disorder, schizophrenia, paranoid schizophrenia, drug and alcohol abuse, paranoid delusional disorder, posttraumatic stress disorder, panic disorder, intermittent explosive disorder, generalized anxiety, impulse control disorder, passive-dependent personality disorder, hallucinogen persisting perception disorder, limited mental capacity). The diagnosis categories were recoded to mood disorders, psychotic disorders, anxiety disorders, mental retardation, personality disorders, no information, and other. Referral source is Adult Probation and Parole Services, County MH/MR, court ordered, or no information; hospitalization during probation period (1 = yes, 0 = no); original crime that led to sentencing and services was measured as misdemeanor, felony, or no information. These categories were recoded from the original, more specific offenses.

Intervening Variables and Critical Inputs

Fines and costs (1 = yes, 0 = no);[6] restitution (1 = ordered to pay restitution, 0 = not required to pay restitution); and counseling services that are either required or made available to the probationer/parolee were examined. These services vary from counseling (drug and alcohol abuse, anger management, sex offenses, other) to day programming and were coded (1 = participated in some form of counseling or day programming, 0 = did not participate). The number of violations and number of new charges, if any, were summed over the course of the SOS supervisory period to create two separate variables representing violations.

The purpose of this paper is to illustrate alternative measures of program success that take into account the needs of offenders with mental retardation or mental illness. We use descriptive statistics, contingency tables, correlation coefficients, *t*-tests, rank-sum tests, logistic regression, and survival analysis to examine the relations between participation in counseling, housing status, demographic factors, and the desired end results. Our inferential statistics document factors associated with some of the alternative outcomes. We do not attempt to provide an exhaustive assessment of explanatory factors that determine program success for every outcome measure.

RESULTS

Offender Background and Status at Sentencing

Of the 50 special offender files that were analyzed, 74% of the offenders were White, 12% Black, and 14% Hispanic. Seventy-four percent of the offenders were men. The average age of the offenders was 34 years. Fifty-four percent of the special offenders were parolees. Seventy percent of the original crimes were misdemeanors, 24% were felonies, and 6% had no information. Forty-two percent of the offenders were ordered to pay restitution. The referral source was primarily Adult Probation and Parole Services (82%). However, 4% were referred by the County MH/MR office, 12% were court-ordered, and 2% of the files contained no information on referral source. Of the 82% referred by Adult Probation and Parole Services, 98% of the cases came from Standard Supervision and 2% were referred by the impaired driver program.

Thirty-two percent of the offenders had more than one presenting diagnosis. Table 1 illustrates the total number of presenting diagnoses. The most frequently occurring diagnosis was a psychotic disorder followed by an assessment of mental retardation. When the offenders' case was opened, 46% were living independently, 34% were living with family, 10% resided in a community residence or personal care facility, 4% were hospitalized, 4% were living in a group home, and 2% were in some other living situation.

Offender Status at Case Closing

By the time the cases were closed, 56% were living independently, 22% were living with family, 2% were living in a personal care facility, 2% were

Table 1.   Presenting Diagnoses.

Clients' Presenting Diagnoses	Number of Diagnoses
Mood disorders	17
Psychotic disorders	20
Anxiety disorders	6
Mental retardation	19
Personality disorders	7
No information	1
Other	5

Note: The total exceeds 50 because the offenders often had more than one presenting diagnosis.

hospitalized, 2% were living in a group home, and 16% were in some other living situation. The average number of housing transitions was 2.94 (s.d. = 3.99); half of the offenders had more than 1.5 housing transitions during the supervision period. Although source of income at the date of sentencing was not recorded in the files, we have information on their source of income at case closing. At this point, 26% of the offenders supported themselves through wages only, 10% relied on Supplemental Security Income, 8% relied on Social Security Disability Income, 44% relied on a combination of those three sources including welfare, and 12% had some other form of income.

Forty-eight percent of the offenders had paid their court costs in full, 14% had the costs remitted, 12% were on administrative probation and still paying the costs, 20% of the files had no information regarding the final status of the costs, and 6% had other provisions. Eighty-two percent of the offenders completed the program, 6% had died, 4% were in jail, 2% had their probation revoked, 2% were no longer eligible for the program, and 4% had incomplete information. Sixty percent of the offenders completed the program without any additional violations. Of those offenders who violated the conditions of their probation or parole, 60% were technical violations. With regards to new charges, 84% had no new charges, 8% had one new charge, and 8% had two or more new charges.

During the supervision period, 34% of the offenders had been hospitalized. Sixty-four percent of the offenders had participated in some form of counseling or day programming. Sixty-six percent of the offenders required medication. Of those offenders who needed medication, 88% maintained their medication, 3% did not, and 9% of the cases had no information regarding the maintenance of medication. Consistency of counseling attendance depended on the type of support services the offender was offered or required to attend. According to Table 2, drug and alcohol counseling was the most common form of counseling. Sixty-five percent of the offenders who attended drug and alcohol counseling attended at least 50% of their sessions. The offenders who were required/offered sex offender counseling, anger management, or day programming attended very consistently. The remaining offenders who attended other forms of counseling had less consistent attendance; however, this may be due to incomplete documentation of these counseling sessions in the case files.

We use inferential statistics to explore factors associated with completing the program without a violation. We use this variable as a measure of recidivism. Although the program staff did not include demographic characteristics in their program theory, we provide these tests to establish a point

Table 2. Participation in Support Services ($N = 50$).

	Support Services				
	Drug and alcohol counseling	Day programming	Sex offender counseling	Anger management	Other counseling
Required of or offered to	30%	16%	2%	2%	18%
Never attended	14%				
Attended <50% of the time	14%				
Attended 50–79% of the time	36%				33%
Attended 80–100% of the time	29%	100%	100%	100%	11%
No information	7%				56%

of comparison for other researchers. We found that demographic factors had little impact on whether the offenders completed their supervision without a violation. Race and sex had no effect on completing the program without a violation (Pearson $\chi^2(2) = 0.346$, $p = 0.84$ for race; Pearson $\chi^2(1) = 0.02$, $p = 0.89$ for sex). However, age of offender was significantly related to whether the individual completed the program without a violation ($p < 0.01$). Using logistic regression, we determined that the odds of completing the program without a violation increased by 8.4% for every 1 year increase in the offender's age at sentencing (95% confidence interval (CI) = 1.02, 1.15). Parole status was a significant determinant in completing the program without a violation. Parolees were more likely to violate than the probationers did (Pearson $\chi^2(1) = 9.07$, $p < 0.01$). Specifically, 59% of theparolees committed a violation during their supervision versus 17% of the probationers who committed a violation during supervision. We found that there is a moderate association between parole status and committing a violation ($\lambda = 0.25$). Among those who re-offended, parolees and probationers were equally likely to commit technical violations.

In terms of our alternate measures of success, we correlated the number of housing transitions, number of new charges, and number of violations to determine whether there was a relation assuming that violations and new charges (as critical inputs) would be positively related to the number of housing transitions (a measure of stability and improved well-being). These numeric measures were positively skewed. When we used Spearman's ρ and a one-tail test, we found moderate, positive associations. As the number of new violations increased, the number of housing transitions increased ($\rho = 0.64$, $p < 0.01$) and as the number of new charged increased, the number of housing transitions also increased ($\rho = 0.39$, $p < 0.01$). We note that causal ordering was theoretically derived and was not determined from the case files.

The number of housing transitions was also affected by the age of the offender. Our bivariate regression analysis using a two-tail test indicates that for every 1 year increase in age, there was a 0.112 decrease in number of housing transitions (95% confidence interval (CI) $= -0.21, -0.01$). Age explained 10% of the variation in the number of housing transitions these offenders experienced. Parolees had slightly more housing transitions than probationers (parolee mean $= 3.63$, s.d. $= 4.62$, probationer mean $= 2.13$, s.d. $= 3.00$); however, the difference was not statistically significant (t (d.f. $= 48$) $= 1.33$, $p = 0.19$) even when the non-parametric, rank-sum test was used. In addition, race and sex were not associated with the number of housing transitions (F (d.f. $= 2$) $= 1.45$, $p = 0.25$, and t (d.f. $= 48$) $= 0.741$, $p = 0.46$, respectively).

We also investigated whether participation in counseling had an impact on completing probation without a violation, maintenance of medication, current housing, and total number of housing transitions. Participation in counseling was marginally related to completing probation without a violation (Pearson χ^2 (d.f. $= 1$) $= 3.71$, $p < 0.10$), but the relation was not what we expected. Offenders who participated in counseling were more likely to violate than those who did not receive counseling (50% vs. 22.2%). We offer two explanations for this relation. First, while studying the case notes, we found that many of the individuals who participated in counseling had been involved in more serious crimes. They were also on probation for a much longer time, which would allow more time to violate. On the other hand, the individuals who did not have counseling had usually been arrested more recently for a minor crime and sentenced to 6–12 months of probation. Most of these individuals did what they needed to do to complete their probation and did not require counseling. Counseling seems to be required of or offered to offenders who are at greater risk for re-offending. There is also a time ordering problem in the data. This statistical test does not indicate which variable came first, the counseling or the violation. In many cases, the violation may have occurred, and then counseling took place. From that time on, the individual may not have violated again.

We found that participation in counseling was not related to whether the offender maintained her/his medication (Fisher's exact test, $p = 0.51$) or the offender's current housing situation (Fisher's exact test, $p = 0.71$). Yet, offenders who participated in counseling experienced more housing transitions than offenders who did not participate in counseling (rank-sum test $z = -2.66$, $p<0.01$). As we reasoned above, offenders who were involved in counseling had committed more serious crimes and may have moved between prison and a residence more often.

To identify factors that are associated with time to next offense, we performed a Cox regression of the hazard for re-offending on sex, age, parole status, restitution, and counseling. We used date of sentencing and date of next offense for the analysis. According to Table 3, for every 1 year increase in age, the hazard (risk) for re-offending decreases by 5% controlling for other factors. Probationers have a 74% lower risk for re-offending than parolees after taking into account demographic and therapeutic factors. Counseling and restitution, which we expected to reduce risk of recidivism, had no effect independent of the other demographic factors.

CONCLUSIONS AND RECOMMENDATIONS

The purpose of our study was to identify, define, and measure alternate outcomes for programs serving special offenders. We argue that measuring success of special-offenders program with outcomes other than recidivism provides a more complete understanding of the organization's effectiveness. The model we designed to explain how these outcomes were achieved came

Table 3. Cox Regression of the Hazard for Re-offending by Demographic Factors and Counseling ($N = 50$).

Variable	Hazard Ratio	Standard Error
Sex (1 = male)	0.65	0.35
Age	0.95*	0.02
Parole status (1 = probationer)	0.26**	0.17
Restitution (1 = ordered)	0.73	0.36
Counseling (1 = participated)	1.20	0.75
Log likelihood	−61.49	
χ^2 (d.f.)	14.58** (5)	

*$p<0.10$.
**$p<0.05$, two-tail test.

from the program theory that the staff members articulated. Even when we measure success in terms of recidivism, few of the Lancaster County (PA) Special Offenders Program clients re-offended. Moreover, offenders who receive services through this program were likely to maintain their medication, attend counseling, pay their court costs, be self-supporting (albeit with financial support from various public assistance programs), and demonstrate a limited number of housing transitions.

We concluded that offenders who participated in counseling were more likely to re-offend and they experienced more housing transitions than offenders who did not participate in counseling. Yet, participation in counseling was not associated with maintenance of medication or time to next offense. The significant associations we found may exist because those who participate in counseling need more support to overcome problems associated with housing transitions and recidivism. The relations between counseling and the alternate measures of success require investigation.

We found a correlation between the number of housing transitions and the number of new charges and violations. Others have concluded that an individual's residential mobility decreases social attachments (Sampson, 1991). Social control theorists argue that weaker ties to conventional social institutions increase the chance of engaging in criminal (deviant) activity. To the extent that offenders with mental illness or mental retardation move often between group homes, co-residence with family members, independent living, the street, and hospitals, they may develop fewer and perhaps weaker social attachments to family, neighbors, and staff. Other researchers have found that exposure to significant life events including a residential move is correlated with affective disorders in persons with intellectual disabilities (Hastings, Hatton, Taylor, & Maddison, 2004).

Residential instability may contribute to greater involvement in criminal activity by exacerbating pre-existing psychiatric conditions. On the other hand, violating the law may result in a temporary assignment to jail or inpatient treatment. Both types of residential moves would appear in our data as housing transitions. We recommend that additional research and data collection strategies establish the time ordering of these variables. By recording the dates and types of residential moves, the researchers and program staff can determine whether the special offender was on a path to greater self-sufficiency. Similarly, if special offender programs can provide services that reduce residential mobility, then the establishment of stronger ties to the community may deter recidivism.

Investigating the influence of demographic factors on alternate measures of success was not our primary aim. However, we found that age and parole status were both associated with the risk of re-offending, whereas, only age was associated with the number of housing transitions. Older offenders had fewer housing transitions and had a lower risk of re-offending than younger offenders. Probationers had a lower risk for re-offending compared with parolees. Our findings with regard to age and recidivism are consistent with Sampson and Laub (2003). We speculate that probationers have a lower risk for re-offending because they have been able to maintain normative social ties without the disruption of incarceration. The threat of incarceration or additional sanctions may not serve as a deterrent for parolees who may prefer the regular meals and relatively safe shelter that the correctional facility offers versus surviving on the street or at the mercy of friends and relatives.

The limitations of our study and other programmatic recommendations relate to data management. The archived probation files were comprehensive, but there was no systematic ordering of the information in the files and the MH/MR case manager's notes were not merged with the probation department's files when they were archived. Hence, we were unable to determine the extent to which the ex-offender learned the costs of breaking the law or the consequences of criminal activity. These more subjective measures would be better analyzed qualitatively.

As data collection for this study was underway, the SOS program began to automate the recording of data for open cases. Automation of case management and data sharing are the wave of the future (Brown, 2003; Henderson, 2004). Probation and parole departments need to be cognizant of this shift. Presently, the United States government is compiling an indexing system that would allow criminal justice data to be maintained at the local level, but accessed across jurisdictional boundaries by using an XML data dictionary (see http://www.it.ojp.gov/index.jsp). The implementation of a global information sharing system certainly poses security concerns that need to be addressed. Of equal concern to researchers and policy analysts who will access these data is the quality of the data maintained at the local level. Some degree of data standardization will be necessary to evaluate individual and organizational success.

We recommend that special-offenders programs include the dates of housing transitions, counseling sessions, and new charges/violations as well as provide the specific diagnoses from the *Diagnostic and statistical manual of mental disorders*, 4th ed. (DSM-IV). Multiple diagnoses are a common occurrence in this population. The actual recording of multiple diagnoses needs to be specific, consistent, and exhaustive. Moreover, a standard, electronic reporting format that enables probation officers and case managers to enter date of contact information and progress notes would resolve some of the time-ordering problems we encountered. We also recommend that probation officers identify the source of income at sentencing to determine whether there has been a change in economic self-sufficiency by the time of case closing. Our recommended measures can be standardized across Probation and Parolee Departments to make data sharing more efficient.

One purpose of articulating the SOS program theory was to determine the mediating processes to the desired end result. Unfortunately, the case files did not include information on some of these paths. We recommend that data collection strategies (electronic databases or case files) be constructed with a program theory in mind so that the paths to success or failure can be evaluated. Involving researchers with an expertise in program evaluation would behoove probation and parole departments so that they can construct data collection instruments that will enable them to more effectively evaluate organizational success.

NOTES

1. Disclaimer from the Court of Common Pleas of Lancaster County, Pennsylvania: "While statistical assessment is helpful in determining the overall effectiveness of a program, it must be emphasized that the individual complexities and challenges faced by the seriously mentally ill offender cannot be easily categorized or truly quantified. This is a very preliminary study of a small sample of clients who were supervised by the Special Offenders Services program of Adult Probation & Parole Services in Lancaster County, Pennsylvania. The definition of success for this population warrants further review and ongoing research will be necessary to evaluate the true effectiveness of the program. The Court of Common Pleas of Lancaster County has approved this research project. The Court wishes to thank Anne Marie Coté, Dr. Kimberly Mahaffy, and Millersville University for their efforts with this project."

2. We acknowledge that factors unrelated to organizational practices may influence whether the ex-offender achieves these outcomes. However, our purpose was to provide baseline data for the agency and to recommend strategies for collecting data of greater relevance to offenders with mental retardation or mental illness. After appropriate measures have been identified, an impact evaluation can be completed to assess whether the supervision and community services "caused" the change in the offenders' cognitions and behaviors.

3. These dates were initially chosen to limit the scope of the project as the intent was to merely provide baseline data. As she began the data collection, the first author realized that most other closed files prior to this time frame had already been destroyed or were unavailable.

4. A violation can be breaking one of the rules of the probation and parole office. For example, the individual may miss a counseling session and fail to report it to the probation officer. In that instance, the violation would be considered a technical violation. However, a person may actually commit another crime. A new offense is another type of violation.

5. Those individuals who exited prison on parole after serving time were defined as "parolees." In addition to those individuals, any person who was sentenced parole without petition or parole with petition was also considered a parolee.

6. All offenders who enter the criminal justice system in Pennsylvania are assessed court costs to pay for the services they receive. However, most special offenders in Lancaster County are not assessed fines because they are economically disadvantaged. Consequently, the measure of fines and costs is a constant for this sample.

REFERENCES

Braithwaite, J. (2000). Shame and criminal justice. *Canadian Journal of Criminology, 42*, 281–298.

Brown, T. (2003). *Functional standards development for automated case management systems.* Lexington, KY: American Probation and Parole Association.

Ditton, P. (1999). *Mental health and treatment of inmates and probationers.* Washington, DC: U.S. Department of Justice.

Council of State Governments. (2002). *Criminal justice/mental health consensus project.* New York: Council of State Governments.

Harlow, C. W. (1998). *Profile of jail inmates 1996* (No.NCJ 164620). Washington, DC: U.S. Department of Justice.

Hastings, R. P., Hatton, C., Taylor, J. L., & Maddison, C. (2004). Life events and psychiatric symptoms in adults with intellectual disabilities. *Journal of Intellectual Disability Research, 48*(1), 42–46.

Henderson, T. A. (2004). Got data? Make sure it is formatted and defined right. Paper presented at the annual conference on Criminal Justice Research and Evaluation, Washington, DC.

Linhorst, D. M., McCutchen, T. A., & Bennett, L. (2003). Recidivism among offenders with developmental disabilities participating in a case management program. *Research in Developmental Disabilities, 24*, 210–230.

Sampson, R. (1991). Linking the micro- and macrolevel dimensions of community social organization. *Social Forces, 70*(1), 43–64.

Sampson, R., & Laub, J. (2003). Life-course desisters? Trajectories of crime among delinquent boys followed to age 70. *Criminology, 41*(3), 555–592.

Weiss, C. (1998). *Evaluation.* Upper Saddle River, NJ: Prentice-Hall.

White, D. L., & Wood, H. W. (1986). The Lancaster County, Pennsylvania, Mentally Retarded Offenders Program. *The Prison Journal, 66*(1), 77–84.

Wood, H. W., & White, D. L. (1992). A model for habilation and prevention for offenders with mental retardation: The Lancaster County (PA) Office of Special Offenders Services. In: R. Conley, R. Luckasson & G. Bouthilet (Eds), *The criminal justice system and mental retardation: Defendants and victims* (pp. 153–165). Baltimore: Paul Brookes Publishing.

THE ORGANIZATIONAL RESPONSE TO COMMUNITY RE-ENTRY

Stephanie W. Hartwell

ABSTRACT

Current thinking suggests that specialized services are needed for the successful community reintegration of ex-inmates with psychiatric disabilities (Hartwell & Orr (1999). Psychiatric Services, 50, 1220–1222; Healey (1999). National Institute of Justice, February; Hartwell, Friedman, & Orr (2001). New England Journal of Public Policy, 19, 73–82). Nevertheless, stable community re-entry after criminal incarceration involves the response of multiple organizations due to the complexity of community re-entry factors. This chapter presents findings from the analysis of secondary data collected since 1998 and a qualitative interview study with ex-inmates with psychiatric disabilities that identified pathways and turning points influencing community re-entry. Using Sampson and Laub's life course theory as a framework (Sampson & Laub (1993). Crime in the making: Pathways and turning points through life. Cambridge, MA: Harward University Press.), the pathways and turning points offer a point of departure for agencies and organizations in responding to ex-inmates with psychiatric disabilities in the community. Pathways related to service needs at release include race, age, education, diagnosis, and criminal history; whether an individual is on probation or parole; and whether an individual has a history of homelessness, mental

The Organizational Response to Persons with Mental Illness Involved with the Criminal Justice System

Research in Social Problems and Public Policy, Volume 12, 197–217
ISSN: 0196-1152/doi:10.1016/S0196-1152(05)12010-9

198 STEPHANIE W. HARTWELL

*health services, and/or substance abuse. Turning points post release in-
clude institutional resource availability, living arrangements, psychotropic
medication compliance, outpatient therapy and substance abuse treatment, and having entitlements and benefits in place at release.*

INTRODUCTION AND BACKGROUND

Recently, there has been increased attention to psychiatrically disabled individuals in correctional custody and their inevitable return to the community at release (Laberge & Morin, 1995; Lamb & Weinberger, 1998; Hartwell
& Orr, 1999; Travis, 2000; Draine, Salzer, Culhane, & Hadley, 2002; Fisher,
2003; Hartwell, 2003a, b). Among prisoners, the rate of psychiatric disabilities is four to five times the rate of the general population (Morris &
Tonry, 1990; Regier et al., 1990; Morris, Steadman, & Veysey, 1997; Rice &
Harris, 1997; Wolff, Diamond, & Helminiak, 1997), and approximately
16% of all those incarcerated in state prisons (16% of all males and 24% of
all females) have some sort of psychiatric disability (Ditton, 1999). Ten
percent (10%) of male and 18% of female inmates are estimated to have an
Axis I major mental disorder of thought or mood (Pinta, 2001). The vast
majority of these inmates return to the community with complicated profiles
and service needs (Rice & Harris, 1997; Lamb & Weinberger, 1998; Lamb,
Weinberger, & Gross, 1999).

Individuals released from prison must manage the transition from long-
term correctional custody to a less structured environment and altered daily
life in the community (Travis, 2000; Taxman, Young, & Byrne, 2002;
Hartwell, 2003). At least one-third of ex-inmates recidivate to correctional
custody (Feder, 1991; Gendreau, Goggin, & Cullen, 1999; Bureau of Justice
Statistics, 2000). Research on recidivism and the community reintegration of
released inmates rarely distinguishes persons with psychiatric disabilities
from the general population of offenders (Vose, 1990; Gendreau et al.,
1999). Furthermore, most models predicting to recidivism emphasize criminal history variables (Kempf, 1989; Loeber & LeBlanc, 1990; Bonta, Law,
& Hanson, 1998; Gendreau et al., 1999).

While criminal history variables are no doubt relevant to individual outcomes post-release, social environment and linkages to the institutional and
service domains are also essential features influencing the community reintegration of ex-inmates with psychiatric disabilities (Sampson & Laub,
1993; Horney et al., 1995). As offenders mature, individuals who learn to

"live by the rules" and make the "right" choices (pro-social connections) and organizational connections have an increased potential to desist from criminality and integrate to the community (Becker, 1963; Sampson & Laub, 1993). Given this framework, desistance from criminality has to do with both pathways including personal/history variables, and turning points – factors that influence re-entry (Sampson & Laub, 1993; Laub & Sampson, 2001). Thus, while current thinking suggests that specialized services are needed for the successful community reintegration of ex-inmates with psychiatric disabilities (Hartwell & Orr, 1999; Healy, 1999; Hartwell et al., 2001), stable community re-entry after criminal incarceration involves multiple factors and particular linkages to organizations that have not been fully substantiated. This paper presents findings from analyses of secondary data collected on ex-inmates with psychiatric disabilities and qualitative interview data collected with a subset of these individuals that identifies several factors that facilitate or hinder stable community reintegration or regression to criminal behavior.

METHODS

Secondary Data Set and Analysis

The secondary data originate from the Massachusetts' Department of Mental Health (DMH) Forensic Transition Team (FTT) program. The primary goal of the FTT program is to provide transitional continuity from institution to community for offenders with major psychiatric disabilities. Objectives subsumed under this goal include identification and client engagement, assessment of needs, service coordination, and monitoring post-release.

Prior to release, the ex-inmates are interviewed by FTT staff while incarcerated/institutionalized. During these interviews, program forms are completed that include information from record reviews to identify community service needs. Program forms help provide psychosocial information to involved agencies and are used to engage social support and public safety personnel; facilitate the insurance process; and coordinate housing, outpatient services, transportation, and medication at release. Data from the program forms are coded and entered into the research database by members of the research team and include information on ex-inmates identified as in need of mental health treatment while they are serving sentences in state prisons and found to be severely mentally ill and eligible for DMH services.[1]

After these individuals are released from correctional custody, FTT staff track them for 90 days post-release. They make contact with the ex-inmates in the community, communicate with collateral providers, attend planning meetings as appropriate, and continue to monitor the ex-inmates. After 3 months, FTT staff begins to transition out of the case as the primary organization offering case management services stabilizes. While ongoing data collection includes information on individual background character-istics on all identified offenders, the short-term outcome information in-cluding community functioning data 3 months post-release has only been collected on the group of ex-inmates with psychiatric disabilities released to the community since 1998 ($n = 703$).

The secondary data are organized into sets of variables. For instance, psychiatric variables include primary mental health symptoms (thought, mood, personality disorders) as well as diagnoses of record determined by mental health clinicians in correctional facilities in collaboration with DMH eligibility coordinators. This is the information that is recorded on individ-uals' medical records and correctional reports and passed on to other or-ganizations and social service agencies, so, at least in some ways, the forms and/or records reflect the individual who is receiving services and/or being treated. Nevertheless, the quality of secondary data is limited because it comprises of only the information that transition coordinators, clinicians, and ex-inmates share and that is recorded on program forms passed to the research team. Additionally, the relatively small sample has limited distri-butional properties and a constrained number of variables due to the pro-gram data. Finally, the data are also limited to those offenders in Massachusetts who have been identified as psychiatrically disabled in cor-rectional custody. Individuals who are not identified in correctional custody or known to DMH prior to incarceration are not included in the data set.

Qualitative Interviews

During the fall of 2003, I conducted 20 semi-structured interviews with FTT ex-inmates who had been released from prison. Individuals who subse-quently recidivated to prison or a locked hospital unit 3 months post-release were approached by FTT staff and those individuals who agreed to meet with me were briefed on the project and completed consent protocols. Twenty-two individuals (11 in prisons and 11 in hospitals) were approached to be interviewed and 20 consented and completed the interview protocol (1 refusal in the prison group and 1 refusal in the hospital group). Ten (10) interviews were completed in prisons with inmates and 10 on locked hospital wards with patients. The interview script, used to guide the open-ended interviews, covered each individual's understanding of their service needs in the present and in relation to previous community integration efforts (see the appendix).

I took extensive notes during the interviews that I transcribed, coded, and, as common themes emerged, sorted by topic for analysis. Using the qualitative analysis tool, *NVivo*, the pilot data yielded 20 reports on common themes related to organizational linkages and community re-entry discussed by the interviewees. Data included the identification of key re-entry variables and respondent narratives on the array of services offenders with psychiatric disabilities access and/or believe they need for community living.

The qualitative data are limited due to the identification and selection of the ex-inmates, essentially those who failed in the community and were subsequently reincarcerated or hospitalized, and the interview style of the investigator. I created the interview protocol, completed the interviews, and created the coding and data reduction schemas, so the primary interview data has the potential to be biased. This bias was reduced at least somewhat by the standardized interview procedures and the analysis utilized throughout the course of the study. Here again, generalizations about the findings generated from these data are limited to the experience of ex-inmates with psychiatric disabilities who spent time in the community, but were reincarcerated or hospitalized in Massachusetts. While, there is some value in examining the patterns that emerge as presented in their own narratives, future research will collect narratives on individuals that have remained in the community over time as opposed to recidivating.

FINDINGS

The findings from the secondary and qualitative data are examined using the framework provided by life course theory (Sampson & Laub, 1993). The secondary data describe the demographic characteristics and profiles of the ex-inmates with psychiatric disabilities that function as pathways – characteristics that influence their organizational linkages and services. The qualitative data highlight socio-environmental variables that the ex-inmates with psychiatric disabilities identify as turning points that also influence their community re-entry experiences after release.

Secondary Data

All identified ex-inmates have major psychiatric disabilities and criminal history (see Table 1). Nearly 70% are white males between 25 and 45 years old with high school education. Their cumulative rates of non-violent crime are slightly higher than their rates of violent crime.

Other pre-existing characteristics influencing pathways, organizational linkages, and service needs for this population at release include having a history of mental health (73%) and substance abuse (70%) services, and a history of homelessness (31%) prior to incarceration. Additionally, less than 10% of these ex-offenders were released on probation/parole.

Table 1.   Pathways of Ex-inmates with Psychiatric Disabilities Massachusetts[a].

Variable	(n = 703)
Gender (male)	557 (79%)
Race/Ethnicity	
White	375 (53%)
Black	145 (21%)
Hispanic	99 (14%)
Other	84 (12%)
Age	
18–26	130 (18%)
27–45	450 (62%)
46+	123 (17%)
Criminal offense	
Non-violent	370 (53%)
Public order	179 (25%)
Property/arson	116 (17%)
Drug defined	75 (11%)
Violent	333 (47%)
Assault and battery	255 (36%)
Sexual assault	69 (10%)
Homicide	9 (1%)
Diagnosis of record	
Thought disorder	365 (52%)
Mood disorder	289 (41%)
Personality disorder	38 (5%)
Other	11 (2%)

[a]Percents may not add to 100 due to rounding error.

The outcomes of the 703 identified ex-offenders 3 months post-release include 322 remaining in the community, 132 immediately hospitalized at release, 29 hospitalized 3 months post-release, 85 lost to follow-up, and 135 reincarcerated. Examining the 486 individuals who remained in the community for some time and whose whereabouts are known (less the lost and immediately hospitalized groups), the variables significantly related to the three remaining outcome categories (community, hospital, and prison), include age and diagnostic category, and are presented in Table 2.

As can be discerned, the youngest and oldest groups of offenders with psychiatric disabilities are less likely to be hospitalized or reincarcerated. In fact the oldest group of offenders (46+ group) is the least likely to be reincarcerated overall. These findings fit nicely within the framework of life course theory and the notion of aging out of criminality. Additionally, the diagnostic data reveal that individuals with mood and personality disorders have a more difficult time making pro-social organizational connections and maintaining themselves in the community, at least in the short-term 3-month post-release period, and subsequently end up incarcerated or hospitalized.

Qualitative Interviews

Based on analysis of the qualitative interview data, several variables emerged as important for community tenure according to the interviewees.

Table 2.　Outcomes 3 Months Post-release $(n = 486)^a$.

Variable	Age						Diagnostic Category					
	18–26		27–45		46+		Thought Disorder		Mood Disorder		Personality Disorder	
	n	%	n	%	n	%	n	%	n	%	n	%
Community	61	19	194	61	65	20	177	55	133	41	10	3
Hospital	4	14	21	72	4	14	11	38	14	48	4	14
Prison	19	14	100	75	14	11	61	45	64	47	8	6
X^2	10.18*						11.29*					
df	4						4					

*$p < .05$.
aPercentages may not add up to 100 due to rounding error, and variables have different totals due to missing data as discussed in the Limitations. All variable in tables are statistically significant.

These variables include connections to organizations, agencies, and institutions that offer needed resources for community living, living arrangements, psychotropic medication compliance, outpatient therapy and substance abuse treatment, and having entitlements and benefits in place at release. Interestingly, difficulties with these same variables pose the greatest challenges to remaining in the community.

Among this population, agency, organizational, and institutional connections are limited due to early criminal careers, which have been lengthened in duration and course by major psychiatric disabilities and substance abuse. Thus, the resources available to them in the community are truncated, and the resources they have come to rely on and discuss are a part of their "institutional circuit." A black woman with borderline personality disorder recently reincarcerated for shoplifting explains her resources as limited:

> Because once you are involved with the system you have higher recidivism because you won't get probation again. If I pick up a case using drugs, selling my body, or shoplifting, I am going to jail…and going to jail is not enough disincentive to change. Jail is not a deterrent to me. Why isn't it? It is not my bottom. There really isn't any deterrent for me.

In this scenario, involvement with the criminal justice system begets increasing involvement, yet the consequences of criminal behavior and engagement with the criminal justice system are familiar and known. While very few of these individuals are released on probation or parole in Massachusetts, the conditions of supervised release could potentially help orient expectations for community living. However, ex-inmates lacking motivation, impulse control, or the resources to meet the mandated expectations of employment, housing, and substance-free living, violate their conditions and subsequently spend more time involved with the criminal justice system (Draine & Solomon, 1994; Solomon, Draine, & Meyerson, 1994; Solomon & Draine, 1995a, b, 1999; Solomon, Draine, & Marcus, 2002). These findings highlight the narrowing of available organizational and agency resources for recently released ex-inmates with psychiatric disabilities.

For ex-inmates with psychiatric disabilities, finding a safe place to live after long-term incarceration can prove difficult. Research has shown that psychiatric symptoms and criminal history are more likely to result in homelessness than lack of family bonds (Tessler, Gamache, Rossi, Lehman, & Goldman, 1992). Many individuals who were homeless or marginally housed prior to incarceration due to a lack of affordable housing and those with attenuated family bonds due to longer-term incarceration are released to homeless shelters, transitional housing, or halfway houses, but these options narrow considerably when taking into account subsidized housing restrictions. Convicted drug offenders cannot reside in public housing in many locations (Taxman et al., 2002). Additionally, many states have federally funded programs to enhance shelter and other support programs for the individuals who are mentally ill and homeless (20–40% of homeless adults) (Mauch & Mulkern, 1992; Schutt & Goldfinger, 1992), but these federal funds often exclude individuals with a criminal history (Taxman et al., 2002; Buck, 2001).

So while living arrangements at release are important, they vary in terms of availability and stability. Nearly a third of the sampling frame for this study anticipates homelessness at release. For many, being homeless and staying in shelters is part of their "institutional circuit."

> Shelters are a place to go when you are homeless – bouncing around until you go back to the hospital.

When not living in an institution, most say they prefer some sort of supportive housing arrangement:

> Maybe things would have gone better that time (first release) if I was released to a halfway house instead of on my own.

Supportive housing such as halfway houses offer structure and an understanding of individual's needs whereas living on one's own can be isolating. Thus, although many of these individuals say they want to live alone, they should not, and living with others in a family or communal setting while trying to manage a major psychiatric disability can be challenging.

Psychotropic medication compliance was another challenge identified. While the general consensus was that many respondents felt they had to take "too much medication," they understood that taking their medications helped to manage their psychiatric disabilities and improved their functioning and pro-social connections in the community. Still, many medications produced socially unacceptable side effects, "they make me drool sometimes." Additionally, many expressed being able to access their medication in the community, but resented having to adhere to strict regimens because it reminded them of being "sick." Finally, when street drugs entered the picture, prescribed medication was usually abandoned.

> I had a case manager and knew how to get my meds, but I wasn't taking them because wanted to use (drugs). He was trying to get me my own place, but I was off my meds and using heroin. Street drugs and meds don't mix.

Even if they were advised to continue their prescribed medications if relapse to street drugs was to occur, acquiring and using street drugs became a primary focus drawing attention away from taking care of other aspects of their lives including medication and symptom management.

Street drugs often helped these ex-inmates escape the sick role and the mandates of that role for a brief time. While nearly two-thirds of this population report substance abuse histories, for individuals with psychiatric disabilities, substance abuse problems pose even greater difficulties for community living and public safety (Swanson et al., 1997; Steadman et al., 1998). Mueser, Bennett, and Kushner (1995) found that persons with major Axis I thought disorders (i.e. schizophrenics) were almost five times as likely to have a history of any substance abuse or dependence and persons with Axis I mood disorders were three times as likely to have a history of any substance abuse or dependence than the general population. Steadman et al. (1998) studied community violence of people discharged from acute psychiatric facilities and found that while there is variation by diagnosis and community setting, the co-occurrence of a substance abuse disorder is a major factor related to violence for patients with mental disorders. Swanson, Borum, and Swartz (1996) and Swanson et al. (1997) similarly examined the linkages among violence, mental disorder, and substance abuse using Epidemiological Catchment Area data and have also concluded that the likelihood of violence is "much greater" when substance abuse co-occurs with a major mental disorder (Swanson et al., 1997). In addition to posing an increased risk for violence, dually diagnosed individuals are less likely to connect with services and resources in the community, at least when they are released from hospitals (Solomon, 1986).

At the time of prison release, individuals with psychiatric disabilities are often identified and referred to community organizations and mental health and case management services for assessment, evaluation, monitoring, and intervention, but these linkages are usually made on a voluntary basis (Healey, 1999). Moreover, mental health counseling may help ex-inmates cope with their re-adjustment to community living and all the expectations therein, including family reunification and behavioral contracting, not all ex-inmates with psychiatric disabilities will access or consistently participate in counseling and/or treatment. Among the interviewees, substance abuse and vocational rehabilitation were the favored treatment regimens whereas day treatment and social clubs were described as a "waste of time."

> I don't really like day treatment. I'd rather go to work. I used to go to the Weymouth social club, the Coastal Club. I went because the court wanted me to...bunch of bull, sit around smoking. I'd rather go to AA (substance abuse treatment).

Support programming is a broad and variable service domain that refers to specialized program needs including, but not limited to, case management, employment and vocational training, and education. The majority of inmates are underemployed at the time of incarceration and a little more than half have the equivalent of a high school diploma (Bureau of Justice Statistics, 2000). Therefore, it is not surprising that a year after release, more than half of ex-inmates remain unemployed and could benefit from employment supports, job training, or educational programs (Petersilia, 1999, 2000). However, here again, it is the prerogative of many job training, case management, and social programs to exclude ex-inmates (Taxman, 1998). Nevertheless, this population views work as a productive way to spend one's time even if most employment described is entry level.

> I like to work, any job, I don't know, I like work it keeps you busy…keep me out of trouble and lines my pockets to keep me from being a thief … I understand there illegal resources and legal resources, I only steal when I am getting high.

While vocational programs, job training, education programs, and all types of treatment counseling and specialized case management have the potential to be beneficial, their influence on community stability over time in the context of longer-term prison release among ex-inmates with psychiatric disabilities needs further exploration.

Conversely, having appropriate benefits in place at release can potentially balance the needs of ex-inmates with those of the community by ensuring funds for health maintenance and subsistence living. For instance, social security income (SSI) can create a buffer zone between homelessness and being housed while unemployed, and Medicaid can assure prescriptions are paid for and renewable (Jencks, 1994). Essentially, benefits can provide the resources for ex-inmates to manage the transition from being dependent to independent, and help overcome the barriers to re-entry many ex-inmates confront (Taxman et al., 2002). Felons face state job restrictions, former drug dealers are unable to live in subsidized housing, and most ex-inmates cannot afford school or healthcare without income supports and/or federal entitlements.

Federal entitlements including SSI, Temporary Assistance for Needy Families (TANF), Medicaid, and food stamps are usually suspended upon incarceration and terminated over lengthening periods of correctional custody (Buck, 2001; Rosen, Hoey, & Steed, 2001; Rubenstein, 2001). Thus, most ex-inmates must reapply for benefits at release and this can be difficult. First, many ex-inmates lack the documentation required to initiate benefit/entitlement paperwork (e.g. proof of inability to work or completed substance abuse treatment programs). Second, once the paperwork is complete, the ability and enthusiasm of ex-inmates to negotiate the federal system varies. These difficulties are pronounced for individuals with psychiatric disabilities who may have more chronic needs and less support (Petersilia, 2000). Ex-inmates who are psychiatrically disabled may not be able to work. They may be eligible for entitlement programs such as Social Security Disability Income (SSDI) if they can provide proof of their disability, which may take months to compile (Buck, 2001). Therefore, although benefit and entitlement programs may be helpful in reorienting individuals as they traverse the divide from prison to the community, questions remain about which benefits in particular and the length of time it takes to reactivate them after release. When full benefits are in place, several of the interviewees described entitlements and benefits as disincentives to work:

> The government pays my load, pays my ticket, and I can't go back to work.

This is particularly ironic given the view by most of the respondents that work is an essential organizational linkage, needed for sustaining them in the community.

DISCUSSION AND CONCLUSIONS

For successful community re-entry, it can be theorized that ex-offenders with psychiatric disabilities need pro-social connections and organizational linkages to agencies and activities that help them structure their time and the transition from prison. This chapter utilizes primary and secondary data collection strategies to help shed some light on the re-entry experiences of ex-inmates with psychiatric disabilities. It highlights the relevance of pathways, background and demographic characteristics, and turning points, service attachments in the ever-changing environment that may improve the response of organizations, agencies, and institutions working with ex-offenders with psychiatric disabilities.

In terms of background characteristics, demographic characteristics are those personal characteristics that seem to affect linkages to services and community re-entry experiences. For instance, female offenders differ from males (Broidy & Agnew, 1997; Veysey, 1998; Daly & Chesney-Lind, 1999). At least half of incarcerated women are minorities, lack high school diplomas, and receive welfare prior to arrest (Bureau of Justice Statistics, 1994). Many are mothers who report being physically and sexually abused during their lives (Seiden, 1989; Jacobson, 1989; Bureau of Justice Statistics, 1994;

Morash, Bynum, & Koon, 1998). They have more extensive social service histories because they have different needs than their male counterparts.

Race and age (found to be significant in this study) tend to be pathways worthy of note when examining the re-entry experience of ex-inmates with psychiatric disabilities. Black people constitute approximately 12% of the U.S. population and account for 50% of all persons in correctional custody (Tonry, 1995). Research has shown no significant differences in the rates of psychiatric disability among Black and Caucasian individuals (Kessler et al. 1994). Nevertheless, their disproportionate confinement in the criminal justice system overall and elevated rates in this sample suggests that special attention be paid to their institutional and service linkages post-release, which may be distinct. Age is also worthy of note in studies of criminal desistance and community reintegration because there is some evidence of maturing out of criminal behavior over time (Sampson & Laub, 1993; Bureau of Justice Statistics, 2000). The majority of all offenders are under 35 (Bureau of Justice Statistics, 2000), and the data presented here do seem to suggest that older ex-inmates with psychiatric disabilities are less likely to be reincarcerated after release than their younger counterparts at least in the short term. Speaking with older ex-inmates with psychiatric disabilities might shed some light regarding whether age has influenced their desistance from criminality.

An important concept to consider, related to pathways and turning points influencing successful linkages to organizational, institutional, and service domains, is stigma. For instance, individuals with lengthy or particular criminal histories (i.e. violent felons, sex offenders) may have a more difficult time accessing services such as housing, treatment, and/or support programming because they are believed to be "dangerous" or "risky" (Hartwell, 2003b). Additionally, while past criminality may not predict future crime, previous adjudications can influence future adjudication outcomes (e.g. three strikes laws). Thus, there seems to be a cumulative effect of involvement with the criminal justice system over time (Hartwell, 2003a). Furthermore, living in the community with the "double stigma" of a psychiatric disability and a criminal history may be exacerbated by the social isolation fostered through lengthy incarceration (Link et al., 1987; Link, Struening, Rahav, Phelan, & Nuttbrock, 1997; Hartwell, 2003b).

Longer-term correctional custody may result in deterioration of social networks and social skills. Thus, potential turning points or linkages to institutional resources, appropriate living arrangements, psychotropic medication compliance and support, outpatient therapy and substance abuse treatment, and entitlements and benefits become more important in providing a network of resources outside the criminal justice system. Psychotropic medications, public assistance (Medicaid, SSI), primary care, substance abuse treatment, and psychiatric hospitals are all essential features of the community continuum of care for this population (Healey, 1999). Thus, the ability to leverage a hospital bed for individuals in need of a hospital level of subsistence support and supervision is worthy of examination as well as the role hospitals play in stabilization and community reintegration. A hospital stay may be a turning point in improving an individual's health as well as interrupting cyclical behaviors that may lead to engagement with the criminal justice system such as illicit drug use (Stohr et al., 2003).

Recently, more individuals being released from prison are released to the community without mandated correctional monitoring or transitional services aiding community reintegration (Porporino & Motiuk, 1995; Healey, 1999; Travis, 2000; Piehl, 2002). Thus, the organizational and service linkages they make are largely voluntary unless they are mandated to supervised release, the sex offender registry, probation and/or parole. Nevertheless, ex-inmates with psychiatric disabilities are expected to have a distinct set of needs from both ex-inmates in general and individuals with psychiatric disabilities without a criminal history. For instance, mental health services research has shown that intensive case management can reduce the risk of violence and hospital use and increase housing stability and quality of life for individuals discharged from the hospital with major mental disorders (Olfson, 1990; Dvoskin & Steadman, 1994; Mueser, Bond, Drake, & Resnick, 1998; Phillips et al., 2001). These findings establish the efficacy of intensive case management for former patients not involved in the criminal justice system (Mueser et al., 1998; Phillips et al., 2001). However, a growing body of literature that examines the impact of specialized or intensive case management programming for individuals with psychiatric disabilities involved with the criminal justice system does not always support this conclusion of efficacy (Draine & Solomon, 1994; Solomon & Draine, 1995a, b; Wilson, Tien, & Eaves, 1995; Wolff, Diamond, & Helminiak, 1997; Roskes, Feldman, Arrington, & Leisher, 1999; Ventura, Cassel, Jacoby, & Huang, 1998). For instance, Wolff et al. (1997) found that assertive community treatment does not prevent contacts with law enforcement and ex-inmates with the most intensive mental health service treatment also had the most law enforcement contacts (Wolff et al., 1997).

So traditional services and resources do not necessarily ease the special re-entry considerations and needs of ex-offenders with major psychiatric disabilities. Community re-entry is often more complex for ex-offenders with major psychiatric disabilities who are caught up in multiple institutional systems and caught out in the community. However, as this chapter shows, particular pathways and turning points pattern their experience and offer guidelines for organizations to respond to their community-re-entry needs and experiences. Nevertheless, organizations often lack the capacity and resources to disentangle and/or share the responsibility of managing these individuals in the community. Still, the environment or community determines behavior and the organizations that respond to these individuals are part of the environment that reproduce their behavior. Ex-inmates with psychiatric disabilities have trouble managing in the community, particularly in the context of unstructured time. They also have strong sentiments about institutional resources and services, housing options, behavioral management medications, and clinical treatment and counseling programming, and how their entitlements and benefits affect their lives. There is a need to further explore their sentiments brought to light in their narratives that are often overlooked – "The hardest thing about this is that the stigma of being mentally ill make my stories seem unbelievable," – by the organizations, agencies, and institutions that have the power to improve their re-entry experience.

NOTES

1. DMH's eligibility process selects individuals with DSMIV Axis I major mental disorders, who have significant functional impairment, and whose condition is expected to be chronic.

REFERENCES

Becker, H. S. (1963). *Outsiders.* New York: The Free Press.

Bonta, J., Law, M., & Hanson, K. (1998). The prediction of criminal and violent recidivism among mentally disordered offenders: A meta analysis. *Psychological Bulletin, 123*(2), 123–142.

Broidy, L., & Agnew, R. (1997). Gender and crime: A general strain theory perspective. *Journal of Research in Crime and Delinquency, 35,* 5–29.

Buck, J. A. (2001). Spending for state mental health care. *Psychiatric Services, 52*(10), 1295.

Bureau of Justice Statistics, U.S. Department of Justice. (1994). *Special report: Women in prison.* Washington, DC: U.S. Government Printing Office.

Bureau of Justice Statistics, U.S. Department of Justice. (2000). *Mental health treatment in state prisons.* Washington, DC: U.S. Government Printing Office.

Daly, K., & Chesney-Lind, M. (1999). Feminism in criminology. In: F. T. Cullen & R. Agnew (Eds), *Criminology theory: Past to present*. Los Angeles, CA: Roxbury Publishing.

Ditton, P. (1999). *Mental health and treatment of inmates and probationers*. U.S. Department of Justice. Bureau of Justice Statistics.

Draine, J., & Solomon, P. (1994). Jail recidivism and the intensity of case management services among homeless persons with psychiatric disabilities leaving jail. *Journal of Psychiatry and Law, 22*, 245–261.

Draine, J., Salzer, M., Culhane, D., & Hadley, T. (2002). The role of social disadvantage in crime, joblessness, and homelessness among persons with serious psychiatric disabilities. *Psychiatric Services, 53*, 565–573.

Dvoskin, J., & Steadman, H. (1994). Using intensive case management to reduce violence by mentally ill persons in the community. *Hospital and Community Psychiatry, 45*(10).

Feder, L. (1991). A profile of ex-inmates with psychiatric disabilities and their adjustment in the community. *The Journal of Psychiatry and Law, Spring-Summer*, 79–98.

Fisher, W. H. (Ed.) (2003). *Research in community mental health: Special edition on community interventions for offenders with severe psychiatric disabilities* (Vol. 12). Oxford, UK: Elsevier Science Ltd.

Gendreau, P., Goggin, C., & Cullen, F. (1999). The effects of prison sentences on recidivism. The Department of the Solicitor General Canada. User Report n.24.

Hartwell, S. W. (2003). Deviance over the life course: The case of homeless substance abusers. *Substance Use and Misuse, 38*(3–6), 477–504.

Hartwell, S. W. (2003a). Prison, hospital or community: Community re-entry and ex-inmates with psychiatric disabilities. In: W. Fisher (Ed.), *Research in Community Mental Health*, Vol. 12. Oxford, UK: Elsevier Science Ltd.

Hartwell, S. W. (2003b). Short term outcomes for offenders with psychiatric disabilities released from incarceration. *International Journal of Offender Therapy and Comparative Criminology, 47*(2), 145–158.

Hartwell, S. W., Friedman, D., & Orr, K. (2001). From correctional custody to community: The Massachusetts Forensic Transition Team. *New England Journal of Public Policy, 19*, 73–82.

Hartwell, S. W., & Orr, K. (1999). The Massachusetts Forensic Transition Team for ex-inmates with psychiatric disabilities re-entering the community. *Psychiatric Services, 50*, 1220–1222.

Healey, K. (1999). Case management in the criminal justice system. U.S. Department of Justice, Office of Justice Programs. *National Institute of Justice, Research in Action, February*, 1–12.

Horney, J., Osgood, D., & Marshal, I. (1995). Criminal careers in the short term: Intra-individual variability in crime and its relation to local life circumstances. *American Sociological Review, 60*(5), 655–673.

Jacobson, A. (1989). Physical and sexual assault histories among psychiatric outpatients. *American Journal of Psychiatry, 146*, 755–758.

Jencks, C. (1994). *The homeless*. Cambridge, MA: Harvard University Press.

Kempf, K. (1989). Delinquency: Do the dropouts drop back in? *Youth and Society, 20*, 269–289.

Kessler, R. C., McGonagle, K. A., Zhoa, S., Nelson, C. B., Hughes, M., Eshelman, S., Wittchen, H., & Kendler, K. S. (1994). Lifetime and 12-month prevalence of DSM-III-R psychiatric disorders in the United States. *Archives of General Psychiatry, 51*, 8–19.

Laberge, D., & Morin, D. (1995). The overuse of the criminal justice dispositions: Failure of diversionary policies in the management of mental health problems. *International Journal of Law and Psychiatry, 18*(4), 389–414.

Lamb, R. H., & Weinberger, L. E. (1998). Persons with severe psychiatric disabilities in jails and prisons: A review. *Psychiatric Services, 49*(4), 483–492.

Lamb, R. H., Weinberger, L. E., & Gross, B. (1999). Community treatment of severely ex-inmates with psychiatric disabilities under the jurisdiction of the criminal justice system: A review. *Psychiatric Services, 50*(7), 907–913.

Laub, J., & Sampson, R. (2001). Understanding desistance from crime. *Crime and Justice, 28*, 1–69.

Link, B. G., Cullen, F. T., Frank, J., & Wozniak, J. F. (1987). The social rejection of former mental patients: Understanding why labels matter. *American Journal of Sociology, 92*, 1461–1500.

Link, B., Struening, E., Rahav, M., Phelan, J., & Nuttbrock, L. (1997). On stigma and its consequences: Evidence from a longitudinal study of men with dual diagnosis of psychiatric disabilities and substance abuse. *Journal of Health and Social Behavior, 38*, 177–190.

Loeber, R., & LeBlanc, M. (1990). Towards a developmental criminology. *Crime and justice*, Vol. 12. Chicago: University of Chicago Press.

Mauch, D., & Mulkern, V. (1992). The McKinney Act: New England responses to federal support for state and local assistance to the homeless mentally ill. In: P. O'Malley (Ed.), *Homelessness: New England and beyond*. Special Issue of the New England Journal of Public Policy (pp. 419–430). Amherst, MA: University of Massachusetts Press.

Morash, M., Bynum, T. S., & Koon, B. (1998). Women offenders: Programming needs and promising approaches. National Institute of Justice, Brief Report, August.

Morris, N., & Tonry, M. (1990). *Between prison and probation: Intermediate punishments in a rational sentencing system*. New York: Oxford University Press.

Morris, S. M., Steadman, H. J., & Veysey, B. M. (1997). Mental health services in United States jails: A survey of innovative practices. *Criminal Justice and Behavior, 24*(1), 3–19.

Mueser, K., Bond, G. R., Drake, R. E., & Resnick, S. G. (1998). Models of community care for severe psychiatric disabilities: A review of the research on case management. *Schizophrenia Bulletin, 24*, 37–74.

Mueser, K. T., Bennett, M., & Kushner, M. G. (1995). Epidemiology of substance use disorders among persons with chronic psychiatric disabilities. In: A. F. Lehman & L. B. Dixon (Eds), *Double jeopardy: Chronic psychiatric disabilities and substance use disorders*. Chur, Switzerland: Harwood Academic Publishers.

Olfson, M. (1990). Assertive community treatment: An evaluation of the experimental evidence. *Hospital and Community Psychiatry, 41*, 634–641.

Petersilia, J. (1999). Parole and prisoner re-entry. In: M. Tonry & J. Petersilia (Eds), *Crime and justice: A review of research*, Vol. 26. Chicago, IL: Chicago University Press.

Petersilia, J. (2000). When prisoners return to the community: Political, economic, and social consequences. Papers from the executive sessions on sentencing and corrections. No. 9, *Sentencing and Corrections for the 21st Century*. U.S. Dept. of Justice.

Phillips, S., Burns, B., Edgar, E., Mueser, K., Linkins, K., Rosenheck, R., Drake, R., & Herr, E. (2001). Moving assertive community treatment into standard practice. *Psychiatric Services, 52*, 771–779.

Piehl, A.M. (2002) *From Cell to Street*. MassINC: Massachusetts Institute for a New Commonwealth. January

Pinta, E. (2001). The prevalence of serious mental disorders among U.S. prisoners. In: G. Landsberg & A. Smiley (Eds), *Forensic mental health: Working with offenders with psychiatric disabilities.* Kingston, NJ, U.S.: Civic Research Institute.

Porporino, F., & Motiuk, L. (1995). The prison careers of the mentally disordered offenders. *International Journal of Law and Psychiatry, 18*(1), 29–44.

Regier, D. A., Farmer, M. E., Rae, D. A., Lock, B. Z., Keith, S. J., Judd, L. L., & Goodwin, F. K. (1990). Comorbidity of mental disorders with alcohol and other drug abuse: Results from the epidemiologic catchment area (ECA) study. *Journal of the American Medical Association, 264*(19), 2511–2518.

Rice, M. E., & Harris, G. T. (1997). The treatment of mentally disordered offenders. *Psychology, Public Policy, and the Law, 3*(1), 126–183.

Rosen, J., Hoey, R., & Steed, T. (2001). Food stamps and SSI benefits: Removing access barriers for homeless people. *Clearing House Review Journal of Poverty Law and Policy,* March-April, 679–696.

Roskes, E., Feldman, R., Arrington, S., & Leisher, M. (1999). A model program for the treatment of ex-inmates with psychiatric disabilities in the community. *Community Mental Health Journal, 35*(5), 461–475.

Rubenstein, G. (2001). Getting to work: How TANF can support ex-offender parents in the transition to self sufficiency. Washington D.C. Legal Action Center.

Sampson, R., & Laub, J. (1993). *Crime in the making: Pathways and turning points through life.* Cambridge, MA: Harvard University Press.

Schutt, R., & Goldfinger, S. (1992). Mentally ill persons in emergency and specialized shelters: Satisfaction and distress. In: P. O'Malley (Ed.), *Homelessness: New England and beyond.* Special Issue of the New England Journal of Public Policy (pp. 407–418). Amherst, MA: University of Massachusetts Press.

Seiden, A. M. (1989). Psychological issues effecting women throughout the lifecycle. In: B. L. Perry (Ed.), *The psychiatric clinics of North America.* Philadelphia, PA: Saunders Press.

Solomon, P. (1986). Receipt of aftercare services by problem types: Psychiatric substance abuse and substance abuse. *Psychiatric Quarterly, 58*((3) fall), 180–188.

Solomon, P., Draine, J., & Meyerson, A. (1994). Jail recidivism and receipt of community mental health services. *Hospital and Community Psychiatry, 45*(8), 793–797.

Solomon, P., & Draine, J. (1995a). Jail recidivism in forensic case management program. *Health and Social Work, 20,* 167–173.

Solomon, P., & Draine, J. (1995b). One-year outcomes of a randomized trial of case management with seriously mentally ill ex-inmates leaving jail. *Evaluation Review, 19,* 256–273.

Solomon, P., & Draine, J. (1999). Explaining lifetime criminal arrests among ex-inmates of a psychiatric probation and parole service. *Journal of the American Academy of Psychiatry and Law, 27*(2), 239–251.

Solomon, P., Draine, J., & Marcus, S. (2002). Predicting incarceration of ex-inmates of a psychiatric probation and parole service. *Psychiatric Services, 53,* 50–56.

Steadman, H. J., Mulvey, E. P., Monahan, J., Robbins, P. C., Applebaum, P. S., Grisso, T., Roth, L. H., & Silver, E. (1998). Violence by people discharged from acute psychiatric inpatient facilities and by others in the same neighborhoods. *Archives of General Psychiatry, 55,* 393–401.

Stohr, M., Hemmins, C., Brown, D., Dayley, J., Gurnik, M., Kjauer, K., & Noon, C. (2003). Residential substance abuse treatment for state prisoners: Breaking the drug-crime cycle among parole violators. NIJ web document. NCJ 199948.

Swanson, J., Borum, R., & Swartz, M. (1996). Psychotic symptoms and disorders and the risk of violent behavior in the community. *Criminal Behavior and Mental Health, 6,* 317–338.

Swanson, J., Estroff, S., Swartz, M., Borum, R., Lachicotte, W., Zimmer, C., & Wagner, R. (1997). Violence and severe mental disorder in clinical and community populations: The effects of psychotic symptoms, comorbidity, and lack of treatment. *Psychiatry, 60,* 1–22.

Taxman, F. S. (1998). Reducing recidivism through a seamless system of care: Components of effective treatment, supervision, and transition services in the community. Office of National Drug Control Policy, Washington/Baltimore United States.

Taxman, F.S., Young, D., & Byrne, J. (2002). *Offender's views of reentry: Implications for processes, programs and services.* Report for the U.S. Department of Justice.

Tessler, R. C., Gamache, G., Rossi, P., Lehman, A., & Goldman, H. (1992). The kindred bonds of mentally ill homeless persons. In: P. O'Malley (Ed.), *Homelessness: New England and beyond.* (pp. 265–280). Special Issue of the New England Journal of Public Policy. Amherst, MA: University of Massachusetts Press.

Tonry, M. (1995). *Malign neglect: Race, crime, and punishment in America.* New York: Oxford University Press.

Travis, J. (2000). *But they all come back: Rethinking prisoner re-entry.* U.S. Department of Justice, Sentencing and Corrections for the 21st Century.

Ventura, L., Cassel, C., Jacoby, J., & Huang, B. (1998). Case management and recidivism of mentally ill persons released from jail. *Psychiatric Services, 49*(10), 1330.

Veysey, B. M. (1998). Specific needs of women diagnosed with psychiatric disabilities in United States jails. *Women's Mental Health Services: A Public Health Perspective.* Newbury Park, CA: Sage Publications.

Vose, G. (1990). The effect of community reintergration on rates of recidivism: A statistical overview of data for the years 1971 through 1987. *Massachusetts Department of Correction, July*(16), 389–421.

Wilson, D., Tien, G., & Eaves, D. (1995). Increasing the community tenure of mentally disordered offenders: An assertive case management program. *International Journal of Law and Psychiatry, 18*(1), 61–69.

Wolff, N., Diamond, R. J., & Helminiak, T. W. (1997). A new look at an old issue: People with psychiatric disabilities and the law enforcement system. *The Journal of Mental Health Administration, 24*(2), 152–165.

APPENDIX

(1) Orienting Question/Discussion (how are things?).

(2) How do you feel about living in the community these days/since your release? (best and worst about it, how it makes he/she feel).

(3) What have you accomplished as of late? Is there anything you are particularly proud of?

(4) What has frustrated you recently? Can you think of the last time you had something that was hard to manage? You were having trouble with something, or something like that. Walk me through some experiences.

(5) How did you get *housing at release*? What were the difficulties you encountered? What helped? Was the housing adequate?

(6) How do you feel about where you are currently living? Is it adequate? What are the good parts, what are the bad parts? Are you getting any *housing supports* or case management related to housing? What does it do for you?

(7) Describe your average day – how do you spend most of your time? Would you describe yourself as busy or bored? Are you *working? In school?* How do you get around when you have to (car/public *transportation*)?

(8) Are you in any *support programming* such as vocational training or GED classes? Do you cook and shop for yourself or do you have support that helps you with those types of activities? Do you find this support helpful?

(9) Who have you been hanging around with? Who do you spend most of your time with? How do you get/stay in contact with these individuals (car/phone/residence)?

(10) How has your use of *drugs and alcohol been*? Do you feel it has been manageable? Has your use or the use of those around you interfered with or improved your community functioning? Are you in any type of substance abuse treatment? How do you find it?

(11) Do you think being on probation/parole has been/would have been a good thing for you? Why? Do you think you would feel more supported in the community if you were under some kind of *criminal justice monitoring* such as probation or parole? Why or why not?

(12) Do you continue to pursue *mental health counseling*? What do/did you like most about it? What do/did you like least? What type of mental treatment (psychiatric services, one-on-one therapy, outpatient therapy, social club) would keep you coming back/engaged?

(13) Are all your *benefits and entitlements* in place? If so what are they? Are they helpful? What are your concerns related to the benefits? If not, why not? Do you experience benefits as helpful in living in the community? *Do you manage your money wisely?*

(14) How is your *physical health*? Are you able to manage it/your condition while living in the community? How do you do it? What does your health interfere with? Have you had any problems accessing your medications or managing them in the community? Do you have any additional/other health concerns at this point?

(15) In the last three months were you *hospitalized* for mental health or physical health problems? How was that experience? Did it help stabilize you in the community?

(16) How do you feel about making connections to institutions and services in the community (i.e. How relevant does he/she think services are in community living?)

(17) If applicable: What happened that he/she ended up re-incarcerated. Did services play a part in their re-incarceration? If so how, could you please walk me through that.

SET UP A CONTINUATION ORDER TODAY!

Did you know that you can set up a continuation order on all Elsevier-JAI series and have each new volume sent directly to you upon publication? For details on how to set up a **continuation order**, contact your nearest regional sales office listed below.

To view related series in Sociology, please visit:

www.elsevier.com/sociology

30% Discount for Authors on All Books!

A 30% discount is available to Elsevier book and journal contributors on all books *(except multi-volume reference works)*.

To claim your discount, full payment is required with your order, which must be sent directly to the publisher at the nearest regional sales office above.